MW01235283

The Que

Extraordinary Family Secrets

& Untold Stories

of America's Farthest North Bag Lady

By Tricia Brown

Tricia Brown
Fairbanks, Alaska

Larson & Larrigan, Publishers

Anchorage, Alaska

For my matchless mother, Phyllis M. Walsh

ISBN-13: 978-0-9657676-1-3

Editor: Carol Sturgulewski
Designer: Tricia Brown
Proofreader: Jennifer Houdek
Cover photos: Front: *Fairbanks Daily News-Miner* Archives; Back: Erik Hill/*Anchorage Daily News*; Epigraph: *Fairbanks Daily News-Miner* Archives

Address inquiries to:
Larson & Larrigan, Publishers
14185 Hancock Drive
Anchorage, Alaska 99515
LarsonandLarrigan@gmail.com

FSC
www.fsc.org
MIX
Paper | Supporting responsible forestry
FSC® C016245

Printed in Canada
First printing May 2024

IRENE SHERMAN, 1911-1995

Her physical disfigurement was very disturbing to those seeing her for the first time . . . Those that didn't immediately recoil at her appearance, and took the time to listen and chat with her, would soon discover she was not the monster she appeared, but rather a very unfortunate, damaged individual trying to survive as best she could.

— Bud Basse, former Fairbanks resident
September 17, 2013

Contents

1. Meeting the Queen 6
2. A Game of Telephone 14
3. Search for Answers 19
4. Why Here? 34
5. Insane Cold and Temporary Insanity 46
6. The Wisconsin Farm Boy 55
7. Married Life 65
8. Trail from the Totatlanika 79
9. The Third Avenue Hotel 86
10. Girl with the White-Blonde Hair 93
11. Whom Do You Believe? 98
12. Mrs. Sherman is Distracted 104
13. Bitter Grief, Brutal Cold 114
14. A Shattered Family 122
15. Outside, Alone 130
16. Another Baby, and Another, and Another 136
17. Agnes Sails South 142
18. Carriage of Justice 149
19. You've Got a Visitor 157
20. Irene Sails North 161
21. First Comes Love 166
22. Father-Daughter Dance 171
23. The Birth of Packsack Annie 176
24. Tracking Frances 185
25. California 'Cousins' 191
26. The Kindness of Pioneers 203
27. Growing Up Georgerene 210
28. What They Had in Common 217
29. The Curious and the Persistent 224
30. A New Life in Centralia 228
31. Simple Faith 233
32. Irene's Way 243
33. What Was and Is 247
34. After All These Years 253
35. Chain of Care 260
36. The Road Home 285
Appendix: Ancestry of Irene Mary Sherman 297
Acknowledgments 301

Prologue
NO FAIRY TALE
Alaska Territory

Once upon a time, a lonely woman married a gold miner. The newlyweds left their frontier town for his far-off mining claim. One year and three days later, the couple welcomed a perfect, blonde baby girl.

Once upon a time, a distraught woman left a remote cabin in below-zero temperatures to follow her husband and dog team. She bundled up her small child and infant, and loaded them onto a dogsled that she'd pull through deep snow. They became lost. She had packed no food, water, ax, or even matches. The next day, the woman managed to find the cabin again and collapsed inside. Her toddler was barely alive. Her baby had frozen to death.

Once upon a time, a thirsty woman decided to spend the day socializing. She added fuel to the stove—it was well below zero—and firmly shut the cabin's front door, leaving three small children behind it. When the stove cooled, the five-year-old tried to restart it. The two youngest were burned to death. The third would wish she had died.

Once upon a time, Irene Sherman might have had a chance at life.

(Courtesy Jim Dau/ADF&G)

CHAPTER 1
MEETING THE QUEEN - Fairbanks 1978
To me, she represented the deepest of human mysteries

Like many parts of my life, my journey to find Irene was long and meandering. Whenever somebody asks me how our family ended up in Alaska, I speak of us like a migratory herd: "Oh, we just followed each other up the highway, kinda like the caribou."

Once I was one of two passengers in a Cessna 180 flying above a herd of caribou in the thousands, the mass of moving dots below us on a Turkish rug of tundra. Over headphone static, the pilot said, "Wait now, wait 'til we get to the front." My forehead pressed against the side window, I watched from this remarkable balcony seat as we outflew the animals to reach the leading edge. The mass had narrowed, from hundreds to dozens, then further on, a handful. And then I spied him, a single meandering creature just moseying along and making his own trail, seemingly unaware of the crush behind him.

"Can you believe it?" said the pilot. "Sometimes you see this. All these animals, this whole herd, and they're following one juvenile. A teenager! Do they even know where they're going?"

Like the caribou, my family did not always move with great forethought or a specific goal. Sometimes just an idea or an invitation was enough for a spark. We'd all started out in the Midwest, but by the early 1970s, my father, his two brothers, their wives, and a bunch of their kids had up and moved to Guam, one man following another in search of a place to thrive professionally and financially. Back in Illinois, I was eighteen, already relishing my newfound adult freedoms of a job, a car, an efficiency apartment, and a boyfriend. I would not be moved.

They did well, those three brothers and their wives. But one aunt hated the tropics and complained bitterly and often. Secretly, ingeniously, my uncle came up with a solution: Posing as his wife, he applied for a teaching position at the University of Alaska Fairbanks and forged her signature on the application, confessing to her only when she was called for an interview. She accepted the job offer in Alaska and became the family's solo advance party to Alaska in 1972, the single caribou at the head of our herd.

The trickling into Fairbanks began in earnest. Next up was a cousin my age who'd been hired to work at a remote camp on the massive Trans-Alaska Pipeline project that was transforming Alaska in a thousand ways. Next my father and his second nuclear family left Guam and pointed north. In August 1975, three other siblings drove the Alaska Highway in a dilapidated '64 Impala. In Fairbanks, all three soon found piecemeal jobs as bartender, gas station attendant, and saloon can-can dancer at a local theme park. That left me and my young family as the last of the clan in Illinois.

Dad's occasional letters from Fairbanks were so friendly, so invitational. "Come on up! There's money lying all over the place!" wrote the top-level Realtor with his back-slapping brand of salesmanship. And now he was selling Alaska to me. Every so often, a scrawled letter told us about the Alaska pipeline, about cabin life, about their Alaskan husky and my half-brother's progress on the tuba.

Dad sent the Fairbanks paper's travel supplement that showed a family sitting at their kitchen table for breakfast by the open window. The thing was, a live moose had its head through the window and looked to be feeding off the same table. I was sold. Another letter ominously informed us that a wolf had killed someone's dog at the edge of town. I was unsold. He wrote again, saying he'd lined up a secretarial job for me, and even named my future boss. The place was perfect for young couples like us, he urged. I began to dream of possibilities.

On July 21, 1978, my then-husband and I, and our two preschoolers, came off a drive of more than three thousand miles up the Alaska Highway, stumbling into town after twelve flat tires, a broken axle, and a broken tongue on our homemade trailer. We were young, resilient, and relentlessly broke, but ready for something new.

One day after our arrival, the city's Golden Days festival celebrating the discovery of gold that launched the boomtown felt to us like a welcome party thrown by the citizens of our new hometown. That Saturday during the festival's Grande Parade, I finished shooting the roll

In 1978, our little trailer wasn't suited for the challenges of the mostly unpaved Alaska Highway. I'd painted "Alaskabound" and a bright graphic arrow on its sides, showing our route north and west from Chicagoland. (Tricia Brown)

of 110 film that was still in my camera, framing Santa Claus atop the North Pole Fire Department truck. I captured the legislator biking on an old-timey wheel and the backfiring antique truck with a smoke-burping moonshiner's still in the back. There were chesty can-can girls and a jail on wheels. More politicians. And soldiers in block formation, marching in their winter white camouflage uniforms.

It was then that I saw Irene Sherman for the first time. She was a solo parade entry on a personal float—a tricycle built for grown-ups. Irene had decorated it and herself. She wore layers of stained secondhand clothes topped by a winter coat and a flouncy hat.

The woman was in her sixties, I guessed, built like a fireplug, round and sturdy, and thickly covered while the rest of us were in short sleeves. It was impossible to know the old woman's actual size under

Irene waves to the crowds during the 1973 Golden Days Grande Parade (Alaska Film Archives, University of Alaska Fairbanks; AAF-10407; Roger Emerson Wheelock, filmmaker)

all those clothes. She assumed a regal air as she pedaled her trike, turning left and right and nodding. "That's not a costume," my stepmom said near my ear. "That's our town bag lady. Whether it's eighty above or forty below, she's wearing a parka and winter boots." Everybody was waving and clapping and I did, too. Like a queen, Irene lifted one hand to gesture back. Stubby, curled fingers extended from scarred hands. When she turned toward us, beneath the brim of her fancy hat, Irene's face was a mask of discolored, uneven burn scars. As the trike passed, I read the poster on the back. "IRENE MARY SHERMAN, THE QUEEN OF FAIRBANKS, FAIRBANKS-BORN 1911." I scanned the faces of the locals stacked along both sides of the street and saw smiles and hints of pride. She was *their* bag lady, their Irene Mary Sherman. Maybe they wouldn't have had her over for dinner, but on this day, it was love.

In time, I would learn more about "The Queen" and this place, her dominion, in fits and starts, watching her clump through downtown streets in loose-fitting men's work boots, noting her annual birthday party picture in the *Fairbanks Daily News-Miner*, mentally filing away hearsay about her scars and what caused them. As I learned about her, I learned about the heart of my new hometown and the guardian angels who quietly kept an eye on her.

I considered her role as the northernmost bag lady in the United States, surviving where seasonal temperatures ranged from minus forty (or fifty or sixty) upward to an occasional eighty-five-plus degrees above zero Fahrenheit. Where she slept, what she ate, how she handled the threat of frostbite—all valid questions for a new person in town. But in truth, very few of the people who applauded her that parade day had answers either. They only knew her as a Fairbanks icon. Local color. But a mystery to most.

Irene was used to walking for miles as she made her rounds among stores, gift shops, yard sales, and many bars. She knew the streets as well as or better than any cabbie. A chronic "collector," she dropped in on construction job sites and garage sales, pulling a wagon for newfound treasures and sticking around to visit. New and old friends were everywhere, and she greeted them coarsely and loudly, especially when she was visiting favorite watering holes. Around Irene's padded waist, a beer mug dangled from a rope, ready for refilling. On good days, she found drinks on the house, or else she might coyly sidle up to a new friend for a refill in exchange for a few Fairbanks history stories.

Back in the 1940s, one of Irene's favorite stops was the Cottage Bar on Second Avenue. But the list of favorites was long. Later, she also haunted the Mecca, Tommy's Elbow Room, Ken's Bar, the French Quarter, Steak & Pipes, the Big I, the Savoy, and Mike's Pipeline Bar. At day's end, she'd ramble over the Cushman Street Bridge to Garden Island and the Immaculate Conception Church, past the bank building and newspaper offices, and onward to her "wigwam." That's what she called her ramshackle site in the neighborhood named Graehl.

Her home, created from the things she carted and dragged here, had a story of its own. So technically, she wasn't homeless, I realized, but she couldn't possibly live inside that junkyard year-round, could she? Not much was visible beyond her border of pallets, chained refrigerators, boxes, and broken washing machines, all positioned just so by the Queen, right at the edge of the street in a neighborhood that knew her, was used to her, helped her.

In 1978, Irene led local author Joan Koponen on a tour of her place, the exterior anyway, while a tape recorder was running. Listening in forty-five years later, I noted the lift in Irene's voice as she detailed her home's features with pride, almost like a Realtor showing a choice property in the Tour of Homes.

"Heck, what you see there is more or less odds and ends that I've been accumulating since '48," Irene said. "Of course, I've stacked things on top of each other and put roofs on 'em. And then there's wood scattered in the doggone conglomeration, and scrap paper that I use for startin' fires in my wood/coal stove."

Irene kept up the chat as she led her visitor around outside, never inviting her in, but instead describing what went unseen, behind that chained row of broken appliances, what lay at the end of the various tunnels she'd engineered as entry points.

"Most of this stuff, it's for a fence, like, so that I can have an inner sanctuary back in the house without anybody scrutinizin' me," Irene said. Clearly, she'd had her share of scrutiny and demanded control of her space. Listening, I could visualize Irene waving her arm, her burn-scarred, stubby fingers pointing at the heap, here, then there.

"I got myself a huge box over there and I've fixed a bed inside of that danged thing so in the summertime I can sleep out there and yet be closed in so nobody can get to me and touch me," she said. She was as fiercely independent an Alaskan woman—or man—as I'd ever meet. Yet surely her independence came at a cost.

Passing Irene in town, we newer folks were repelled by *and* attracted to her strangeness. Some chose to give her no more notice than a heave in a sidewalk, wary and aware, merely maneuvering around a problem. Others gave her a hearty greeting, matching hers.

To me, she represented the deepest of human mysteries. *What had happened to this woman? What was her story? Where were her people?*

Irene slips into her fortress through one of several possible entries. In 1988, her lot was full, but she vigilantly prevented her collection from creeping into the street. (Erik Hill/*Anchorage Daily News*)

CHAPTER 2

A GAME OF TELEPHONE - Fairbanks 1979

Even her contemporaries were subject to weaving hearsay with fact

Irene was used to reactions like mine the first time I first met her up close. A little jolt of a shock—*Oh!*—soon dissipated as I tried to focus on her lively eyes and the person behind them. It was an embarrassing, unwanted response. Her eyes were wide, and shiny, discolored scars crossed her face and neck. Hidden beneath layers of sleeves were newer scars of grafted skin—donated by her own father, I'd later learn. Missing teeth slurred her speech somewhat. The only other visible part of her body, her hands, were likewise afflicted with new scars on top of old, the result of multiple release surgeries to keep her stunted fingers from permanently curling inward and becoming less useful.

Irene's adult-sized tricycle, which she often rode, came to her as part of a 1968 out-of-court settlement after Irene charged the *Seattle Post-Intelligencer* and a local radio personality with libel. Steve Agbaba was a verbose man nicknamed "Agblabba" or "the Mouth." Irene claimed injury when the Seattle paper published Agbaba's derogatory remarks, among them calling her "pack sack Irene" and that she made her living by "making people pay her to stay away." Agbaba had no real hard feelings toward Irene, and likely had let his mouth just run to a reporter. In the settlement, which amounted to between $4,000 and $5,000, Agbaba also proved his contrition by buying her the three-wheeler. The trike's spacious baskets made her copious collecting so much easier. When she was on foot, Irene often pulled a little wagon to shop garage sales, fingering goods and paying in cash.

Cruising around town, she was forcefully friendly, almost assaulting people with hearty greetings at a foghorn decibel. "Hiya, baby!" But a warm greeting could turn sour in a heartbeat, depending on her mood. Or crossing paths with a large rock in the wrong place might end with a loud scolding and a toe kick. "Git back where you belong, you sumbitch!" Later I'd learn that a good reason may have lain behind

For generations, Irene (with her Oly stein on her belt) was a common sight around town. (*News-Miner* Archives)

what seemed like erratic behavior, like her fixation for out-of-place rocks. Her weird responses suddenly became clear when I read a transcript of Koponen's 1978 taped interview: " . . . when I'm at somebody else's place, I try to do somethin' for 'em, like kick the doggone rocks under the porch, because, boy, I've got it in for the rocks. I went and messed up this instep with 'em one time; I stepped right on top of the damn thing and it tore my instep up. Jeez, I was sure disgusted with that."

As many others told me, even in the best of times, Irene didn't seem entirely checked-in. How long she'd been that way, I didn't know. Was it dementia, had she suffered brain injury, or was it a coping mechanism adopted through years of trauma? There were as many opinions as there were mosquitoes in this town.

Every so often, somebody would drop a story about Irene's burns. As an elder, she'd already lost many peers—those who knew her life story more accurately—but even her contemporaries were subject to weaving hearsay with fact. Those who remained offered conflicting memories as time passed. That's what stories do, what people do to them. Anyone who's played the old game of "Telephone" knows that change is inevitable and laughable in the space of just minutes. Stories about Irene had been passed along for decades. There'd been plenty of time to mutate.

Irene was the hero in most of those stories. There'd been a house fire, they'd said, and she'd rushed in and saved her baby sister. Another remembered that she'd rescued her children. No, no, someone would correct. She wasn't even old enough to go to school yet. Okay, there was a death, or maybe was it two people, but it could have been her, too. It was all her mother's fault, someone asserted. A cabin fire. Nope, she fell into a campfire. Bad luck.

That's all I'd heard. No more detail than that. But in my eyes, and in the eyes of Fairbanks, she carried nobility on her shoulders along with that dirty parka cinched by a leather belt. Irene had been elevated, had elevated herself, in her self-titled "Queen of Fairbanks" role by surviving unimaginable pain and ongoing danger. My sweeping interest focused as I learned ways that this street person had become an essential thread in the fabric of this community.

My first mild summer of 1978 would give way to cold so piercing and painful that I couldn't imagine how a physically impaired senior citizen who was essentially camping could handle it on a daily basis. And yet she carried on, year after year.

While Irene was a pioneer, I was a *cheechako*, the Chinook jargon word for a new arrival or greenhorn. In the late 1800s, Chinook developed as the mixed-bag language, enough for an Alaska Native and non-Native to just get by in communicating. *Skookum* meant "very strong and able." That was Irene. As an old-time non-Native pioneer, she was also a labeled a *sourdough*, a group named for the yeasty bread or pancake starter that "Trail of '98" stampeders carried with them along to the goldfields. Many of the earliest Fairbanks settlers were experienced sourdoughs who'd arrived from other gold camps; the remainders, the hopeful *cheechakos*, had a rocky time figuring out how to survive, let alone make money—something like the rough arrival for my little family even seven decades after the stampeders swept in.

Stories swirled around how and when Irene was so severely burned. (Erik Hill/*Anchorage Daily News*)

Pictured with her ever-present Olympia beer stein. (*News-Miner* Archives)

In 1904, Presbyterian missionary Reverend Dr. S. Hall Young landed here to find a camp town populated by about five hundred people scattered in log cabins, a handful of frame buildings, and "plenty of tents," he wrote later. Dr. Young also observed two busy sawmills and that "the sounds of hammer and saw were heard on all sides." Population numbers increased when you counted the thousands more who lived in clusters along the creeks with Fairbanks as their hub city.

Dr. Young chose a lot on the edge of town, on the corner of Seventh Avenue and Cushman Street, to build the first Protestant church in the Interior. Wrote one church historian, "By 1905, the church had twenty-three members, only eight of them Presbyterian."

In the church's founding records, two charter members stood out to me: Mrs. Minnie Eckert, former member of the Baptist Church of North Seattle, and Mr. John H. Patten, a respected prospector-turned-hotelier who was among five men elected as trustees. The document revealed the depth of the bag lady's roots in Fairbanks. Mrs. Minnie Eckert was Irene's maternal grandmother, who'd come to Fairbanks in 1905 with two teenaged children following a divorce from Fred Eckert back in Seattle. Minnie became acquainted with John Patten during their work to establish the new church, and they married in 1908.

Together, the Pattens became essential players in the development of early Fairbanks, in business as well as the town's vibrant social life. If only their family life, or rather that of Minnie's children and grandchildren, were not so public and scandalous, they might have spent the rest of their lives there.

CHAPTER 3
SEARCH FOR ANSWERS - July 1988

I got the damnedest habit for pickin' up
scrap—nuts, bolts, knickknacks.

Watching Irene in the 1978 Golden Days Parade had planted a seed of uncommon curiosity in me. In pondering the life of this solitary child-woman, I joined the ranks of Fairbanks residents, present and former, who would view her protectively, with warm, nostalgic feelings, a celebrated figure in our personal histories. She was rooted in a place that called itself the "Golden Heart City," not just for its location at the center of a supersized state, but also for its generosity in spirit and deed. The more I learned about her, the more I discovered just how fitting the tagline was for both the town and its people.

By the summer of 1988, a decade had passed since I'd come off the Alaska Highway and first laid eyes on Irene. In that stretch, I'd earned a journalism degree at the Fairbanks campus of the University of Alaska, and I was hired to write and edit feature stories at the local paper, the *Fairbanks Daily News-Miner*. After a few years, I relocated four hundred miles south to Anchorage while still making frequent drives up north to see my extended family. Irene and the mysteries surrounding her were still sparking my imagination when I proposed a freelance assignment to the *Anchorage Daily News* for its Sunday magazine, *We Alaskans*. Enough of the rumor mill, the imaginings of townspeople who'd heard this or that about Irene's childhood, that terrible fire, and who helped keep her alive today. Send me to Fairbanks for this year's Golden Days, I pitched, and I'll chase down Irene and those closest to her for in-depth interviews. I'll hit the university archives and library for confirmation in the paper trail, and make additional calls as needed. It was the time to get her story straight; she was approaching eighty and still in crude living conditions.

On the third Saturday of July 1988, I parked myself on the curb along the Golden Days parade route and relished this small-town tradition, watching and waiting for Irene to pass on her adult-sized

In July 1988, Irene was cruising through the parade in a sports car instead of her usual three-wheeler, like true Golden Days royalty. (Tricia Brown)

tricycle. But this year she surprised us regulars. Instead of pedaling her three-wheeler, Irene was riding atop the backseat of a classic convertible like a beauty pageant winner. The poster on the bumper still boasted her claim to fame: "Irene Mary Sherman, 1911, Fairbanks-born, Queen of Fairbanks." She sparkled in the sun with a glittery purple cape slung over her parka, a red boa, and a wide-brimmed pink hat decorated with a beat-up plume. A red Gay '90s garter was slipped over the dirty sleeve of her blue parka. She joyfully waved to friends and strangers alike, and we all clapped and waved back, smiling broadly, as if she'd summoned us all here for this purpose, on this day.

According to plan, I would interview Irene the next morning over breakfast, but I worried whether she'd show up. Setting a specific meeting time seemed dicey, because she operated on a different clock than others. What time is "good and early"? Wally Burnett, the Fairbanks businessman who was currently looking after Irene's affairs, had taken care of the particulars. We were to rendezvous at the Black Angus, the restaurant in the lobby of the Polaris Hotel, which Burnett owned and operated with his wife, Ruth. At eleven floors high, the

Polaris had been the tallest downtown building since 1952.

That Sunday morning, I was burning up some time a block away in Golden Heart Park, along the Chena River by the Cushman Street Bridge, when I spied Irene marching around the plaza on her own. Irene was used to people asking for a photo, and I was just one more. I introduced myself and posed her by the landmark "Fairbanks' First Family" statue at the center of the fountain. An impish, closed-mouth smile brightened her face. "I've Got My Irish Up!" her pin exclaimed. Across the river behind Irene, I could see Immaculate Conception Church and the bank that once had been an annex to St. Joseph's Hospital. The landmark buildings, I would later learn, were landmarks in Irene's life story, too.

When it was nearly time for our meeting at the Black Angus, I suggested we head over, pausing as we walked so she could loudly hail her friends on the sidewalks. Irene had not changed her clothes in the twenty-four hours since I'd last seen her. She was still aglow in purple glitter and pink ribbons over a thick parka and whatever else was under it. Sliding into the booth across from me, Irene said, "I guess you're wondering why I'm still in my get-up and all. I want 'em to know I'm still one of the wheels."

At that moment Wally Burnett walked in, smiled at me, and greeted Irene, "How ya doin' baby?!" with a light touch on her shoulder. "You're looking awfully sharp today. How'd you get to ride in that big car yesterday?" There was nearly a generation between them, and they treated each other like a favorite aunt with her favorite nephew.

"They bamboozled me and stuck me in the hotel so they could catch up with me," Irene answered brightly. Who "they" were, she didn't say, but clearly somebody wanted to give Irene an extra dose of honor. And that's how it was in this town, I learned. People helped her without crowing about it to others. It had always been like that. There'd be no falling through the cracks for Irene. But in this stage of her life, Wally was the principal player.

Over eggs and toast, I asked Wally to please explain, again, how he was related to Irene, because I'd heard there was a connection.

I just couldn't untangle it. He launched in—"My Aunt Frances was my father's adopted sister and . . ." *Wait, wait.* I slowed him to catch up. Okay, Aunt Frances and Irene had the same birth mother? But Frances had been adopted out to Wally's grandmother? Got it.

Irene loudly jumped in, "So that makes us in-laws, right, Burnett?"

"That's right," he volleyed back.

"By the way, Wally, where in the devil is she?" More than once during this breakfast, he would remind Irene that her birth sister, Frances, was living in Van Nuys, California. She had been for years.

"What the nuisance is she doing down there!?"

"She's retired down there," Wally said. "She hasn't been back to Alaska in about thirty years."

"Well, doggone it, that's no good."

Turning to me, Wally said that likewise, Irene hadn't traveled Outside (as Alaskans termed anywhere that's *not* Alaska) in about thirty years.

She broke in: "Well, I don't intend to go Out, if I can help it!"

". . . and your sister doesn't intend to come back either, so I guess we're gonna have to do something. We're gonna have to get a common meeting around somewhere."

And then Irene grabbed a pause in the conversation to answer a question that I hadn't yet asked: *How many siblings did she have?* "I think there were about seven of us . . . I've forgotten how many."

Wally quietly added his postscript: "Just Irene and her sister are still around."

"Where are the others?" I asked Irene directly.

"I haven't got the slightest idea."

The Polaris Hotel was one of the few "skyscrapers" on the downtown Fairbanks skyline. On the top floor, the Tiki Cove was the going place for outstanding Asian cuisine and stylish décor. I'd been there on dinner dates while in college. In an earlier life, the popular restaurant had been nestled below the Mecca Bar, on Second Avenue, which Wally also owned. After he acquired the Polaris, he'd moved the restaurant to make the Tiki Cove a crown atop the building. Between the lobby and the top-floor restaurant, dozens of rooms were filled with

The Queen posed for me in Golden Heart Plaza downtown near the statue titled "Fairbanks' First Family." (Tricia Brown)

tourists in the summer months. Naturally, in winter, there were fewer occupied rooms. But regardless of season, Wally Burnett made sure his "aunt" had a rent-free room ready for occupancy anytime she wasn't up to walking home.

Irene knew the streets and shortcuts around Fairbanks by heart. In her mid-seventies, however, her sense of direction was beginning to fail. The familiar paths to home became like new ground—dangerous at twenty below. Wally had urged her to stay full-time during the previous couple of winters, with hit-and-miss results.

"That's why we've got her here, because she gets lost," Wally said quietly. In summers, Irene was free to roam and could stay at the hotel or "over in my wigwam," as she called her tumble-down quarters across the river. It was equipped with power, but lacked running water.

And she didn't want anybody trespassing or messing around with her set-up. And no upgrades, either. Just leave her be.

"But it gets kinda rough there," Irene admitted. "I get my ice and what have you and use that. 'Course I've got radio and one thing and another, and I turn it on and see if I can get some music."

Irene told me she used a small wood/coal stove for heat. Given her history and considering the fire danger—all that paper and wood in close proximity to the stove—I winced as I thought about it, but it didn't feel right to ask about it in this moment.

Wally said he was happiest when Irene was safely ensconced at the Polaris. Care nurses could come in twice a week to bathe her, and doctors would see to the spots of skin cancer on her face. She'd also had another surgery on her fingers, cutting away the binding scar tissue that kept them curled. According to Wally, Irene was living better than ever. He was serving as Irene's chauffeur and accountant, too. He paid her bills and issued her fifteen or twenty dollars a day from the five to six hundred a month she got from Social Security and the state's senior benefit program at that time, the Alaska Longevity Bonus program. Whenever he could, Wally took her to her home place, "so she can see what's there," and brought her along on drives.

It was obvious that Wally and Irene had a unique relationship. His quick comebacks put her in a giggly mood. And he answered every question—even if she was interrupting another conversation of his.

"Hey, Wally, pardon me."

"Yes, honey."

Irene was curious about a man in the hotel lobby who seemed to be just hanging around. He was pacing and looking out the window.

"Is he with you?" she asked Wally. His eyes cut in the direction she'd nodded her head.

"No, he's waiting on a trip to Mount McKinley."

"Well, he's looking like he's trying to get something goin'. . . . I didn't see him packing any valises or anything."

Wally spoke under his breath, so low that I barely heard him: "She watches *everything*."

Strolling with Wally by her home place, Irene was bundled up on a warm July day. No matter the temperature, she donned many layers every day. (Erik Hill/*Anchorage Daily News*)

For me, the breakfast interview was anything but casual. Understanding how rare this opportunity was, I was hungry to take in every word, every nuance of Irene's face, hands, and voice, and wishing I had more time. This was my first chance to rope her in and actually sit for direct questions about her life, or at least what she could remember, but she was as restless as a kindergartner. As a journalist, I knew this was a one-sided relationship. I was the taker, harvesting for my story needs, sensing where there might be holes, looking for more grounding, worrying about errors, ready for her to bolt.

Could I trust what she said? What was she leaving out? What was unsaid because long ago she'd stopped looking at, talking about, the most painful times of her life? I wanted to arrange another rendezvous, but she was all about "skedaddling" and getting back out.

Wally and I were standing, ready to leave, when Irene announced, "I want to shanghai somethin'," and folded her paper placemat with its map of Alaska and facts about the Last Frontier. She asked the waiter to wrap up her cold eggs and leftover toast, but Wally stopped him. "No, we'll get her some fresh food later on."

Minutes later, Irene plopped into the passenger seat of my 1982 Escort, and I drove to her place on the dead-end street on the other side of the Chena River, near Noyes Slough. I was not invited inside.

The last I saw of her, Irene was climbing over narrow steps made from uneven wooden blocks shored by newspaper stacks. She briefly crouched for a tunnel-like opening before her purple spangled cape disappeared from view. Some kind of inner court lay inside, beyond the wall of chained appliances and pallets. As awful as it looked, for Irene, this was her place of safety, security, and stability. She had made it what it was with her own hands.

"I got the damnedest habit for pickin' up scrap—nuts, bolts, knickknacks," she'd said years earlier to Joan Koponen. "Because you never know, you might want to have something' like that, and you'll need to attach that to somethin' else, and . . . that's the pack rat in me." She'd paused and laughed. "The damn G.I.s used to call me Packsack Annie. I used to have one of them packsack things."

Seems she was fine with the G.I.s calling her Packsack Annie, but took umbrage when local radio personality Steve Agbaba used the term (hence the awarded adult-sized tricycle). You could never tell what might light her up. I later learned that Irene had started a few fights, quite a few actually, especially in bars and especially if someone was picking on a friend. And that she never ran from one.

"I'm not sayin' I'm a pal of everyone," she said. "There was this goofball that raised hell with some of my railroad buddies in the territorial days. So I says, 'Damn you, you're goin' to put an end to this in a hurry.' I shoved him back a few steps, and then I give him a good one, and boy, he went down like a ton of bricks and cracked the back end of his head." Irene did not stifle her laughter at that memory.

"Of course, the gang wasn't too happy with me for that deal, but dang it, I told 'em, I says, 'When someone goes botherin' my friends,' I says, 'they ain't goin' to get nowhere.' Because hang it, I practically broke my teeth on the railroad when she was startin' to come through, and those fellers mean a lot to me."

Back home in Anchorage, I transcribed notes and printed them out at the *Anchorage Daily News*. (Those green-and-white striped dot-matrix printouts that went into a file drawer more than thirty years ago are back on my desk.) I drove to the Anchorage Public Library and immersed myself in the Alaska Collection's microfilmed newspaper archives and books about early Fairbanks. And I worked the phone to check facts and go beyond my single-source interview. I raked in more answers. Some of them broke my heart.

Irene had lived through growth spurts, booms, and busts of this town, a gold camp that had grown into Alaska's second-largest city, from gold discovery through the military influx of World War II, into the post-War boom, and further to the Trans-Alaska Pipeline construction years, and beyond. She'd been judged for her speech, appearance, morality, or lack of it—and enjoyed for her fun-loving company—but it seemed few had tried to really learn about her. Why had she made certain choices? Which ones were out of her control?

For the most part, I found her forthcoming, a natural-born storyteller, albeit occasionally unreliable, enough to throw doubt into a journalist's best efforts. I researched and traced some of Irene's absent family, drawing from a tangled mess of disordered story fragments Irene herself had offered. Finally, my finished magazine piece was published in Anchorage and again in Fairbanks, in *Heartland*, the Sunday magazine that I'd founded several years earlier.

Far from boilerplate, Irene's profile held shocking, poignant details about nearly eighty hard-lived years. It seemed to satisfy Alaskan readers' insatiable appetite for pioneer stories, but more importantly, laid out facts that blew apart long-held myths about how and when Irene had acquired her physical and mental disabilities. I also named some of the guardian angels who looked after her without fanfare. The profile won awards, and I happily took my moment in the sun, and then went on to the next assignment, and the next.

But Irene lingered in my mind, especially whenever I heard that Fairbanks temps were taking another deep dive. Was she at the Polaris tonight? In 1995, Irene reached the end of her incredibly hard trail, and generations in Fairbanks mourned her absence. Many raised a glass of Olympia beer—Irene's brand—in her honor.

As decades passed, the profile I'd written appeared online in pdf form and later, in the Facebook era, the administrator of a Fairbanks memories group pinned the story to her page. A mere mention of Irene's name would elicit hundreds of comments from those who'd grown up around her. Now they were scattered all over the country, or still in Alaska, ready to share Irene memories that were infused with both fear and respect. At one point, I counted nearly six hundred comments, all from one person's two-word seed post: "Remember Irene?" Inevitably, tales of those burn scars crept into the anecdotes, some diving back into speculation, just like the days when the message was carried and warped by word of mouth instead of electronic messaging. Quickly, the page administrator usually injected a note directing members to read the old *Heartland* story. I realized that somehow I'd become the authority on Irene Sherman. In time, I discovered there was so much more that I didn't know.

※ ※ ※

Irene had been in her grave for twenty-five years on January 3, 2019. Late that evening, I was at home, scrolling through my phone while watching TV, when an email from a stranger popped into my inbox.

"My name is Michelle Moore," the note began. "We got your name from your article on Irene Sherman, aka 'Queen of Fairbanks.' My son and I are doing a little research. We are happy your name was clear on the article. My husband is John Moore. He is the son of Georgerene Sherman . . . Irene Sherman was eleven years older than Georgerene, so she didn't endure that fire, when Irene was four or five. I can tell you Georgerene's adoption story."

Her words revived my memory of talks with Irene and that open-ended sentence: "I think there were seven of us . . ." In 1988, I knew of two siblings who'd died as babies in horrific circumstances, and there was Frances, the one who'd been raised by Wally Burnett's grandmother. This woman was saying there were other siblings that I didn't know about, raised by other people in other places. I hadn't planned to dive back into Irene's story, but the undertow was powerful.

I knew Irene's childhood had been stunted by words and deeds of absentee or negligent adults around her. More than one pioneer had told me that Irene's parents "didn't do right by her." I guess that's how child abuse used to be termed. Some knowledge had been kept from the damaged little girl. And her own powers of recollection were suspect.

Enjoying a cold Oly at RJ's Bar, 1988. (Erik Hill/*Anchorage Daily News*)

She'd glibly retold certain versions of stories so frequently that fact and fiction had merged. (Upon reflection, not too different from your average adult.) But an extra layer of difficulty impaired her. She was saddled with unknown degrees of mental illness that colored her thoughts and memories. Were there seven kids? Was that her memory or what she'd been told? And most of all, what had happened to the others? All I knew now was that that thirty-year-old profile I'd written was incomplete.

"Irene and Georgerene never got to meet," Michelle Moore continued. "My mother-in-law, Georgerene, started really searching for her sister . . . but she was too late. They were so similar. Big coats, used big belts to hold up their clothes, wore wool sweaters, lived like Alaskan survivors, proud to be born in Alaska . . .

"I see that we are too late, too, to find people that knew Irene," she wrote. "There must be a sibling of Georgerene's left, or a child of one of her siblings?? They were long livers. . . ."

I paused here and chuckled. *Too late to find people who knew Irene?* She still possessed a wide fan base among a generation who were now nostalgic grandparents, always ready to share their remembrances of the Queen. Some good encounters; some not so pleasant.

"Well, can we talk soon?" Michelle wrote. "You will be amazed when you see Georgerene's photo. Even more amazed when you learn of how she lived."

My brain was supercharged. It was late or I'd have called Michelle Moore immediately. But I needed to find my old notes and prepare for such a conversation, so I decided to wait. I slept poorly. The next morning, I dug out those green-striped dot matrix printouts of interviews and notes from 1988. Once again, I studied photos that Erik Hill had taken of Irene and her junkyard castle. Her expression was inscrutable. And then I called Michelle. My phone in one hand, with the other I rustled up a used notebook and started scribbling on its few empty pages as she talked.

Michelle was warm and curious, asking what Alaska was like and interested in all that her late mother-in-law Georgerene had missed because she'd left as a child. At what age, Michelle didn't know exactly. Just that the girl's birth parents, Agnes and James Paul Sherman, had named her Pauline Agnes. It had been changed at adoption. Georgerene knew nothing about Irene until later in life, when she was a grandmother herself, and deeply disappointed that they'd never connected. Now they were both gone.

Michelle told me there were other siblings, too, other children who either died in their mother's care or were adopted out. I could check off a couple of those names, but there were other blanks. Still, what I knew so far was profoundly sad.

That afternoon I headed to the library with a plan to begin by building out Irene's family tree. I needed a sense of the landscape.

Within a week, I'd unearthed family details that John and Michelle never knew. We began exchanging photos. There was another story here. A second magazine piece? A book? Something more, anyway. I decided to apply to Alaska's Rasmuson Foundation for a fellowship to help support my research and writing. To my joy I received the grant, giving me the freedom to widen my search, allowing me to fly to Idaho, to meet Irene's long-lost nephew and his wife in person, and to examine Georgerene's photos and papers. Later, I flew to Juneau and dug in the Alaska State Archives, all the while exchanging emails and texts with the Moores. What I'd found; what they'd found. As we crossed off each question, two more arose.

※ ※ ※

With some effort, I finally tracked down Linden Staciokas, Irene's last court-appointed conservator. In the early 1990s, she was charged to make decisions for Irene when she could no longer care for herself. A long-time Fairbanksan, Linden had witnessed Irene's wanderings about town and how locals had interacted with her through the years. I wondered if she could cast light on questions that eluded me, like *Why would a whole town celebrate a somewhat deranged bag lady? Why were they honored if she showed up at their garage sale? Why would a reporter ask how she was voting in an upcoming election? And did her story matter today?*

Did any of this matter, beyond the fact that Irene had been a living curiosity in one of America's rarest places?

Linden and I traded stories about ways Irene had been present in each of our lives. She reiterated that although she was fond of the old woman, she really couldn't be called a friend. The truth was, the court had pulled Linden's name from a pool of potential conservators, so it was merely her job to look after Irene's affairs during her last years. After learning that I was researching the Queen for a book, Linden had sent a message that to me rang with truth:

"I am glad Irene will get another presentation to the public," she wrote. "I have always felt that she was dehumanized by people, like some pitiable icon of Old Tyme Fairbanks. She was not pathetic. She had agency and managed to carve out a life after a hard start and in a harsh climate. She could be bawdy or prim, nasty or kind, truthful or full of exaggerations, if it would buy her a drink."

Was Linden right? Was Irene more icon than an ordinary woman with flaws? Had the people of Fairbanks helped seal that image of a rootin'-tootin' Last Frontier gold-miner gal? I guessed the answer depended on whom you asked.

At Golden Days celebrations, Irene proudly presented herself as an enduring piece of history, carrying the mantle of the pioneer generation. That was her public face. People pointed her out to their visiting relatives as "our" bag lady. Took pictures with her. The press covered a bridge opening as Irene cut the ribbon shoulder-to-shoulder with the governor. Most birthdays, she posed with her baker friend, Peggy Goldizen, and a sheet cake donated by Market Basket.

But for many others, she was just another neighbor lady. As a girl, Kristine Castillo liked to fish the Chena River near her Graehl home, and Irene often joined her just to watch and chat. In winter months, Kristine walked by Irene's junk-filled home going to and from school.

"She was a great person," Kristine recalled in a social media thread about Irene. "One time stands out, when my sister didn't want to go to school." It was twenty below zero, Kristine wrote, and her little sister, a first-grader, had been zipped into an orange, one-piece jumpsuit parka for the walk to school. But this morning, she stopped and broke into tears right in front of Irene's place. The child threw herself down in the empty street, a sobbing, orange blob. "She wailed," Kristine recalled.

And then . . . "Irene came out and said that I was a good big sister, and I needed to take my baby sister home because she 'needed more night-night.'" With the kind neighbor-lady's advice, the older sister collected the younger, and they walked back home.

※ ※ ※

Irene's final conservator was in a position to cast back over the decades and assess Irene's lifeline. Linden Staciokas asserted and I agreed on one important point: Irene's freedom to live as she did could not have happened in any other place or time. In this isolated city at the center of an isolated state, an island within the "island" of Alaska, the population looked out for her, while not imposing so-called protections that would have removed her freedoms.

Outside of Fairbanks, Alaska, Irene likely would have been institutionalized early on, rather than enjoyed. So proud of its transient pioneer roots, Fairbanks offered a true live-and-let-live atmosphere, lending authenticity to the beloved bumper stickers: "We don't give a damn how they do it Outside."

For Irene, it was the code she lived by.

In an image titled "Sluicing a winter dump," two men use muscle and high-powered water to shovel and wash away overburden into sluice boxes that will sort the gold from other material. A sluice box angles away from their work on each side. In winter, miners accumulated a mountain of soil and rock, waiting to process it when the rivers were running again. (Archives, University of Alaska Fairbanks, Albert J. Johnson Collection, UAF-1989-166-6)

CHAPTER 4
WHY HERE? - A Bend on the Chena River, 1901
He hurriedly spread some advantageous lies about
how much gold could be found.

Felice Pedroni had come all the way from Italy to Alaska and Yukon Territory to dig for gold and get rich. Muscular, compact, and richly mustachioed, Pedroni was known among his fellow miners as Felix Pedro. He'd worked the 1892 gold rush based in Circle City, Alaska, on the Yukon River, and then joined the Klondike stampede before returning to Circle and widening his prospects to other creeks in the Tanana Valley. As the nineteenth century turned to the twentieth, Pedro found a wealth of color in one outlying creek, but upon his return, he was unable to find that choice spot again.

Felix Pedro is credited with the gold discovery that started the stampede to Fairbanks. (Archives, University of Alaska, UAF-1966-9-7)

Fairbanks historian Terrence Cole told the story in his 1991 book, *Crooked Past: The History of a Frontier Mining Camp.* In late August 1901, Pedro and his partner, Tom Gilmore, prospected other creeks as they searched for their lost creek. Pedro couldn't find it, but he and Gilmore liked what they did find. The partners were low on supplies when, providentially, they spotted the smoky discharge of a paddle wheeler nearly twenty miles away on a bend in the Chena River.

On board, entrepreneur E. T. Barnette had failed in his attempt to bully the captain into pressing further upriver. Captain Adams insisted it was too shallow, and pointed to their contract. He wouldn't risk his craft. The dispute ended when Adams directed his crew to help move Barnette's goods to the riverbank—at the edge of raw wilderness—and

By late 1906, Fairbanks had been built up, and then much of it burned. The town was rebuilt by the time this photo was made on August 22, 1907.

assist with throwing up a few structures for a trading post and shelter. Here then would be the site of a settlement that Barnette briefly called "Chenoa [Chena] City."

Pedro and Gilmore became Barnette's first customers, replenishing their supplies while speaking conservatively about their work on the nearby creeks. But they'd lit a fire in Barnette. He hurriedly spread some advantageous lies about how much gold could be found. (I could almost hear my father: *Come on up! There's gold nuggets lying all over the place!*) With that, the ever-mobile, ever-hopeful band of sourdoughs who advanced from strike to strike—Circle City, Rampart, the Klondike, Nome—poured in. Another river settlement a few miles downriver ultimately claimed the name "Chena," while Barnette (and his friend Judge James Wickersham) found advantage in renaming this place for an Indiana politician.

(Archives, University of Alaska Fairbanks, UAF-1958-1026-02047)

Harry Badger, one of the early stampeders who came in from the Klondike, remembered it took him and a partner thirty-three days to drive their dog teams from Dawson, following the frozen Yukon River to the Goodpaster, the Tanana, and finally to the Chena. Interviewed by Al Bramstedt of KFAR radio in 1974, Badger remembered when they arrived, food was "very, very scarce."

"Captain Barnette had some food—had a lot of flour among other things, and that's one thing we were all short of. And he offered to sell that at $5 a sack, provided we'd buy a $75 outfit. In that $75 outfit we were required to take three cases of canned vegetables consisting of cabbage and beets and some other thing that was mostly water; it wasn't fit for food, any of it. . .

"So we called a 'miners meeting,'" said Badger. "We had no marshals, and we had no soldiers, we had no lawyers. Nothing else excepting the 'miners' meeting' was the law of the land; whatever (we) they said, went. So we served notice on old 'Cap.'" Badger recounted that the miners demanded Barnette "turn that flour loose," or they would simply take it. The very next morning, flyers appeared advising that flour was available at five dollars per sack.

"There was an immediate line formed on Front Street that walked in one end of the store and out the other with each man with a sack of flour on his back," Badger remembered, "until his stock was pretty well depleted."

The hopeful, inexperienced miners, the *cheechakos*, were learning on the job, but many new arrivals were knowledgeable, able-bodied sourdoughs like Badger and his partner, who'd streamed in from the Klondike and other gold camps.

Meanwhile, tramping in from the south with others, Irene's father, J. P. Sherman, was fresh off the trail from Valdez. As it turned out, Barnette's grandiose words about the golden ground around his town were inadvertently truthful. There really was abundance in the region. Felix Pedro and Tom Gilmore found their paystreaks, as did others in their wake. But not all. Some gave up early, like one Swede named John Nelson. By 1902, Nelson was among the stampeders who decided to up and leave Fairbanks about a minute before the boom-town really took off. The why is unknown, but someone later wrote that he'd gone south to become "a resident of the Outside." The term "Outside" was commonly used then, and still is, for anywhere beyond Alaska, but mostly pointing to the continental United States.

Twelve years passed until 1914, when John Nelson returned by steamship to Valdez on the Gulf of Alaska. Then, extraordinarily, Nelson mushed three Great Danes on the well-established 365-mile Valdez Trail to Fairbanks, a route that one day would be paved and formally named the Richardson Highway. As new pioneers in a 1978 Chevrolet Blazer, our drive from the Alaska border to Fairbanks had covered a hundred miles of the Richardson.

When Nelson last stood here, E. T. Barnette's log cabin trading post and outbuildings had been among few structures and the only store. Since then, the Northern Commercial Company had purchased Barnette's

One of the earliest photos of E. T. Barnette's trading post is dated April 1903. Without proof, Barnette boasted about the gold to be found near his post, and Fairbanks exploded in population. (Alaska State Library, Wickersham State Historic Sites Photo Collection, P277-011-003)

business and held a strong presence on the riverfront as well as in the local economy. What is now Alaska's largest community, Anchorage, wasn't yet on the map—it would come to life as "Ship Creek" in 1915, just a tent camp along the anticipated U.S. government railroad route.

Coming off the trail in December 1914, Nelson paused his dog team on Cushman Street, stepped off his sled runners and approached a stranger. "Where can a man find quarters for his dogs?" he asked, and took directions to a nearby hotel. Most of the hostelries could now lodge visitors in comfortable rooms, even with heat and running water, and stable their dog teams or horses in a barn or a basement.

By the time Fairbanks town was a teenager, its people were buying tailored clothing in modern stores, spending at bakeries and restaurants, bars and clubs, and enjoying running water and telegraph-telephone services. At least a couple of times a week, one or two of a dozen fraternal orders hosted a dance with Victor Durand's four-piece orchestra, or a ladies' group gathered for tea and charity work.

Entertainments such as roller skating, ice skating, curling, shooting, parades, and children's events were sprinkled throughout the calendar, along with plays and formal-dress balls. Men dropped by the row of tiny cabins behind discreet fencing off Fourth Avenue, where the so-called "good-time girls" did business. Newspaper reports kept all up to date on who was visiting in town, which hotel they'd checked into, and who was leaving by trail or steamer.

Before heading for his hotel, John Nelson turned back to the friendly stranger on Cushman Street. "I stampeded to this country twelve years ago, before the name Fairbanks was even thought of," he said. "A fellow feels a little lost when he arrives in a town which stands on a site which was all wilderness the last time he saw it."

Then he went on his way.

※ ※ ※

Irene Mary Sherman was born in Fairbanks only because her migratory European ancestors had first moved to Canada in the previous century. They'd come from France, Germany, England and Scotland, traveling by wagon, ship, and railway, and pausing in separate journeys that to me required an unimaginable level of courage and stamina. Decades before I first watched Irene pedaling down Second Avenue during Golden Days, her father, maternal grandparents, and one set of great-grandparents had separately entered the United States from English-speaking Ontario and French-speaking Quebec. Did they have a plan, or was this possibility born of inspiration, hope, and little more? My mobile father and his brothers came to mind. My own journey, too.

I'd become somewhat obsessive about studying my own ancestry in 1997, when by coincidence, two oversized envelopes arrived in the mail within two weeks of each other. One from Illinois; one from Indiana. Unknown to each other, a cousin from each side of my family mailed me the results of her own genealogical inquires, an introduction to my place in a tree that was ever-widening above me, a canopy that was fascinating, especially coming from ignorance as I had. With so many

In 1910, the first federal census for Fairbanks included John and Minnie Patten and her two Eckert children, followed by a long list of Third Avenue Hotel lodgers, including J. P. Sherman Jr. (U.S. Census Bureau)

early deaths and divorces in my ancestry, I had emerged with few touchstones to the past. I didn't even know my maternal grandmother's first name.

So it was only natural that I created a map to see how Irene fit in her own family tree, beyond what she'd told me. Toward the end of her life, she seemed to be on her own, with only far-away Frances, who didn't seem that warm to her birth sister. *Who had raised Irene and what had happened to them? How many siblings were there, really?*

Through birth and death documents, letters, records, and oral histories of other pioneers, I expanded my knowledge, but there was the matter of Irene's own memories. In other press interviews through the years, she'd never mentioned that her grandmother was one of the earliest settlers in Fairbanks, coming north in 1905 with two teenaged children. Or that her gold miner father had arrived earlier still.

As pro-Fairbanks as she was, I couldn't imagine why she wouldn't have brought that up, but she *had* memorized something of her own ancestry and stood ready to recite it.

I noticed that if a question touched painful or uncertain areas, Irene handily deflected what she didn't know or didn't want to talk about, whipping out standard phrases to cover a multitude of answers, *What happened to your father? Did your parents get along? And where was your mother then?* Instead, she answered in rat-a-tat form: "Well, Dad was Irish-wooden-shoe-Holland-Dutch and English, and my mother was German-French Canadian and Scotch. And ye god, I'm scrambled 'til hell won't have it. And then I'm Alaskan-born on top of it. . ."

More than once, she rattled off that speech. More than once, she ended with, "I'm pretty well-satisfied . . ."

Knowing a fraction of what she'd lived through and how she now lived, I found that hard to believe.

※ ※ ※

The 1910 federal census, the first-ever census for Fairbanks, was taken less than a year before Irene's birth. Its pages told stories of the town's immigrant population. It also lent clues as to how Irene's parents crossed paths here and married shortly after that census was taken.

I find census records fascinating because they're so much more than lists of names, details about the people building a community's society and economy. Deciphering its shorthand in columns, you learn where individuals were born, where their parents were born, who else lives with them, and if and how they're related. The census lists their occupations, ages, marital status, and race (a column which in 1910 Fairbanks was nearly filled with Ws for white). Seemingly invisible to the census takers in 1910 were the Athabascans, the first people. More likely they just preferred to *not* live among the newcomers, still seminomadic within their homeland. Once or twice, I saw "Ath" or "Ind" for an Alaska Native, or "Jap" written for a Japanese family.

So many foreign-born people lived in 1910 Fairbanks that on paper neighborhoods looked like the United Nations: Sweden, Ireland, Poland, Germany, Holland, Scotland, Norway, Japan, French-speaking Canada and English-speaking Canada. More than half of the states were represented. No surprise, but in the "Occupation" cells of the census, I found a preponderance of "miner" with the occasional note about whether a married miner was alone. There was that word "Outside" again: "Wife Outside" or "wife in Oregon."

Irene's Quebec-born grandmother, Mina "Minnie" Jenott Eckert, and her grandfather, Frederick Henry Eckert of Ontario, Canada, had migrated south through Michigan and Wisconsin, and later west to Seattle as part of an extensive band of family members from each side—Eckert and Jenott—who shared housing and supported each other.

Both families had traveled thousands of miles to get there. And what timing! To be swept into the Klondike Gold Rush by sheer

In spring 1905, the year Irene's grandmother arrived, a devastating flood struck Fairbanks. An observer wrote that the Chena "took out the bridges, cut away the banks, and did serious damage to all the property around." One man poling, this party drifted past downtown businesses. (Alaska State Library, Wickersham State Historic Sites Photo Collection, P277-011-026)

coincidence. When a shipload of Klondike gold sailed into Seattle on July 17, 1897, a few Jenott and Eckert men jumped onto northbound ships headed for the American port of Skagway, ready to take the Chilkoot Pass to the Klondike. Several of Irene's first cousins were later born in Skagway; an uncle was sheriff for a while.

Of the many thousands who joined the Klondike Gold Rush, only a rare few were lucky enough to get rich and return Outside to live well on their gold haul. One of Minnie's brothers, Joseph Jenott, was a lucky one. He bought homes and property in the Seattle area for himself and other family, then later traveled and saw the world. Others, like Irene's grand-mère Minnie, would look for riches in the surge of business in an Alaska boomtown. Mining the pockets of the miners.

The 1910 census stated that Minnie and John Patten had married two years earlier and were proprietors of the Third Avenue Hotel.

A string of names—family and lodgers—followed. The record showed Minnie had given birth to six children; five were still living. Two were with her, and three were in the "States." Minnie's father was born in France; her mother in Scotland. Having grown up in Quebec, her first language was French, and her English was heavily accented.

Minnie had come from the other side of the continent to reach this unique spot on the American frontier, so unlike her own culture as to be otherworldly. Born in 1869 Ottawa, a historically Francophile province, she was christened Mina Elizabeth LaChappelle dit Jenott. Her parents were Francis "Frank" LaChappelle dit Jenott and Jeannette "Jennie" Frances Giroux. According to the French naming convention, Minnie and her siblings all possessed the middle name of "LaChappelle." By 1884, the elder Jenotts and some of their children set out for the U.S., pausing for a time in East Saginaw, Michigan. There, when Minnie was only fifteen, she married Frederick H. Eckert, twenty-four, a lumberman now based in northern Wisconsin. A first-generation Canadian from Chelsey, Ontario, Fred did not intend to grow old there.

I traced the newlyweds' westward migration by the birthplaces of their children, among them Irene's mother, Agnes, who was born in Hayward, Wisconsin, in 1889. By the time Minnie was twenty-one in 1892, she had delivered five children, now ages seven, five, four, three, and two. Next, Fred and Minnie pushed westward to Seattle, where they welcomed their last child, Bessie Mae, in 1895.

As 1899 turned to 1900, the Eckert house at 2611 Elliott Avenue, Seattle, was filled with a passel of English-speaking Eckerts— Fred, Minnie, and their six children—plus Minnie's parents, Jeannette and Frank Jenott. The elders had immigrated in 1898 and 1899, one before the other. It's hard to imagine the kind of journey they had experienced, each traveling with an adult son or daughter. Had Jennie and Frank Jenott come around the Horn by ship like their eldest son had? Or did they cross the continent to reach Seattle via railway like some others? Either way, it was a monumental decision and task. No comparison to my cry-baby stop-and-start trip up the Alaska Highway.

In 1904, Minnie and Fred buried their seventeen-year-old

daughter (also named Minnie) in a Tacoma, Washington, cemetery, and then divorced. Afterward, Minnie made her big move to Fairbanks, bringing along Agnes and Clarence. Her youngest, Bessie, stayed behind, presumably with her father or Jenott relatives. The two eldest Eckert children were grown and gone. Another son had run away from home as a boy and taken to the high seas, rarely to be heard from again.

Minnie and Fred's divorce and all the events that had led to it had all but destroyed the Eckert family. The Jenotts' family ties seemed stronger. Minnie's eldest brother, Joseph, had gotten wealthy on Yukon gold. Back in Seattle, he filled his immense house with relatives: daughters, sisters and their husbands, a bachelor brother, an Eckert niece, mother Jennie, and even an extra roomer. Caring for family was a powerful Jenott tradition, so fresh from the "old country" and unwavering in Minnie's generation. In the next generation, while the use of the surname "LaChapelle dit Jenott" dissolved, first names were carried forward in their American babies: Frances, Jeanette, Irene, Agnes, Elizabeth, Frederick, Joseph, and John Joseph.

While Irene Sherman would claim Alaska as her forever home, seemingly a solo act, there were aunts, uncles, and cousins on both sides, many Alaska-born, who settled in Washington, Oregon, and California. So did several of Irene's great-aunts and uncles. However, by the late 1960s, with the death of Irene's father, she alone held down the fort in Fairbanks. Other blood relatives were in their graves or absent.

It grieved me to learn that Irene and several siblings were never cherished as an innocents, something we wish for every child. As Minnie looked on and wrung her hands, the children of her daughter Agnes—those who survived infancy—endured terrible hardship in the care of an abusive father and an addicted mother with untreated mental illness. Then I made a discovery that offered insight into enduring bonds within the Jenott family: Two of Minnie's sisters, both of them childless and living Outside, would step in as essential supporters—rescuers, really—in a family safety net that kept its secrets. If not for their sacrifices through the years, the great suffering of Agnes Sherman's unfortunate children would have been greater still.

CHAPTER 5
INSANE COLD AND TEMPORARY INSANITY
Fairbanks 1979

'Inside, Outside, or Morningside.'

In Fairbanks, I discovered that Mother Nature wanted to kill me. What happens at forty-five degrees below zero is this: the flesh of bare fingers is easily "burned" or even detaches when you touch a metal handle, doorknob, or key. Walking outdoors, your sinus cavity at eyebrow level becomes the epicenter of a monumental headache, as if a 16-penny nail had been driven into your skull. Oil thickens (and so does blood, it seems) into sludge, and bearings (likewise human joints) resist movement. Burning lungs resist expansion. Rubber seals and faux leather becomes brittle and can shatter. The tires of cars parked outdoors acquire a flat spot on the bottom, so if and when the car rolls forward, it takes a few minutes of great bumping around—like driving Fred Flintstone's car —before the friction heats and rounds out the tires again. A cup of

Student parking on the University of Alaska Fairbanks campus, winter of 1979-80. Each outlet required a working fuse; students were strongly urged to carry extras, along with an extension cord. (Tricia Brown)

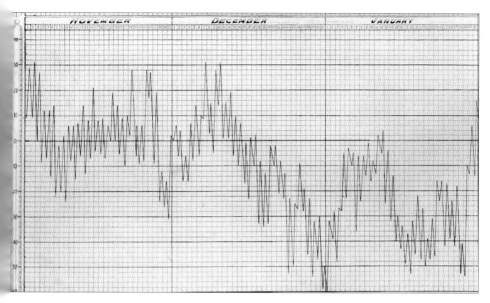

Temperature charts maintained by the Red Cross Drug Store recorded a low of -60°F on January 1, 1913, and it dipped into the -50° range again before the end of the month. (Archives, University of Alaska Fairbanks, Albert J. Johnson Collection, UAF-1989-0155-00447)

boiling water, flung into the forty-below air, instantly transforms into crackling ice crystals with a gentle, sparkling *whoosh*.

Twenty, thirty, or even forty degrees below zero does not stop Alaskans from layering up and going about their business. There are jobs and day care and church. Got to get groceries and gas and go to appointments and club meetings. Recess for the kids is still outside unless it's twenty below or colder. The joggers jog, walkers walk, and the city promotes bus rides or car-pooling to reduce exhaust particulates in the stagnant air. Cold does not stop animals from hunting for prey, peeing in the snow, or tiptoeing around a set laid by a trapper. And below-zero temperatures do not prevent a fire from burning. It only hampers those trying to put it out as flowing water turns to layers of glacial ice in minutes, transforming a smoldering building into a fairy castle with a true, but tragic story. Exposed flesh around rescuers' eyes is reddened, and beards, eyebrows, and eyelashes are coated with rime from exhalation.

Not once during my first winter did I ever wonder where Irene Sherman was sleeping at night. I only cared that my oil pan heater was functioning correctly, or my vehicle would become a piece of large, frozen yard art.

I'd heard about "cabin fever," the unpredictable behavior that crops up in humans forced to live in confined spaces, as in during a long, very cold winter. In the early days, old mining partners, once friends, had been known to tip over and attempt murder or suicide, sometimes succeeding. Others who crossed an undetectable line went out in the snow in their long johns and froze to death. A missing man might not be found until spring, dug out of a snow drift without hat or gloves, frozen in a position as if he were floating in unseen water.

I learned a new phrase that had its roots in early territorial days, and it was directly tied to the mental health challenges that everybody faced, sourdoughs and cheechakos alike. If a person hadn't been seen for an extended period, there were only three places to look: "Inside, Outside, or Morningside." It was the shorthand version of saying they're still here, inside the territory. Or they're Outside, not in Alaska. Or they've been committed to Morningside Hospital for the Insane, an institution in Portland, Oregon, that was the landing place for many a suffering Alaskan. Later, someone added a fourth word to the old saying: Inside, Outside, Morningside, or Suicide.

A trip to Morningside required identifying and arresting a person as possibly insane, jailing them (often with the real criminals) for an indeterminate amount of time, during which one's sanity would be questioned before a panel of jurors. If found "really and truly insane," the guilty party would be transported to Morningside with a paid travel companion. Names of the accused routinely appeared in newspapers Was the person really and truly insane? What constituted grounds for admission could well have been alcoholism, epilepsy, depression, brain injury, delayed cognitive development, birth defects, or simply aberrant behavior.

In 1904, Fairbanks had a wood-frame jail and courthouse, which was dedicated in a July 4 speech by federal Judge James Wickersham. There was little else around it in the archival photo I examined. The structure burned later and replaced by a poorly constructed substitute.

In 1915, the judge expressed his criticism of how insanity suspects were jailed there, in particular the women. He wrote the U.S. attorney general that January 6: "In this stinking hole the United States of America keeps the insane women who fall into their clutches at Fairbanks, Alaska. . . . Some innocent woman who becomes insane is arrested as if she were guilty of a crime and chucked into one of these dirty holes over this old rotten foul-smelling jail filled with the stench and curses of prisoners and kept there for months at a time."

While the practice of jailing insanity suspects did not cease— Irene would experience that firsthand one day—the "rotten, foul-smelling jail" was finally replaced in 1932 with a solid concrete structure that rose up on the same site as the one that Wickersham had dedicated in 1904, now with multiple levels housing federal and territorial offices, courtrooms, jail, and the post office. The grand art-deco style "federal building," as it was known, faced Cushman Street between Second and Third Avenues.

In 1913, in a move to save the federal government some money, U.S. Secretary of the Interior Franklin K. Lane asked Alaska's attorney general to change how "insane persons in the territory" were examined. The new idea involved deportment. "It is requested that the nativity of the insanity suspect be determined here, in order that deportment may be made from here direct to the person's native country, thus saving the government from a great deal of unnecessary expense." The district attorney's office had been advised that Morningside asylum in Oregon, which held the government contract for Alaska's insane, had ninety-five foreign-born inmates.

In those early territorial days, those arrested for insanity, if not jailed with criminals, might dally in a government-funded "detention hospital" as they waited for their trip to Morningside. In hindsight, we know that some of those who were arrested may have been insane in that they were a danger to others or themselves. Perhaps they lacked the ability to perceive and function in society-approved ways. Just as often, those sufferers were wrestling with temporary, situational mental health challenges, like circumstantial struggles, postpartum depression, or seasonal affective disorder. Or, in the case of Irene Sherman's mother, Agnes, a lethal combination of several.

※ ※ ※

I'd heard that many of society's runaways and independents pointed north because Fairbanks was an end of the road, a place where they might outdistance Uncle Sam's reach. Bucking the government. And that's the irony: Look at a map and you'll see a jigsaw puzzle of state and national parks, refuges, and reserves that nearly covers Alaska. Subtract the Native lands, too, and that leaves a puny 3.9 percent of the state's total acreage in private ownership. And, more than 25 percent of all employed Alaskans work for the government—the highest percentage per capita among all states.

From the climate to the landscape, wildlife, seasons, and people— everything around me was new, wondrous, and challenging. (Lynette Clark Collection)

This is a place where extremes are normal: extreme cold, extreme beauty, extreme daylight, extreme opinions. Then we become extremely Alaskan. I'd never heard of another state where everyday people knew the words to their state "Flag Song." Here, if you begin with, "Eight stars of gold . . ." someone nearby will reply ". . . on a field of blue." They might even sing it. Those of us who come up become something of cartoons to those we left Outside. Stories about us are overblown at both ends of the Alaska Highway that wends through Canada. The AlCan, as the route is still called by some, remains the primary way to reach Alaska by road. After a while up here, we tend to forget where we came from, and we start believing the Last Frontier hyperbole ourselves. Rough, tough, wild and rugged. Different. On the other hand, a lot of the time, it's the truth. We also learn that individualism has a price.

To me, Fairbanks remained a wilderness in July of 1978, even though early on we'd partaken of the McDonald's on Airport Way. There was the Gavora Mall, a much-admired strip of adjoined stores, but the newest wonder was the Bentley Mall, the town's first *enclosed* one-story shopping experience. Every car and truck had a stub of an electrical cord sticking out of its grille to plug in when it was below zero, to warm thickening oil in the engine block; the auto grilles often were covered with aluminum foil or a scrap of cardboard wired into place. Helps the car warm up faster, I was advised. I saw rows of stunted power poles at the heads of parking places, ready for drivers to plug in. Lengthy power cords hung in loops from side mirrors, like a cowboy's ready lasso. So many bearded, flannelled, booted men! So many capable, braless, forward-looking women! "How long have you been here?" was routinely asked of me. My short-timer answer did not elevate me in their eyes.

Early in my makeover as an Alaskan, my father drove me through a couple of miles of undeveloped land on a road that linked the newer part of town with the downtown core. This stretch was still a blank canvas, undeveloped. Just scrub black spruce on each side, their roots struggling to gain purchase in the ice-riddled soil. And once more, I wondered about the possibility of wild animals lurking. I was primed with fear thanks to those letters from Dad (*family dog killed at the edge of town*). And there were my sister's stories of her escaped pet surely being eaten after an AlCan roadside pee stop in the Yukon. Cat was probably dead before she pulled up her pants. It wasn't that I expected a bear to jump me any minute. It's just that I thought, yeah, it could.

I couldn't stretch my imagination far enough to picture what this place was like when the first white stampeders began arriving in earnest. How brash yet clearly stupid and misdirected they must have appeared to the Native Alaskans of this region, the Athabascans, masters of staying alive, even thriving, in this place of extremes. I learned that the traditional Athabascan homeland stretched across many thousands of acres inside Alaska and into Canada, covering more ground than any other Native tribal lands, from ancient times to today. These first Alaskans were not inclined to settle in communities in the western way, but moved in groups as need demanded, returning seasonally to fruitful spots. Taking care not to overdraw their resources at hunting camps, fish camps, trapline camps, the people followed lifelong patterns. Traditional knowledge and experience told them how and when to hunt, fish, and trap. The values of sharing, respect, and self-identity, the art, dance, and survival skills, they taught their children, handed down generationally for thousands of years.

If they were smart, the newcomers learned survival techniques from the Alaska Natives. For Natives, the gold rush here, as it was in the Klondike, was nothing more than an invasion, theft of resources, racist domination, interference with cultural norms, and ignorance of the first peoples' connection to their homeland. While virtually all of the non-Natives had come from another place, the Natives ably lived on land that their ancestors had walked since prehistory. The depth of that connection and the ancient knowledge that went with it was inconceivable to anyone except a Native.

※ ※ ※

I'd grown up in the Midwest, so I knew cold from standing in a skirt at a school bus stop, while prairie winds lashed my red thighs. But I'd never imagined this kind of cold. More dreadful that first Fairbanks winter was the chill that struck my very wellbeing. Our apartment was a "daylight basement," so we lived subsurface with narrow windows near the top of each wall. And those were nearly obscured by snowbanks.

Worse still was the bitter cold and waning light. We stopped going to church. It was too much work to corral the toddlers, bundle them up, and get the truck started and warmed, always in the dark. So we went to work and stayed home, rearranging the antennae on our little portable black-and-white TV, largely isolated and hardly missed. I watched as glorious daylight was sucked away in five-minute chunks, then two minutes, then seconds, day by day, leaving us with three hours and change, just a sliver of gloomy light, by winter solstice. We juggled debts, missed payments, worked while broke, and we shared a single vehicle to take our toddlers to day care, then me to work, then him to work. And play it all in reverse in the late afternoon. All in the dark.

If I didn't look out the single window in my shared office between about eleven in the morning and two in the afternoon, I'd miss an opportunity to see the sun hovering above the horizon. The yellow ball did not blast light into the room, did not produce heat, and never tracked overhead. It lazily lifted above the jagged edge of the distant mountains and bumped above the line before listlessly ducking out of sight. With it went my fruitfulness, my tenderness, my care for others, my own self-care. This was SAD, or Seasonal Affective Disorder, a problem so common it had an acronym, but so new to me that I thought I was the only sufferer. Coworkers told me that after winter solstice on December 21, things would be better. We'd be gaining daylight, little by little. "You've gotten through the worst of it!" they chirped.

Then came a rare February, weeks of forty-below temperatures coupled with "ice fog." The dense fog was comprised of ice crystals and unhealthy particles suspended in dead air, much of it expelled by cars and woodstoves. It covered the entire town and made it impossible for a driver to see more than a foot in front of the headlights. Traffic crawled. For people with dicey lungs, the ice fog that nestled into the geographic "bowl" that was Fairbanks was a health hazard, more toxic than Los Angeles smog at its worst. The inversion of cold air in low spaces, with slightly warmer air above it, would change the way I thought about where I lived. If you drove to the surrounding hills after midday, you could be in the sun, looking down at that fluffy blanket of foul air obscuring the town. What was I doing down here in this toxic soup?

The sun did return in my first spring, and it dazzled during the glorious days and nights around summer solstice that June. I looked up and wondered again about the people who'd come before me, who had managed and who had not. In the years to come, I learned that if I stayed focused, creative, purposeful, I could ride out the brutality of the climate and the stretches of weather-related sadness. Yes, I sagged. But like that yellow ball that always came back, so did hope.

Noting the incremental loss of sunlight each day after experiencing the longest day of year is still disheartening after all these years. (Tricia Brown)

CHAPTER 6
THE WISCONSIN FARM BOY - Fairbanks 1903

No, no, I don't want to marry you!

In 1900, James Paul Sherman Jr. was twenty-one years old and ready to strike out on his own. He'd left the family farm in Kilbourn, Wisconsin, and was selling boots and shoes in Evanston, Illinois, while briefly boarding with a teenaged cousin and elderly aunts. How and when he responded to the call to the Far North, I don't know—his daughter Irene believed it was about 1900—but he came in through Valdez on the Gulf of Alaska. There he stayed for a while and "learned the ropes," she said, before he eventually made his way to the Interior, that enormous geographic basin between the Brooks Range in the north and the Alaska Range in the south.

J. P. was among the earliest to land in Fairbanks, as early as 1903. Even the name "Fairbanks" was new that year, following a political maneuver by founder E. T. Barnette and Judge James Wickersham to gain the favor of U.S. Senator Charles Fairbanks. The Indiana senator was about to share a ticket with Theodore Roosevelt and eventually would serve as vice president from 1905 to 1908. Charles Fairbanks would never step foot in his namesake town, but from the first day he arrived, J. P. was anchored.

Fairbanks was just a baby boomtown when J. P. made it his jumping-off place to investigate mining and trapping opportunities in outlying areas. He wasn't a large man—medium build, medium height, with brown eyes and light brown hair—but he was tough. He loved roughing it, living the cabin life, running dogs, eating what he hunted and fished, reading the land for evidence of gold-bearing soils, and reading tracks in the snow as he decided where to lay his traps. He was free, an ambitious bachelor with nothing to tie him down.

These were prosperous years for Fairbanks, when the population swelled with gold output exponentially. In 1903, some three hundred inhabitants brought in $30,000 in gold; a year later, three thousand people lived in town and the outlying creeks during mining season, and the output was $350,000.

Photographer Albert J. Johnson captured the first minutes of the fire that destroyed much of downtown Fairbanks in 1906. (Archives, University of Alaska Fairbanks, UAF-1989-166-255)

By 1909, the population was holding steady at twelve thousand residents, and gold production had reached $10.5 million. Celebrating the tenth anniversary of the camp, the *Fairbanks Sunday Times* printed an "Industrial Edition" that boasted, "Where else has a handful of penniless pioneers, with nothing but grit for capital and a remote and isolated wilderness as a field of operation, within so short a time brought into existence from nothingness an annual export trade of more than $10,000,000 and an import trade of $3,000,000?"

Fairbanks had survived floods and occasional fires and had rebuilt with vigor, yet disaster would continue to strike, crushing but not breaking its citizens. In 1906, nearly the entire business district was destroyed in a fire that, for decades to come, was considered the worst in Fairbanks history. The boilers of the Northern Commercial Company provided steam to power the fire hoses, but firemen ran out of wood in the midst of the catastrophe. When the pressure began to fade, the N.C. Company store manager ordered a ton of bacon thrown into the boiler fires, reviving the power and ultimately saving the town. Over on Cushman, on the block south of the courthouse, the Third Avenue Hotel hunkered between Third and Fourth Avenues in an area that was spared. Hotel owner John Patten was grateful. The ashes of downtown had barely cooled when friends and competing businesses pooled their resources and manpower, and the sound of the saw and hammer rang again for weeks. Temporary quarters in tents predominated for sawmills, bars, and restaurants. A developing fire department sprouted from all-volunteer to both paid and volunteer crews, and the city purchased more sophisticated equipment.

A few years after the town was rebuilt, the *Fairbanks Times* supplement of April 3, 1910, bragged about their growth. In a piece titled *An Empire Out of Wilderness*, the writer advanced, "In less than a decade, a few thousand pioneers have converted the haunts of the wild beast into a factory of wealth."

Like most miners from outlying creeks, when J. P. came into town on business, he roomed at a local hotel. He was lodging at Third Avenue Hotel in 1910, when that first census was taken, listed among twenty-three male lodgers, two servants, and a hotel clerk. Owners John and Minnie Patten also were living on site with her children, Agnes, now twenty years old, and Clarence, nineteen. Youngest daughter Bessie was on her way.

There at the Third Avenue Hotel, J. P. Sherman met Agnes Eckert, a crossing of paths that descendants generations later would examine with great interest, principally asking "What if?" and considering various other outcomes.

J. P., as he preferred over James Paul, was a junior. His father, James Sr., was born in Chicago in 1846, and briefly farmed in Kansas before settling his family—wife Jennie, daughter, and son—in central Wisconsin. In 1864, the elder J. P. had mustered into the Civil War, serving in Company D, 134th Illinois Infantry for one hundred days, from late May to early October. His regiment was one of those called "Hundred Days Men," joining the service at the height of the war to take over routine jobs and free experienced men for the warfront. From captains to sergeants to corporals, privates, even the company musician and wagoner, every man served the same time.

By 1878, the family was living in Kilbourn City, named for its founder. The town lay north of Baraboo at the Prairie Dells, an area of forests, fertile farmland, and an extraordinary sandstone gorge carved by the Wisconsin River. At Kilbourn—today's Wisconsin Dells—J. P. Sherman Jr. was born on December 15, 1878.

Even before the birth of his son, in 1871, the senior Sherman was declared disabled and receiving treatment and pay for medical infirmities. His primary condition was hemiplegia, a partial paralysis that affected the right side of his face, indicating damage in his brain's left hemisphere. His doctor also reported that J. P. Sr. suffered from neurasthenia, described as "popularly called nervous prostration."

Since 1906, the veteran had been in and out of the National Home for Disabled Volunteer Soldiers in Milwaukee, Wisconsin. Records describe him as five feet, six and a half inches tall, with a dark complexion, hazel eyes, and gray hair. He was still married, but living apart from Jennie when he died there at age sixty on April 8, 1919, from heart disease. At his death, he left no assets to his wife. Instead, he instructed that his estate valued at $328.35 go to his next of kin, J. P. Sherman Jr. of Fairbanks, Alaska. I wondered about the ways the elder Sherman's prolonged health issues affected his son's work and family life. J. P. Jr. likely took on the brunt of the physical labor on the farm. He seemed eager to escape and make his own way to Alaska well before his father's death.

By the winter of 1909-10, J. P. was thirty-one years old, single, and well-established when he booked into the Pattens' Third Avenue Hotel. There was another Sherman in town, Alaska-born Ben Sherman and his family, but the men were not related.

Intent on thriving in one of the harshest climates in the country, J. P. had done well living off the land, mining and trapping in Alaska's Interior for the last seven years. He'd traded the gains of his labor for plenty of money, enough to make himself rich and soft. But he never seemed to get rich or soft. Everyone knew that fallbacks were inevitable,

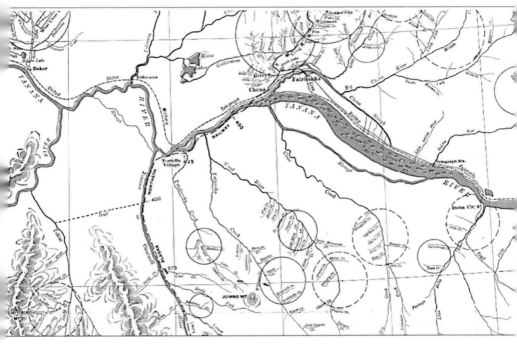

J. P. Sherman's claims were on the Totatlanika River and Platt Creek, near "Jumbo Mt." shown in the low center of this 1910 map by D. H. Sleem. (David Rumsey Map Center/Stanford University)

but even as a young man, J. P. was respected as a successful miner out in mineral-rich Totatlanika country, a broad region south of Fairbanks between the Tanana River and the northern foothills of the Alaska Range. J. P. actively mined in summers and ran a trapline in winters. He was also one of those hardy men who drift-mined in winter months, regardless of temperature. To reach and follow the paystreak, drift miners used wood-fired boilers and "steam points," metal rods that were pounded into the frozen soil so steam could be forced in to melt it. Some operators used a boiler-powered windlass to bring up their mucked-out material from the drift-mine shaft. Lacking those tools, a man could build a roaring campfire, melt the frozen soil, dump out the buckets to one side, and build another fire in the shaft, repeating the process to follow the gold. But shafts sometimes caved in, leaving many men injured, some fatally.

In spring, when rivers were liquid once again—a season called Breakup in Alaska—drift miners ran the contents of their dump through a sluice box and learned the return of that winter's labor. Was it worth it?

With Felix Pedro's gold discovery northeast of Fairbanks, hundreds of miners fanned across streams north of town, including above and below his discovery claims. With so many men "out on the creeks," a narrow-gauge railroad went into service. The Tanana Mines Railway, later called the Tanana Valley Railroad, connected the hub town to the outlying mining communities. Twice daily to the creeks, trains paused at Ester, Big Eldorado, Goldstream, Engineer, Pedro, Gilmore, Cleary, Fairbanks, Vault, Treasure, Dome, Little Eldorado, and Chatanika. TVRR's president Falcon Joslin advertised that trains worked in connection with teams of horses, so freight could be delivered "promptly on the claim or at the store."

On November 12, 1910, the assay office announced the region's gold production for the year. The Tanana District had produced about half of what it had the previous season, yet the new camp of Iditarod found gold quantities "much greater than it was ever expected to be." Bear in mind that $1 in 1910 was equivalent to more than $32 in 2024. "The returns for the [1910] season from Alaska have just been published," reported the *News-Miner*. "They show that the output of the Tanana was $4,125,000; Nome $3,500,000; Iditarod produced $787,000, and the remainder of Alaska produced $802,000."

Rather than follow the crowds to the streams north and east of town, J. P. Sherman chose to prospect in the lesser known Bonnifield District to the south, a vast region that held intriguing possibilities. Miners had been pulling gold out of a twenty-mile stretch of the Totatlanika River in the Bonnifield since 1905, and J. P. was among them, even then. By April 1910, he was named as one in a handful of operators in an *Alaska Citizen* story about the district's untapped resources, as the editor salted the story with hyperbole.

Waxing that "limitless wealth beaconed" from the Bonnifield, the paper questioned why any operator or prospector would be drawn to over-explored areas when, right under their noses, with sixty miles of decent trail to reach it, was a place "sufficient to stagger the imagination and make one wonder whether it is possible for such fabulous riches to be gathered in one spot . . . a veritable storehouse of treasure."

As for communications, reported the *Citizen*, ". . . operators and prospectors in the district have to go several miles below Nenana to send a letter or message to Fairbanks. Much valuable time is thus lost as it is almost as far to Nenana as it is to Fairbanks."

Projecting the cost of prospecting this close to Fairbanks, a region teeming with fish and game, the editor was certain it would cost far less than in other remote sites. "It has been estimated that with the aid of his gun, a prospector's expenses should not exceed 50 cents a day. Therefore, $300 would be sufficient to buy an outfit and keep a man in the field for over a year."

In 1910, J. P. was one of about thirty "outfits" putting at least one hundred and fifty men to work throughout the Bonnifield. The top producers among them included the largest, Berry-Hamil, plus others with multiple partners, such as the Gustavson brothers, Cook & Murphy, and Johnson, Stell, & Co. Only two individual miners were on the short list of successful operators in the Bonnifield: John Haraman was one; J. P. Sherman was the other.

※ ※ ※

In the winter of 1909-10, J. P. came into town from Platt Creek, about fifteen miles northeast of Healy, to room at the Third Avenue Hotel. There he caught the eye of a petite young woman named Agnes Eckert, who was almost eleven years his junior. He was very nearly a contemporary of her mother.

The recorded remembrances of a Fairbanks pioneer named Clara Rust fill in some blanks in the courtship of J. P. and Agnes. Arriving in Fairbanks in the fall of 1908, Clara would have been Agnes's peer. Yet I knew better than to take everything she said as fact. After all, she was an elder when she was interviewed many decades later, so it was a long reach back in time.

J. P. and Agnes had gone out dancing one evening, Clara recalled, and when J. P. took her home, Agnes announced to her mother and stepfather that they were engaged. In shock, J. P. stammered: "No, no, I don't want to marry you! I don't want to marry *any* woman. I'm out in the backcountry most times. That's no place for a woman."

But Agnes was in a hurry, Clara remembered. In particular, Agnes wanted to beat her fifteen-year-old little sister to the altar. And Bessie Mae had recently announced her engagement to a bank clerk. Clara suggested that Agnes had targeted J. P. and may have insinuated they'd been intimate. That would be enough for the Pattens. An alternate theory presents a series of questions, however. Is it possible that her parents pushed the marriage because Agnes was a problem daughter? John Patten had been a widower until his 1908 marriage to Minnie. Maybe he was ready for his stepdaughter to fall into the arms of a successful gold miner. Or just maybe Agnes already had been showing signs of mental health issues that would plague her—and her family—for all of their days.

On December 20, 1909, the *News-Miner* related that Agnes and J. P. would soon wed in the parlors of the Third Avenue Hotel. J. P. had

Advertising its luxury offerings in the local papers, the Third Avenue Hotel on Cushman was a successful enterprise for John and Minnie Patten.

left for Platt Creek, the paper reported, "intending to return this week with dogs and sled, with which he will take the outfit of his bride to his home on Platt." The Reverend James H. Condit, who had recently replaced Dr. Young as pastor of First Presbyterian Church, would officiate. The date was set: December 23. The paper advised, "The wedding will be solemnized in the presence of relatives and a few intimate friends of the couple. Mr. Sherman will leave here New Year's Day for Platt Creek with his bride."

The newspaper announcement was premature. When the wedding day arrived, all the arrangements had been made, but the groom was absent. Some miners who'd recently returned from the Susitna Valley region, a couple hundred miles south, told Agnes and the Pattens that J. P. was actually down there. He'd been delayed doing assessment work on several of his other claims. Plus the weather was turning. "Owing to the heavy storms which were reported from the Susitna, some fears were felt for Sherman's safety," the *News-Miner* reported on January 8, two weeks after their missed wedding date.

"It is expected that [Sherman] will telegraph when he reaches Nenana," offered the paper. "This is the nearest telegraph station to the country he is in. In the meantime, the word brought back by the prospectors has allayed the fears as to the safety of the groom."

As it happens, the wedding didn't take place until January 26. The next day, headlines read "Popular Local Couple United in Matrimony at Third Avenue." Reverend Condit officiated at the hotel with few witnesses, despite the couple's implied popularity. "The bride has a wide circle of friends in the camp as has also the groom. They will make their residences in Fairbanks for the present. Mr. Sherman has extensive interests in the Totatlanika country."

The original honeymoon plan was to whisk away by dog team to the Platt. But J. P. had delayed the wedding while enlarging the dumps on other claims. Perhaps he was also having second thoughts. After his wedding day, J. P. couldn't run his dirt until the streams thawed. On his own, he might have gone trapping while he was paused from mining. Instead, the couple began their wedded bliss in Fairbanks—Agnes was a city girl, after all—and waited for Breakup.

※ ※ ※

Minnie Patten's youngest girl, Bessie Mae Eckert, had stayed in Seattle when Minnie, Agnes, and Clarence came north in 1905. Now they were reunited. If Agnes was Minnie's wild child, then Bessie was trouble in training. At fifteen, she'd maneuvered a proposal out of a hapless bank clerk. Clara Rust suggested that act had fueled Agnes's rush to the altar with J. P. Yet Bessie's dream of marrying was not fulfilled. Not yet, anyway. Minnie did what so many anxious mothers would have done: she sent her daughter to boarding school. By late April 1910, Bessie was writing from the Annie Wright Seminary for girls in Tacoma, Washington, reporting about what a good student she was.

Among so many life changes, the arrival of Minnie's beloved sister in Fairbanks brought her great comfort. One of four sisters, Elizabeth came up after her own divorce in Seattle. It was natural that she'd gravitate to her eldest sister. When Agnes was born, Minnie had named her Agnes Elizabeth. And Agnes adored her namesake aunt, having grown up around the extended Jenott family in Seattle. This Elizabeth would play an important role in Agnes's future.

Elizabeth's route to Fairbanks took years. During the Klondike Gold Rush, when the immigrant Jenotts were based in Seattle, she was a "washer woman" for the White Star Laundry. On December 12, 1900, Elizabeth married a German bartender named Frank Goreska in a home ceremony witnessed by brother Charles and sister Irene Jenott. However, the marriage ended within four years. Elizabeth stayed in Seattle for a bit, and then decided to go north. In Fairbanks, she found love again and married Lewis N. Markle on May 10, 1910, at the First Presbyterian Church, just four months after the same minister tied the knot for J. P. and Agnes. A generation apart in age, the two couples' entries are separated by only two lines in the church's marriage registry. However, the vision of fresh starts for Elizabeth and Lewis, and J. P. and Agnes, was not as rosy as any of the parties might have imagined.

CHAPTER 7
MARRIED LIFE – Fairbanks, Winter 1910-11
If he don't come back after me,
he'll surely come back after his coat

After the belated Sherman wedding, the newlyweds stayed in town for several weeks, and then left by dog team for Totatlanika country during what is typically some of the coldest times of the year. The mercury often sat at minus twenty degrees or lower. For Agnes, the comforts of the Third Avenue Hotel, with its soft beds, running water, and attendant social life, would be sorely missed. She joined her husband on Platt Creek and entered the "not fit for a woman" life, sleeping and keeping house in a remote cabin, melting snow and ice for water, and tending the woodstove for cooking and heating. away from the restaurants and dances that she adored. Once the big rivers thawed and water flowed in

Fairbanks swiftly emerged as a hub of year-round social activity. Here, three-legged racers compete in the July 4, 1911, games on Front Street. (Archives, University of Alaska, UAF-1989-155-185)

the Platt again, J. P. would begin running his dump pile, falling trees for stove wood, and bringing home fish and game for Agnes to prepare. Was it blessedness? Apparently not for Agnes, because she wasn't gone from Fairbanks for long.

In no time, Agnes was back inside the social swirl that she'd so missed, and her peers were noting the absence of her groom.

"I remember people were kiddin' her about her husband, you know," said pioneer Clara Rust. "She would say, 'If he don't come back after me, he'll surely come back after his coat.' Because she was wearing . . ." Clara paused to clarify: "He had one of these his big wolf coats that everybody was wearing at that time. . . . And she'd wrap that around her and come down and she would say, 'Well, if he don't come back after me, he'll surely come back after his coat.' And talk that way. So then the first thing you know, why, she was pregnant. And he came down once in the time, and I guess he left some money there for her, or something. She was staying at the hotel with her parents."

One year and three days after the Shermans were married, on January 29, 1911, their firstborn entered the world at St. Matthew's Episcopal Mission hospital. The first hospital in Fairbanks, the two-story building stood next to the log church facing the Chena River on Front Street, later called First Avenue. The good news appeared in the *Alaska Citizen* the next day under the headline "One Little Girl Arrives." The couple named their daughter Irene Mary Sherman. Her first name honored another of Minnie's French Canadian sisters, Irene LaChappelle Jenott of Seattle; the baby's middle name was for J. P.'s mother back in Wisconsin, Jennie Mary.

The paper reported, "An eight-pound baby daughter was yesterday morning at 8:30 born to Mr. and Mrs. J. P. Sherman at the St. Matthew's hospital. Dr. Sutherland waited on the stork and yesterday evening, Mrs. J. H. Patten, Mrs. Sherman's mother, stated that the little lady and her mother were doing finely."

Over at the competing newspaper, the *News-Miner*, a write-up announced that the thrilled new grandmother would be hosting a party on Wednesday at the hotel. I found it interesting that they would publish news that Minnie was "now engaged inviting the friends whom she

Irene was born January 29, 1911, at St. Matthew's Hospital, built in 1904 as part of the Episcopal mission on Front Street, now First Avenue. The log church and neighboring hospital faced the Chena River. (Archives, University of Alaska Fairbanks, Albert J. Johnson Collection, UAF-1989-166-170)

wishes to have present on that occasion."

About that time, John Patten wrote a warning letter to the city council, suggesting that "a number" of local businesses were operating with unsafe wiring. The 1906 fire was still fresh in the minds of the locals. Unease amplified during the winter cold, when stoves and furnaces were operating nonstop. But it was defective wiring that concerned Patten. He urged the council to take action.

The matter was advanced to the city's fire committee to follow up. While they were on the subject, the mayor also appointed a committee to find and purchase two forty-foot ladders for future use. The Third Avenue Hotel wasn't the only building surpassing two stories in the fast-growing city.

Patten's ominous warning, as it turned out, was prescient. Within three years, those new ladders in the fire department's arsenal would be put to use at his own hotel.

※ ※ ※

When Irene was little, there was already consensus among Fairbanks old-timers that her mother Agnes was unstable. In 1988, when I first started making inquiries into Irene's life for that magazine profile, pioneer Frank P. Young was ninety-five years old, yet I found him tack sharp and conversing like a man half his age. As a little boy, he'd crossed the Chilkoot Pass in 1899 with his family, and had been one of the people who'd helped shape Fairbanks into a community. His memory of Agnes was somewhat benevolent.

"The way she acted, the way she talked . . . not exactly right," he told me. "She had the type of insanity, if that's what you want to call it, that's not dangerous to anyone."

History would prove that Frank P. Young was dead wrong. Agnes was a serious danger to her children and herself, and yet back then, who was around to do anything about it? Who would step in and interfere in another person's family, especially if there were multiple stories around? Yet somehow Agnes had not been tried for insanity, bundled up, and escorted to Morningside in Portland. Why not?

Back in 1988, I was wondering whom I could trust as a reliable source for my magazine profile research. Clara Rust's faded memories, which were heavily salted with gossip? Irene's own memories? I'd taken copious notes as we talked—but later comparing her stories to the paper trail, I found irregularities. No surprise there, I guessed, considering her age and the depth of trauma she'd survived from so young. And now it seemed Irene was entering dementia.

※ ※ ※

I could sense how Minnie Patten must have felt in 1911, considering her firstborn granddaughter soon would be leaving during deep winter for the Totatlanika region. J. P.'s closest claims were more than a hundred miles south of Fairbanks on Platt Creek, near Jumbo Dome. The Bonnifield Mining District was laced with gold and other valuable ores, and J. P. had gotten in early. He had numerous claims along the creek, each one

Prospectors test the contents of their dump by running it through a rocker box. (Archives, University of Alaska Fairbanks, Albert J. Johnson Collection, UAF-1989-166-635)

homestead-sized at one hundred and sixty acres. As a bachelor, he had no problem living in primitive conditions. He was fine with no roads, no telephones, no running water, no electricity, and little interaction with people. But for Agnes, the adjustment was unimaginable, especially with a newborn. She made her preference clear to her new husband, and J. P. took her and the baby back to Fairbanks, and then returned to the Platt, coming in only sporadically.

At first, Agnes and baby Irene stayed at the Third Avenue Hotel. Less than a block from the hotel and across Cushman Street stood the formidable Eagle Hall, facing Fifth Avenue. The famed gathering spot was not only used by members of the Fraternal Order of Eagles, Aerie No. 1037. It was also the primary location for several other fraternal organizations and their own formal meetings and celebrations, including the Pioneers of Alaska, Igloo No. 4, and the Moose Lodge. The Eagles were famous for their grand parties, dances, generous feasts, and lavish decorations for holiday gatherings.

And Agnes hated to miss one of their dances, which often included orchestral music led by violinist Victor Durand with pianist Victor Mente, cornet player William Gorbracht, and Gene Huckins on drum and trap. Young Agnes was a regular when she was single; as a wife and mother, she remained a regular.

Tongues began wagging about the Sherman woman, according to rumors that Clara Rust retold in 1975: "And then [J. P.] went away, and he went off on his trapline or wherever he went, and Agnes was alone all the time. . . . While he was gone, she used to come up to the dances at Eagle Hall . . ." By Clara's reckoning, Agnes was among the worst mothers she could conjure. "She would bring her baby in a little [Carnation] cream case to the dances," Clara said. "She'd shove the baby down in there and come and dance all night. . . ." The little wooden Carnation box was fastened to a sled, Clara explained, which Agnes pulled with a rope.

"She'd pull that into the restroom, and the attendants there, they were after her all the time, because she'd leave that baby in there crying. It was smelly and dirty, you know . . . and the attendants would say, 'You need to change that baby,' but she didn't seem to have much to change her with." Finally, the Eagles told Agnes that she couldn't come to the dances unless she got a babysitter for Irene.

I knew Clara's memory was fallible, as is everyone's, plus she was casting back almost seven decades. While her stories were intriguing, it was wise to be cautious about hearsay, yet a bad reputation does have a way of sticking. And it stuck to Agnes.

Still ahead, I would discover compelling proof of Agnes's negligence, and if local stories were true, fueled by alcoholism and infidelity. From what I knew so far, J. P. was the hero, the hard-working father who didn't give up on his family. Later, I wasn't sure about that assessment either.

When I first heard about Agnes coming to the dances with Irene in tow, I found it hard to be neutral. I formed opinions about her without a complete picture. But even as I looked into her life with that bias, more than once I was blindsided by a new piece of information that challenged preconceptions. One such time was when I was trying to figure out the birth order and ultimately, the whereabouts of other children born to Agnes. Irene had said, "I think there were seven of us." That phrase would haunt me as I searched for names, birthplaces, and ultimately, what had happened to Agnes's other babies.

※ ※ ※

The year of Irene's birth was significant for Fairbanks in another way. By 1911, founding father E. T. Barnette, who'd been dumped on the banks of the Chena as a trader and entrepreneur, had served as postmaster, muscled his way in as mayor, founded the Fairbanks Banking Company, and then purchased the Washington-Alaska Bank. Merging the two banking institutions, his personal wealth grew along with his town. And yet in early January 1911, just three weeks before Irene's birth, the Washington-Alaska Bank closed its doors, declaring bankruptcy and leaving investors out of a million dollars. Later, Barnette would sneak out of town in the dead of night, headed for Los Angeles, California, with $500,000. In time, he was located and charged with embezzling only $50,000, but in December 1912, his well-greased political and business connections helped him elude serious punishment.

The trial took place in Valdez, where only a misdemeanor charge stuck for falsifying a financial report. He was required to pay a $1,000 fine. A *News-Miner* editorial writer called the proceedings "the rottenest judicial farce the North has ever witnessed."

Fairbanks did not forget. Even two years after the trial, Barnette's memory was again smeared in the *Douglas Island News*, where the editor projected his desire that the territory's legislature—soon to meet for the very first time—would better protect investors: "A man at Nome raised a check from two to twenty-two dollars and was given five years in the penitentiary. Captain Barnette, who was charged—and the charge was sustained, of robbing the depositors of the Washington-Alaska Bank at Fairbanks, out of nearly half a million dollars, was

In October 1958, E. T. Barnette's original home on First Avenue was still structurally sound shortly before it was razed and later replaced by the Christian Science Church. A *News-Miner* Progress Edition bemoaned the loss of the historical structure. (*News-Miner* Archives)

permitted to go on payment of a nominal fine. It is hoped the present loose and unfair laws under which Alaska is living will be remedied when her first legislature meets at Juneau early next month."

So despised was Barnette, the man who bilked Fairbanks, that his name became a slur for thieving, as in "Barnetting." Saloon owner John Moe took a swipe at Barnette's leave-taking in his newspaper display ad: "One of the Good Things that Captain Barnette overlooked and did not grab, but left behind him, was the barrels of 11-year-old OVERHOLD RYE at the Globe Bar," Moe asserted. "It is still there." Also still there, a downtown street that was named for Barnette.

※ ※ ※

It had been a tough year for Minnie Patten. Here was Agnes carrying on right under their noses, plus Minnie had been compelled to install young Bessie at a Tacoma boarding school for young ladies. In her first year away, Bessie wrote her mother that things were going well. As her second year of school came to a close in June 1911, Bessie prepared to come back home, with a plan to visit family in Seattle for a few days. She'd stay with a couple of Minnie's sisters, her beloved Jenott aunts: Elizabeth, Irene, Margaret, and Louisa. After an agreeable visit, Bessie continued north. She had just sailed into Canada when her world shifted on its axis. As reported later in Washington state's *Tacoma Ledger*: "Miss Bessie Eckert, a 17-year old girl of two years' standing in the school, got as far as Vancouver, B.C. There she married a man five years her senior, whom she had known only a week."

While Minnie was imagining her daughter traveling by ship to Valdez, then onward by trail to Fairbanks, the reality was that her minor daughter had disembarked and eloped with an older man. Bridegroom Lorne McAllister was a Scotsman who'd settled in Canada and worked as the assistant customs house inspector in Vancouver. The newspaper account went on, ". . . immediately after the ceremony he and his young bride took apartments in that city." Describing Bessie as "very girlish in appearance," the reporter inquired about how her mother Minnie would react to this news.

"I really don't know what mamma will say when she hears of this," Bessie told him. "We have wired her, and I expect some of the family will come down to look me over. I have a couple of aunts in Seattle with whom I stayed for a few days directly after school closed, and they threatened to take me away from Lorne, but I am going to sit tight. I like my husband's people very well, but I guess his mother wishes we had waited a while."

The report that reached Minnie and later appeared in the Fairbanks paper stated they'd eloped in Skagway, Alaska. Actually the marriage was in Vancouver, but eventually the couple did set up housekeeping in Skagway. Minnie was both horrified and heartbroken.

By August 10, no one as yet had notified the Annie Wright Seminary that Bessie would not be returning to school.

The horse-drawn fire brigade was stationed in City Hall's street level on Third; beyond it on the corner, the three-story Third Avenue Hotel faced Cushman. (Archives, University of Alaska Fairbanks, UAF-1979-41-175)

For the Pattens, community pillars with stellar reputations, Agnes's behaviors, and now Bessie's, were a stain. In the spring, John Patten ran for the City Council with the endorsement of the *Alaska Citizen*, who hailed him as "vitally interested in the welfare of the town. He has always taken a keen interest in civic affairs, although heretofore he has refused to run for the council." When John did not win office, the necessary and mundane propelled him and Minnie through the calendar. Minnie stayed involved with a ladies society for Bible study, volunteered at fundraisers, and hosted meals and parties frequently. The hotel was a moneymaker and always full, even in winters, when miners and other single men took up long-term lodging. Thankfully, a kitchen blaze there was doused on April 11 that spring of 1911, just six years after the catastrophic 1906 fire. In Fairbanks, any fire struck fear.

"The [fire] department was quickly on the scene and in a very short time the fire was gotten under control by the use of the chemical and the water," the paper reported. "Some of the . . . stock in the back of the store was slightly damaged but little harm was done to the building." After Breakup, John fixed up his "White auto" and offered passengers transportation to the creeks via an alternately dusty or muddy summer trail that wended north and east along what is now the Steese Highway. Striving to keep the community apprised of Fairbanks comings and goings, one paper announced in late July, while news of Bessie's elopement was still spreading by word of mouth, that Minnie had taken some friends berry-picking out on the Fox road in "the auto." Life had to go on.

※ ※ ※

J. P. had good reason to be gone as long and as often as he was during his first year of marriage. He had a debt to repay, and those scheduled payments weighed heavily. Just a few months after his January wedding, an optimistic J. P. had taken out a $2,000 loan from E. R. Peoples, a local merchandiser with several large warehouses across the Chena from the main business district, on the side called Garden Island. On March 24, 1910, J. P. signed promissory notes for repayments beginning with $750 by July 15. The second $1,000 was due August 15, and the final $250 by September 1. Each note also specified 12 percent interest on the principal per annum until paid. As security, J. P. put up title and interest to his four placer mining claims on the Platt River. The loan and repayment agreement was witnessed by Louis K. Pratt and Ed Stroecker of Fairbanks, notarized, and duly recorded in the mortgage books for the territory's Fourth Division of the District Court in Fairbanks.

For a newly married man with a pregnant wife, the pressure was on high. That spring, he needed to focus on the intense work of "staying on the pay." Bucket after bucket of soil and rock had come up as he drift-mined through the winter, and J. P. had conducted the occasional test pan to ensure he was following the paystreak. Soon a mountain of rocky dirt—the dump—developed.

Breakup was clean-up time, when the water was flowing freely and miners ran their dump contents through their sluice boxes. That April, J. P. was confident that his winter work had set him up for a healthy start on repayment. While J. P. seems to have been a lone wolf, it's likely he partnered with at least one other man for the labor-intensive work of running his winter dump. Typically, one man was situated at the top of the sluice box, a wooden trough set up on stilts. "The box" was carefully angled to make the water do the sorting work, but not so tilted that the gold would wash out with the mud and gravel. At the top, he sorted and tossed large rocks as he shoveled, else they damage the box.

Gravity directed the water downward, carrying material with it. Crosspieces, called riffles, were nailed in place along its length, interrupting the flow and allowing the heavier gold to be trapped while smaller rocks and soil flowed out. By blocking or redirecting the water flow at the top, miners could pause the action, and then scrape out the material trapped along each of the riffles. In a one-man operation, the miner could use a cradle-like contraption called a rocker box to do the work of a sluice box in miniature. In the final step of a clean-up, miners manually panned the concentrates at streamside, swirling and tipping the gold pan in shallow water until only glittering gold remained.

For most of J. P.'s spring and summer of 1910, the gold did not present itself. He missed his first payment to Peoples in July entirely, but managed to pay $1,250 in gold coin on August 11, when Irene was eight months old. And then the money stopped. Peoples tried to collect the remainder of the debt as the months rolled by, but failed.

With the court case lingering, and another winter waning in March 1912, J. P. was headed in to Fairbanks, still referred to as a "camp town" as it reached its tenth birthday. As always, the comings and goings of local people made the newspapers: "J. P. Sherman, who has been busied recently locating a number of claims in the Totatlanika country, returned to camp early in the week." On April 8, the Sherman family—J. P., Agnes, and little Irene—left Fairbanks by dog team for Platt Creek. At that time of year, it was a race against the elements.

J. P. was savvy at reading the land. He knew he'd need to cross the Tanana before the trail across the frozen river was destroyed by Breakup. While the annual event delivered the awesome sight of grinding ice moving out of the rivers, it was accompanied by bone-crushing sound as cabin-sized ice cakes jammed against each other, piling up and blocking the current or riding up on the riverbanks to decay. Travelers knew that once Breakup started, river crossings by dog team or horse-drawn sled stages were done. They'd have to wait until all of the danger had passed. Only then was it safe to ferry across. Breakup often caused flooding in villages and settlements along the rivers, and still does.

As Agnes rode in the dogsled toward Platt Creek with her husband and fourteen-month-old Irene, she didn't know that she was already a month into her next pregnancy. Coincidentally, her litle sister Bessie was pregnant at the same time. A few months later, on June 29, the *Fairbanks Daily Times* reported, "Mrs. J. H. Patten was advised during the week that her daughter, formerly Miss Bessie Eckert, of this city, and now Mrs. L. McAllister, of Skagway, had given birth to a ten-pound boy at the windy town. Mr. McAllister is engaged in customs work on the international boundary."

In the case of E. R. Peoples vs. J. P. Sherman, by March 23, 1915, five years after Peoples accepted J. P.'s promissory notes, he had no choice but to foreclose on Sherman's claims. Through his attorney Albert R. Heilig, Peoples demanded the remaining $750 with 12 percent annual interest accruing from March 24, 1910, plus $150 attorney's fees and his costs. As the law provided, Peoples also demanded the sale of J. P.'s four mortgaged mines and any associated equipment on each. Proceeds from the sale would apply to what was still owed Peoples, along with fees, and Peoples would have the right to purchase the mines himself if he chose. J. P. or anyone representing him was barred from redeeming any rights, equity, or claims to the property in any way. Yet another year would pass before J. P. was finally summoned before District Court Judge Charles E. Bunnell, and even then, J. P. claimed to have lost or accidentally destroyed the first summons. U.S. Marshal Lewis T. Erwin sent a deputy marshal to serve a second copy, an "alias summons," after J. P. was finally located in Fairbanks on June 3, 1916.

It was a year that would nearly destroy J. P. Sherman.

Pictured in 1908, Lewis T. Erwin hauled a record seven and a half cords in one trip as a Fairbanks "wood dealer." In 1912, Erwin was delegate to the Democratic National Convention and later served as U.S. marshal for the Fourth Judicial Division, when he became familiar with J. P. Sherman and his financial woes. In 1919, the marshal was one of three members of the territory's Board of Children's Guardians, making decisions about J. P.'s family. (Library of Congress, Carpenter Collection)

CHAPTER 8
TRAIL FROM THE TOTATLANIKA
Bonnifield District, February 1913
She had given no thought to packing food, water, an ax, or matches

Just two days before Christmas 1912, the Sherman family enlarged when a second baby girl was born to Agnes, this time at St. Mark's mission hospital near Nenana. The log buildings—the church, hospital, and boarding school—had been erected on a bend of the Tanana River as part of an expansive Episcopalian missionary outreach to Alaska Native people. Established in 1907, it was among four mission churches in the Interior. Across the river, an Athabascan settlement was called *Toghotthele*, for "mountains that parallel the river," a name that had been westernized to Tortella. Where the Nenana River joined the Tanana, a group of cabins first called Tortella sprouted around 1902 as a trading post and telegraph station. Later named Nenana, the community experienced explosive growth as a railroad construction camp. Although Agnes was not an Alaska Native, St. Mark's mission hospital would serve her, too.

The couple's baby was delivered on December 23, 1912, and named Jeanette—one "n" shorter than Minnie's Quebec-born mother, Jeannette Frances Jenott. The matriarch had recently died in Seattle.

By the cold month of February 1913, baby Jeanette was seven weeks old, and Irene had just turned two. The family was hunkered down at a relay cabin on the Totatlanika River. On the morning of February 15, J. P. hooked up his string of dogs and prepared to take the winter trails to Nenana and onward to Fairbanks. He likely carried a bundle of furs for sale or trade. Primarily he was planning to replenish his outfit and freight it back, filling their personal needs and those of the mining operation beyond what he could hunt or make himself.

J. P. never shied from hard work, yet earning a living the way he'd chosen took a toll on even the strongest body. On that Saturday, bad weather was not giving him a break. The temperatures were below zero and a sharp wind effectively drove it even lower. Still, he needed to go.

A couple of miles from the railroad boomtown of Nenana, St. Mark's Mission with its hospital, church, school, and dormitory primarily served Athabascan families. (Archives, University of Alaska Fairbanks, Walter and Lillian Phillips Collection, UAF-1985-72-99)

He'd follow the Totatlanika River to its mouth at the Tanana River, about ten miles east of Nenana. The river trails were well-used, but blowing snow could easily wipe out visual markers.

Later, when J. P. wrote about the events of those days, he said that before leaving, he'd chopped plenty of stove wood and stocked the cabin with other necessities for his wife and children. But Agnes did not want to be left behind. She was anxious and upset about his leaving and may well have been suffering from post-partum depression, further magnified by the isolation during the season's coldest, darkest months.

Not long after J. P. mushed away, Agnes concluded that she had to follow him. Frenzied, she dressed in layers of warm clothes from top to bottom and likewise wrapped up Irene and Jeanette. Agnes placed the bundled children in the hide-covered basket of a dogsled and laid fur robes over them. J. P. had taken the dogs, so she alone pulled the sled through the snow, trying and failing to follow J. P.'s tracks. In her unstable state of mind, Agnes was fixated on somehow catching up. The unrelenting wind drove biting cold into every seam, every fold of her clothes. She had given no thought to packing even the basics, such as food and water, an ax, or matches. She just left. Later newspaper accounts would wonder at her strength considering she was just a "frail wisp of a woman."

Soon Agnes became disoriented as she traveled, more uncertain when she could not see anything familiar. Panting as she dragged the sled, her exhaled breath formed thick frost on her eyelashes and the stole around her face, like a white wreath. If one of the girls whimpered, Agnes stopped to comfort her and tried to warm the baby at her breast. She was already thin and increasingly dehydrated, so she wasn't providing much nourishment.

Agnes kept moving, wandering through the bitterly cold night and well into the next day before finally stumbling back to the relay cabin. It was now five o'clock on Sunday evening. Some thirty hours had passed. Every limb was numb, and Agnes could barely walk. Unwrapping Jeanette, Agnes saw that her baby's tiny face and lips were blue. She had frozen to death. Little Irene was hypothermic, but somehow the toddler had survived. Carrying the baby, Agnes staggered toward the cabin, half-dragging Irene before collapsing inside. She managed to start a fire and melt snow for the two survivors to drink. They were barely functioning.

On Tuesday, February 18, J. P. mushed into camp to find a desperately weak and distraught wife, a two-year-old who was hanging onto life, and a dead infant. Agnes had been unable to do much for herself or Irene, and had simply kept her baby's body wrapped and in the cabin to keep animals from getting to her. J. P. tried to take care of his family while considering his next steps. He knew he'd need to notify authorities. Finally, he penned an explanatory letter to the U.S. marshal, who received it in early March. In it, J. P. recounted the events—as best he understood—that had led to Jeanette's death. For reasons he could not explain, his wife was imbalanced. Irene was still alive. The baby was dead. He did not know exactly when Jeanette lost her life, but she was

J. P. Sherman drove dogs, like this unnamed man (and miners all over the Interior), hauling gold and furs to town, and returning with replenishments. (Library of Congress, Carpenter Collection, LC-DIG-PPMSC-01558)

deceased when he'd arrived at home. He made February 16 her official death date.

The Alaska Citizen pulled heart-wrenching details from J. P.'s letter for its March 17 story, titled "Infant Dies in Mother's Arms." The article began, "Seldom in the stories of hardships and battle with the elements does such a sad tale of death reach the public as the one disclosed in a letter received at the marshal's office last week telling of the death of an infant child of Mr. and Mrs. J. P. Sherman of the Totatlanika district." At the close of the brief story, readers were informed that the baby's corpse was still at the cabin and probably would be buried at the Nenana mission cemetery. The reporter also noted, "Mrs. Sherman is the eldest daughter of Mrs. J. H. Patten of this city." Minnie Patten's grief was great, but the next few years would bring even more heartbreak.

Community newspapers across the territory picked up the story and in the retelling, it became more and more dramatic, highlighting

Agnes's frailty and detailing the struggle as she tried to share her own warmth by "clasping the slight infant to her breast." The accounts were shattering, especially for those who knew the family: "Caught by darkness on a drifted and windswept trail on the Totatlanika river . . . a two-year-old daughter and two-months-old infant in her charge . . . a one-sided struggle with the elements . . . a greatly weakened condition," reported the *Fairbanks Times*.

Word of their family's tragedy out in the Totatlanika reached the Pattens, who no doubt were grappling with profound grief in a gamut of emotions. Once J. P.'s letter reached the U.S. marshal, the stouthearted Pattens found themselves reeling from sorrow and very public family problems. It's unclear, but possible, that the terrible events of that February influenced their decision to leave town for a while. They escaped to John's mining claims in the Tolovana district. They'd be back after clean-up.

❈ ❈ ❈

Trouble kept coming for J. P.—or else he kept looking for it. On December 8, 1913, while out on the creek, J. P. drew a bead on another Totatlanika miner named John J. Murphy. The man was part of the association Murphy Brothers and Cook, a competitor. J. P. shot him, injuring but not killing the man. On the spot, Murphy demanded an explanation, to which J. P. responded, "I thought you were a caribou." A month later, newspapers said Murphy "evidently accepted the explanation at the time, but has since had reason to believe otherwise."

In January, Murphy appeared before Commissioner Dillon and swore to the complaint, asserting that Sherman had demonstrated "intent to kill." A warrant was issued for J. P.'s arrest; he was found on the Totatlanika, and brought into town. Just a few weeks later, in early 1914, a brief follow-up in the *Alaska Citizen* simply said, "The Fairbanks grand jury exonerated J. P. Sherman whom John Murphy had arrested for shooting at him in 1912. The shooting occurred at Totatlanika." J. P. was freed from jail.

A pattern of arrest followed by exoneration was beginning to

DECEMBER SUN.

Shooting this image across the Clay Street Cemetery, A. J. Painter recorded the arc of the sun on winter solstice 1915, opening the camera's shutter every fifteen minutes. Baby Jeanette had been buried there the previous year. (Archives, University of Alaska Fairbanks; A. J. Painter, Buzby and Metcalf Photograph Album, UAF-1963-71-10)

set up, without fallout. J. P. had been in Fairbanks for the grand jury hearing at the same time Minnie was doing her best to carry on despite the continuing and very public family turmoil. That first week of January, she hosted an evening gathering in the hotel parlor for the Young People's Society of the Presbyterian Church. The *Alaska Citizen* called it "one of the most healthy and delightful social events of the winter." Thirty young men and women spent an evening playing games, enjoying music and food, and experiencing "the larger joy young people find in mingling together in such a wholesome way. . . . The young people unite in pronouncing Mrs. Patten a royal hostess."

※ ※ ※

J. P. had written the marshal that he and Agnes expected to bury their baby at the Nenana mission graveyard, but that spring, she was interred in the pioneer cemetery that bounded the southeast edge of Fairbanks. At three and a half acres, the Clay Street Cemetery had been the town's burial ground since 1903, but it was rapidly filling. By 1918, it would necessarily close to regular burials, and formally shut its gates in 1938, when the new Birch Hill Cemetery opened a few miles away.

Grave diggers would have had to use a pickaxe and shovel to dig the tiny grave. Sometimes they employed "steam points," those metal shafts that drift-miners used to melt frozen ground. When Jeanette was interred, the Shermans probably put up a wooden marker, yet over the years, evidence of her resting place was erased. At least it was recorded in a book.

Jeanette was the first child to die among those that Agnes Sherman carried to term, but she would not be the last. By early 1914, in Nenana, Agnes was pregnant again with a baby she didn't want.

CHAPTER 9
THE THIRD AVENUE HOTEL - Fairbanks 1914
I told them not to take time to dress, but to run for their lives

John H. Patten's grand Third Avenue Hotel on Cushman was regarded as
one of the town's finest structures. Advertised as "the first modern hotel
built in the city," it boasted running water and baths, radiant heat from
basement furnaces, and a warm stable for dogs or horses.

When the hotel was new in 1904, the *Fairbanks Weekly News*
reported on its modern amenities and its owner's forward-thinking
perspectives: "Mr. John Patten, of the Third Avenue Hotel, has solved the
water and fire protection question as far as his premises are concerned.
He secured a sand point and pipe, and having previously penetrated the
frost limit, had no difficulty in forcing the point down a distance of
twenty feet when a splendid flow of pure water was encountered. Mr.
Patten intends to place a large tank in the attic of his building, and by
using pipes he will be able to supply water to any portion of the
premises." So successful was Patten that just a year after opening, he
added a third floor of rooms.

John Patten was already among the best-known pioneers in the
Tanana Valley, and he had been profiled in a special newspaper edition
featuring the movers and shakers of 1904. "[Patten] is a rustling Alaska
pioneer, who has achieved success through his ability to make things
move whether they would or no." He'd been living in Washington state
when he first came north in 1897, bound for Skagway, where he launched
a freighting business over the White Pass. Patten made good money,
enough to open his own mercantile at Atlin, British Columbia, partnering
with Frank Bishoprick. Again, the profits rolled in, and after a while, he
moved into Dawson. In the winter of 1902-03, Patten, like so many
others, got wind of the big strike in the Tanana Valley and joined the
stampede to Fairbanks. He immediately secured several claims of his
own and invested in claims on several other creeks that had not yet been
tested. He was an ambitious man.

Although Patten relied on his claims, it was the hotel business that built his wealth. With his marriage to Minnie in 1908, the couple offered modern, stylish digs to short- and long-term lodgers. Just two blocks away from the riverfront, the ground floor included the hotel office and lobby, parlor, restaurant, storerooms, and on the corner of Third, an outside entrance to the popular Globe saloon. The back of the Globe was the tongue-in-cheek "Democratic headquarters." Hotel rooms filled the upper stories. They advertised both the "American and European Plan." American Plan rates included meals provided by the hotel kitchen; lodgers under the European Plan paid for their dinners on a separate tab, allowing diners to explore other meal options in town. The place was a landmark, standing strong, even though it had been threatened by fire several times over the years.

On August 1, 1911, when baby Irene was six months old, John and Minnie Patten decided to lease their hotel's management to H. D. Fountain, a Dawson stampeder and former "hotel man" from the East who'd come to Fairbanks in 1908. Fountain was a bachelor who'd lived in many hotels, "enough to know the needs of a hotel guest," he told a reporter. First employed at the Northern Commercial Company, then in the court clerk's office, Fountain was glad to be back working as a "boniface," a hotelier. Taking up residency in the hotel, that summer Fountain made a few changes, including repapering and painting the office in an effort, he said, to "prevent the dingy and rundown appearance that has such a habit of coming over a mining town after a few years." Further, he advertised rates of $1 to $5 per day, American or European Plan, and offered auto rides to the creeks north of town twice a day. The option was enticing. Rather than spending hours on the stop-and-go schedule of the narrow-gauge Tanana Mines trains to Gilmore City and onward, a one-way trip of two and one-half hours, passengers could get to their destinations much sooner taking the auto on the summer trail to Fox. Fountain also upgraded his personal life when he married in the hotel parlor in 1913, surrounded by friends.

So the Pattens were not running the hotel in February 1913, when baby Jeanette died on the trail, nor did they resume management until the Fountains' lease expired on December 1. During those two and a half years, they had other options. The couple kept their home on

Cushman Street, not far from the hotel, but John still had those mining claims in the Tolovana area. And in spring 1913, John decided to take up ranching in an area north of town known as Birch Hill (acreage that two decades later would become the new city cemetery).

On May 12, 1913, John Patten was clearing the land with his horse and plow when Frank Eckert (no relation to Minnie's former husband) approached him in the field. Patten had hired the German immigrant a week earlier to help. After a few days, Eckert decided to quit. Patten had informed him about how to pick up his wages from C. H. Woodward, who was Patten's agent for collecting rents and other business transactions. A week passed and Eckert had not yet made contact with Woodward. Eckert very much wanted Patten himself to pay his wages. Angrily, he went to Patten's tent on the ranch, grabbed Patten's own shotgun, and approached his former employer out in the field. Eckert pointed the shotgun at Patten's head and commanded, "Drop those lines, and come on into town. I want that money. Do it now, or I'll blow your head off." Taking the man's instruction seriously, Patten left his horse and plow and walked ahead of Eckert for the three miles to Graehl, an area across the Chena River from the Fairbanks business district. There, Patten's friend C. T. Hinckley advanced the money. Once Eckert was handed his $23, he began unloading Patten's shotgun, when one of the shells accidentally exploded, shaking up the men without harming anyone.

The next day, the *Fairbanks Times* reported, "Frank Eckert is now lodged in the federal jail, awaiting examination as to his sanity." Patten told the newspaper that Eckert had been acting "strangely" for some time, including talking to himself. At the formal hearing, however, Eckert presented as totally sane, so he did not receive a free, escorted trip to Morningside, and the insanity charges were dismissed. He would serve sixty days in jail, however.

The Pattens had had their share of trials. They'd taken repeated hits with the Shermans' reputations sullying their own, and Bessie's elopement had landed hard, so it's easy to imagine that they wanted to get away from town. But their difficulties were far from over. Two months after the expiration of the Fountains' management lease on the

A photo taken from First and Cushman looking south shows the Third Avenue Hotel down the block at center right. It had stood for ten years before that disastrous day. (Archives, University of Alaska Fairbanks, Falcon Joslin Papers, UAF-1979-41-174)

Third Avenue Hotel, the Pattens carried on their roles as proprietors. And John and Minnie would face yet another extraordinary challenge.

One lazy Sunday morning in late January 1914, U.S. Signal Corpsman William J. Callahan entered the hotel and took the stairs with a telegram for Robert Sheldon, a roomer on the top floor. Sheldon was sleeping in at 10:00 A.M., keeping warm against the extreme cold outside his window. After finally rousing Sheldon and delivering the telegram, Callahan stepped back into the hallway. Only about five minutes had passed, he recalled later, but in that brief time, fire had broken through the ceiling of the top floor. Callahan began shouting "Fire! Fire!" and ran to Sheldon's door, where he found the man back in bed.

"When I rushed back to his room, he didn't seem to think there was any need of hurrying to escape the fire," Callahan said later, "and I pulled him out of bed. He went out of the window, and it was my idea first that I would have to go the same way, but I finally managed to reach the stairway." Callahan jumped to the second floor without injury. When he saw that the stairway was not burning, he went back up to the third floor, hurrying through the smoky hallways and calling *"Fire!"*

"People came to their doors and looked out, but few of them seemed to get excited," Sheldon said. "It seemed that many roomers were taking things too easily, and when they started back into their rooms, I told them not to take time to dress, but to run for their lives."

Finally, the boarders grasped the seriousness. They began running down the stairs, jumping out windows, or dropping over stair railings to the next floor down, then shimmying down a ladder. Many were injured, from J. Tod Cowles, whose hair was burned away, exposing his scalp, to Ernest Foster, who suffered third-degree burns on his hands and forearms. The worst off among the survivors was Cyrus "Doc" Medile, who'd jumped from the third story. Some thought he'd broken his back. His survival was still uncertain a day later. Others, a few of them miners, would heal from their injuries. But one Patten employee, Carl Larson, was missing and presumed dead. Larson had been hired to keep the furnaces going through the night. He'd finished his shift and was deep in sleep when the first alarms went off. Witnesses said the place was "a seething mass of flames" within moments of discovery. However, it was not a furnace malfunction, nor could Larson be blamed in any way. The fire had started in the third-floor ceiling or the roof.

"If that telegram had not come for Mr. Sheldon just at that time," the messenger Callahan told a reporter, "I am sure that many people would have been burned to death. It was the first delivery I made since being assigned to that work."

In subsequent reporting, the "fire of an unknown origin" was referred to as the most dangerous fire since the disaster of 1906. It had displaced about twenty hotel guests and lodgers (oddly referred to as "inmates"). But the meaning was clear. All of them were now homeless, and most had lost everything they owned, including clothes, furs, currency, invaluable papers, and other material goods.

Newspapers declared that the building was "doomed before the fire department was summoned." Flames were shooting out of the windows minutes after the first alarm.

"That the entire business section of the city was not destroyed was due to the activity of the fire department and to the work of a number of citizens who volunteer their services," the *Alaska Citizen* wrote. "It was nearly two hours after the first alarm was given before the fire was thoroughly under control."

Among the boarders was F. S. Gordon, a former mayor of Scottish origin and well-known proprietor of a nearby dry goods store on Cushman. One of the first to escape, Gordon had managed to wrap himself in an overcoat before dropping from a second-story window to the sidewalk. Shaken, but not injured. In shock, Gordon didn't realize that he was shoeless in the snow until someone pointed it out. Presumably he hurried off to dress at his nearby store, because Gordon was fully clothed when he returned. A reporter overheard street-side conversation and made notes: "Some of his friends jokingly declared that being a Scotchman, and therefore probably accustomed to kilts, he naturally would not feel the cold on his bare limbs."

Besides the loss of the hotel and the Globe saloon's fine cigars, liquor, and pool tables, the messenger office was destroyed, too. But the Pattens suffered the greatest financial loss. The hotel had cost $30,000 to build, and they carried only $5,000 worth of insurance.

"Mr. Patten said last night that he was uncertain what he would do with the property, but would make up his mind in a few days. He intimated that he may rebuild the hotel on its old site, but would make it two stories in height instead of three, its original height."

Through the newspaper, John Patten publicly thanked all who'd worked to save their hotel. In his opinion, the fire did not spread to neighboring businesses because it had been constructed with double walls and insulated with sawdust. In Minnie's interview, she spoke on behalf of the female guests. She believed all had escaped.

On January 28, with temperatures reported at thirty-three below zero, the public learned that the charred body of Carl Larson was discovered in the hotel's ruins.

With the loss of the Third Avenue Hotel in the middle of winter, there were few opportunities for John and Minnie to find other revenue sources, and their 1913 city taxes became delinquent. The *Fairbanks Daily News-Miner* sent a reporter to the March 13 city council meeting for what was described as a "get the money" meeting, or "bringing in the sheaves." Councilmen agreed that all delinquent taxpayers would have their names advertised in the *Fairbanks Times* for four successive weeks, and then the chief of police would begin seizing property, including woodpiles if need be. John Patten, whose name appeared on the delinquent list, faced the humiliating prospect of covering his tax bill by selling a safe to the city. For three weeks, that very safe had delayed Patten's efforts to file his insurance claim. He'd been unable to open it and physically access his policy.

Three days later, Patten's finances man, C. Harry Woodward, received a wire from San Francisco confirming that a draft for $5,000 was in the mail. By April, with the fire three months behind him, John finally received his insurance check, and they could breathe again. John targeted December to finish debris removal and start rebuilding. Before Thanksgiving, Minnie was back in the saddle with her charity work, cooking and directing helpers for the annual St. Matthew's Hospital fundraiser. And on December 21, the shortest, darkest day of the year, John began work on a new two-story office/retail building on the hotel's footprint, now referred to as "the Patten Block."

It was the beginning of a new ending.

CHAPTER 10
GIRL WITH THE WHITE-BLONDE HAIR
Fairbanks 1913-14

She tried to put the baby in Agnes's arms, but Agnes would have nothin' to do with it

The ground was still snowy on March 24, 1913, but winter's grip had loosened, so Agnes left for Fairbanks, conveying baby Jeanette's body for burial in the Clay Street Cemetery. Escorted by a Mr. Fisher, who operated a roadhouse on the lower Tanana River, Agnes traveled with Irene and baby Jeanette's coffin to the community of Chena, where they caught the train. Readers of the *Fairbanks Daily Times* were reminded in a timely update, "The infant froze to death on the trail a month or so ago, when the mother was caught by nightfall in a storm, some distance from shelter. Fisher left his roadhouse Monday and reached Chena at two o'clock yesterday with Mrs. Sherman, her two-year-old daughter, and the body of the infant. Mrs. Sherman will be up from Chena this morning on the train." There was no mention of J. P.'s presence or intent to join them now or later.

Gravediggers had chipped out Jeanette's grave, and after her interment, they covered it with small chunks of frozen overburden. Who was there to witness the burial? The baby's mother, sister, and grandparents? No service was announced in the papers. If J. P. did show up, he'd soon returned to his claims in the backcountry of the Totatlanika. Agnes reckoned with the shattering loss of her baby while, if rumors are to be believed, behaving unpredictably. Surely the Pattens were grieving, too, living in town and working the farm on Birch Hill. They must have been at odds as to how to help—or control—Minnie's mourning daughter.

※ ※ ※

J. P. and others were accustomed to crossing the Tanana River ice with sleds or horse-drawn sleighs at Tortella on the way to Fairbanks. After Breakup, stages would replace sleighs, and a scow or ferry transported travelers crossing there. Tortella evolved into the boomtown of Nenana, a railroad camp that forever altered the lives of local Alaska Natives.

For centuries, Athabascan families had lived and worked in this region, and they well knew the land and seasons as they hunted, fished, followed ancient trails, and gathered for communal events. In a few short years, all semblance of normal life for the Athabascans was upended as non-Natives—whether missionaries, railroad workers, or town-builders—flooded their homeland. In 1907, Episcopal missionaries planted St. Mark's Mission upriver, a compound that included a boarding school for Native children from throughout the region, orphans or not. Some Athabascan parents who wanted a book education for their children resettled next to the mission, creating a second Native village. In a few short years, Nenana would explode into a bustling railroad camp.

In fall 1914, Irene was nearly four years old and Agnes was heavily pregnant. It would be easy to assume that this baby, like Jeanette, would be born at the mission hospital that October. But varying stories were filled with non-verifiable information. Those who carried first-person accounts passed away long ago. However, one of those stories was still in circulation sixty years later when pioneer Clara Rust recorded details about Agnes's delivery, and how her child ended up in the care of another family entirely. Listening to the 1974 recording, I weighed the content as some parts truth and some parts hearsay, or purely about-town gossip.

Irene's new sister was born on October 11, 1914, under difficult circumstances and, given some stories, questionable parentage. But exactly where was she born?

Clara's account spun out this way: Agnes was back in Fairbanks and "hanging around," she said. "And then her oldest, this girl [Irene] got to be about five years old. If she had any other children, I can't remember, all I know is just this one baby. So I don't know whether the husband gave up on her and left her or what happened to him, but nobody heard of him around, but Agnes was around here all the time with this little five-year-old girl. . . .

"She went down to Nenana, and she lived down there, and most of the men said that you'd wake up in the morning and find her in the bed with them, something like that. Because she became just a tramp down there. And she was running around." (I half expected to hear a *tsk-tsk* next, but it never came.)

Clara offered a lengthy, detailed story of Agnes's home delivery in Nenana with a woman named Blanche Burnett in attendance as midwife. Although Blanche was from Fairbanks, Clara said, she was briefly living in Nenana so her teen-aged sons, Dewey and Searl, could work for the railroad builders. Clara said that on October 11, local leaders came to Blanche's door and asked for help on Agnes Sherman's behalf. After the baby was born, Blanche tried to put her in Agnes's arms, but was refused, Clara asserted. "She said, 'It don't belong to me, I don't want it, I won't have it.'" Instead, Agnes begged Blanche to take the newborn herself.

When I did the math, I realized the story was off. The baby was born in 1914, but Nenana wasn't even a city until town lots were auctioned in 1916. In later interviews, Blanche's descendants told me they were surprised to hear that Blanche had ever lived in Nenana.

A brief news item in the September 24, 1914, *News-Miner* informed that two weeks before Agnes's baby was due, the Shermans were in Fairbanks at the Nordale Hotel (what with the Third Avenue Hotel in ruins). I'd heard only Clara's story—that the birth was in Nenana, so I wondered why they'd risk returning by dog team in her advanced pregnancy. The answer was, they didn't.

Clara's rendering was amazingly detailed, but in error. The truth was, like Irene, Frances was born at St. Matthew's Hospital and delivered by Dr. James Sutherland, the same man who'd attended Irene's birth. The *Alaska Citizen* of October 12 verified the facts—and added a bit of a surprise—in its birth announcement: "To Mr. and Mrs. J. P. Sherman a baby girl was born yesterday noon. . . . Mr. and Mrs. Sherman came here recently from Totatlanika, but Mr. Sherman is still not aware of the arrival of his little daughter, for the day before her birth, he went to hunt caribou and has not returned." *Wasn't that just like J. P.?* I thought. *You can't make up that stuff.*

Agnes named her third daughter Frances Marguerite Sherman.

Her first name represented both sides of her family tree. Agnes's father was Francis Eckert, and grand-mère Jennie Jenott's middle name was Frances. The baby's middle name honored another of Minnie's sisters, Marguerite, also known as Margaret.

Agnes had loaded up Frances with family names, but the child would not carry the Sherman surname for long, if at all, because one part of Clara Rust's story was true: Blanche Burnett did take the infant and raised Frances as her own.

※ ※ ※

In the twenty years since Blanche wed John "Jack" Franklin Burnett, the family grew as they moved from Kalama, Washington, to Dawson, Skagway, and Fairbanks, chasing gold and adventure. In Skagway, Jack was an "expressman," ensuring safe delivery for gold coming out of the Klondike on the White Pass & Yukon Route.

Blanche was the square-jawed, no-nonsense matriarch of the family, the dependable rock whenever her husband was away and engaged in mining enterprises, which was often. In 1914, she was forty-one, and while the eldest of her five children was grown and married, the youngest was five. She thought her baby days were behind her—until Agnes Sherman asked if she'd take her newborn. Blanche wasn't hasty, Clara Rust remembered. She talked it over with her teen-aged boys, Dewey and Searl, who liked the idea. One of them declared, "Yes, let's keep her!" and that sealed the decision.

Decades later, Connie Burnett, Searl's daughter-in-law, told me the family story this way: "Frances was the daughter of this other couple. They were going to go Outside or something. They went to Blanche and asked 'Would you watch this child for a day or two?' And then they never came back. After two years, they finally came back and they wanted her back. And Blanche said, 'No, she's ours now.'"

The varied versions all landed in the same spot: Frances stayed with the Burnetts. The darling baby was the apple of their eye. Blanche treated Frances as her own and dressed her like a doll. In a rare family photo, little Frances stands with others in front of a house that once belonged to Judge James Wickersham. In her frilly white dress, an oversized white bow in her white-blonde hair, the child looks angelic.

The challenge for Blanche now was how to keep the little angel that she had fallen in love with, because just as Blanche feared, Agnes did change her mind.

A day in court lay ahead.

Frances, left, poses with her adoptive sister, Laura Rynearson, and cousins Kate and Jack Dwyer. The Burnett family had purchased this house from Judge James Wickersham. In 1967, the historic building was moved to city property now called Pioneer Park. (Burnett Family Collection)

CHAPTER 11
WHOM DO YOU BELIEVE?
Bonnifield District 1915

. . . printer's ink cannot paint [Sherman's] character black enough

One day I made another sweep of an archival newspaper database, just in case I'd missed anything. That's when a sensational front-page story popped up, published on November 1, 1915, about J. P. Sherman and his mentally unstable wife, who were living in dire circumstances with their sorry child, Irene, out on the Totatlanika. In all the time I'd combed the papers of that era, the article had never surfaced.

Just over a year after Frances was born, Irene was now four years old and living with her parents as their only child, what with Jeanette's death and Frances fostered by the Burnetts. Agnes was six months into another pregnancy—due in January 1916—when the hair-raising story was blasted on page one of the local paper.

The Shermans and other distant mining neighbors along the Totatlanika River were known to each other, as remote as they were, just as folks know each other in Bush Alaska today. One day a married couple and another single miner stopped at the Sherman cabin when J. P. was not at home. During their visit, the trio heard and observed life as Agnes and Irene knew it. What they learned alarmed them, and they resolved to report it to authorities. The trio gathered signatures from other miners in their area and submitted their story and the signed declaration to the *Alaska Citizen*, which published the inflammatory account on November 1.

No doubt the dramatic details were the talk of the town. The story also led to charges of neglect, J. P. Sherman's arrest, and his transport to Fairbanks to face the judge . . . and more talk about town.

I was well aware that it wasn't unusual for early newspapers to print rumor and slander, and yet, as my eyes scanned the article, I rediscovered sympathy for Irene's troubled mother and wondered again about the reliability of my sources.

The story began under a sensational headline.

Prospector Accused of Misusing Wife
Woman Slowly Starving in Totatlanika

A story of a man's inhumanity to a woman: a story of destitution which in all of its details is so revolting to ordinary human nature as to be absolutely unprintable in most respects, is that told by Mr. and Mrs. Harry G. Cloes and J. A. Lilly, who recently returned to Fairbanks from the Totatlanika country. The story concerns Mr. and Mrs. J. P. Sherman and their little four-year-old girl, the latter a mite who knows nothing of a mother's care beyond kicks and curses, for the reason that the mother is dominated by the father, who is nothing more than a brute, if the stories are true. And it would appear that they are true, as the marital life of the Shermans—how he has kicked and beaten his wife; how he has failed to provide either food or clothing for her either in winter or summer, has long been a subject of gossip among observing Fairbanksans and people of the Totatlanika.

It has been asserted locally that Mrs. Sherman is weak-minded. While in the presence of her husband she is dominated by him entirely, according to the stories, but when he is not around she tells just enough of her life story with the man Sherman to convince her hearers that he is everything which he is said to be and that printer's ink cannot paint his character black enough.

Sherman is the owner of considerable mining ground in the Totatlanika country, and has made his headquarters there for a number of years past. About five years ago he married Lois [sic] Eckert, a daughter of Mrs. J. H. Patten of this city and took her with him to the Totatlanika country on his periodical trips there, mostly in the summer. They usually leave here in the spring of the year just before the breakup and return late in the fall, spending the principal part of the winter in Fairbanks.

During these five years seven born and unborn children have come to the couple, according to the stories told by Mrs. Sherman.

Of these two are living, the youngest, about two years of age, having been left with the Burnette [sic] family last spring when Mr. and Mrs. Sherman went to the Totatlanika country. It is stated that Mrs. Sherman is again to be confined in January, and that with her husband, she will arrive in Fairbanks within the next few days.

When Mr. and Mrs. Sherman came to Fairbanks two years ago from the Totatlanika, they lost one of their children. At the time the story told was that the child froze to death, but it now develops that the mother has stated times innumerable that it starved to death at her breast for lack of nourishment, and that she herself nearly died. The only food the Shermans had at the time, it is stated, was rabbits, but, when the supply gave out, they sustained life until they could reach human habitation by gnawing the bones of a malamute dog, which, it is reported, had been killed by Sherman.

That Sherman is attempting to starve his wife and child to death and that he is slowly succeeding in doing so, is the opinion of those who know the details of how they have lived during the past summer. Mrs. Sherman was bedridden a great deal of the time and had nothing more nourishing to eat during her illness than beans and rice. None of the common, ordinary necessities of life found their way to the Sherman cabin on the Totatlanika, according to the stories told, such commodities as sugar, milk and fresh meat being unknown quantities.

The man lives in the same manner as he compels his wife and child to live. Dirt and filth abound in their dwelling place. Most of the time the child is said to be almost entirely without clothing of any kind, and the only clothing worn by the mother is that cast off by her husband. He, in the meantime, being provided with the best that there is to be had in that line.

In speaking of the matter, Mrs. Cloes said that it is not on account of the parents that she is telling the story, but for the sake of the child now with the Shermans, the other here in town and the one as yet unborn. She says that, contrary to her expectations, she found the child now with its parents very bright. She had previously been informed that it was an imbecile and that it could not talk, but states

*that Totatlanika men have told her the latter was true for a time for the
reason that every time the child opened its mouth to laugh, talk or cry,
its father would throw a cupful of cold water in its face.*

The child now in the Burnette [sic] *home here is very bright, and
is the pride of the household. It could stay there forever as far as the
Burnette* [sic] *family is concerned, but it is stated that the deranged
mother says that she will take it away as soon as she reaches town. It is
understood that Mrs. John Patten, the children's grandmother, would
take care of the one now with the parents if its mother would let it come
to her, but that the mother will not consent to such an arrangement.*

*It is rumored that the Woman's Civic club of Fairbanks will look
into the matter of the destitution of the Shermans. As far as can be
ascertained it would seem that the man had always had enough for
himself, but his wife claims that he never had enough to purchase
stockings or underwear for herself and their baby.*

*It is known to be an absolute certainty that Sherman had more
than $1,000 last fall.* [The value of $1,000 in 1915 was worth more than
$30,000 in 2024.] *In spite of this fact, however, his wife was compelled to
beg practically everything she had to eat or wear last winter, according
to all reports.*

*It is possible that a complaint charging insanity will be lodged
against Mrs. Sherman as soon as she arrives in town, and also charges of
non-support of his family may be made against the husband and father,
although no statement to that effect has been made.*

*Sherman is declared to be particularly brutal in his treatment of
dogs or other animals belonging to him. He usually manages, however,
to be kind to them when anybody is around, reserving his ill treatment for
a time when there is no one to see and hear. On one occasion he is said
to have left a horse tied to a tree for two or three days with nothing to
eat, the story being to the effect that a man came along and mercifully
shot the beast, after it had got down on the ice and could not get up.*

*A slight idea of Sherman's unpopularity in the Totatlanika may
be gained from the following: We, the undersigned, miners of the
Totatlanika, do hereby affirm that J. P. Sherman, to our personal*

knowledge, is dishonest, unreliable and unscrupulous, and is held in disrepute by the entire community. (Signed) William McCarty, Charles Anderson, H. G. Cloes, Fred Thiesen, James Larson, Nels Stol, John Cook, Charles Nelson, James Murphy, J. A. Lilly.

❋ ❋ ❋

As I read, I inhaled sharply and rolled back from the screen. How could I have been so wrong about Agnes? How could J. P. have been such a monster? Or had the newspaper capitalized on selling the hype, slander be damned? That was not unusual in frontier journalism, I knew, and yet, those eye-witness accounts . . .

On Friday, December 3, 1915, Deputy Marshal John C. Wood returned from the Totatlanika with J. P. Sherman in hand on a charge of non-support of his wife and child the previous summer. Agnes and Irene accompanied him on the trip to town, and J. P. was released on a $500 bond. The following Monday, J. P.'s case came before the Commissioner's Court. And then about a week later, without issuing further details in public, on December 13, the District Attorney dismissed the case for lack of evidence. J. P. was free to go.

He returned to the Totatlanika with his very pregnant wife and daughter Irene. Dismissed. So if the signed testimony of a group of neighbors was not enough, then the courts believed J. P., not Agnes.

Once again, I asked myself, how did Minnie handle the knowledge that Agnes and Irene were dwelling amid such squalor and violence? Was there nothing she could do without being sucked into the whirlpool herself? Returning to the newspaper archives for more information, perhaps in the timeline of events, I found the answer in the February 7, 1916, edition of the *Alaska Citizen*. The fire that had destroyed the Third Avenue Hotel had been a breaking point for the Pattens. The couple decided to clear out of town, selling the "Patten Block" building while it was as yet unfinished.

By March 1916, about two years after the hotel burned, $15,000 had changed hands, and terms of the sale were leaked to the public. With his insurance payout, Patten would about break even.

John Moe had run the Globe saloon in the old Third Avenue Hotel. After the fire, he opened for business out of a tent until he found temporary quarters. In the new Patten building, Moe's modern bar with the same name would attract his old clientele and more. With attorneys and physicians reserving offices upstairs, and other small businesses filling the ground level, the Patten building was sure to flourish. Everybody won. Most importantly, the Pattens were free to leave, and initially, they were headed Outside.

"According to their present plans," the *Fairbanks Daily Times* informed its readers, "Mr. and Mrs. Patten will leave for the States sometime next month. How long they will be away from Fairbanks they do not know, but they will not return for a year at any rate, according to the statement made by Mr. Patten last evening."

Their plans did change. The Pattens' exit route took them first to Petersburg, Alaska, before they eventually moved "down to the States" for good.

CHAPTER 12
MRS. SHERMAN IS DISTRACTED
Fairbanks 1916
'Where is their mother?' was on everybody's lips

The miners of Totatlanika country had tried their best to protect Agnes and Irene. After neighbors visited the Sherman place in the summer of 1915, subsequent charges against J. P. had been dismissed. I searched for more details, but without a case file number, and with so few surviving court records from the early territorial days, it was a lost cause. I'd contacted the National Archives in Seattle to no avail. They sent me to the Alaska State Archives. I flew to Juneau to search their records in person, but even with the very able help of the archivists, only a fraction of the early court records were in storage. I would have loved to lay my hands on the letter that J. P. had written to the U.S. marshal when Jeanette died. Was there an inquest? And I wanted to read the actual charges against J. P. in this non-support case. Through floods, fires, and purges, those records no longer existed. I'd have to rely on newspaper accounts and other histories.

In the negligence case against J. P. Sherman, U.S. Attorney Roth may have concluded that Agnes was not telling the truth or that in general, she wasn't a reliable witness. She'd have told him that she'd given birth to Irene, Jeanette, and Frances, and explained why only one child was still with her. She had been nearly six months pregnant when that trio of visitors carried the story to the newspaper office. Agnes had also claimed that she'd lost as many as three other babies to stillbirth or miscarriage in her first five years of marriage. And that her husband routinely beat her and mistreated their daughter. True or false?

Even though the charges against J. P. were dismissed, life with this man would be no different. I wonder how he'd reacted to his dirty laundry airing in Fairbanks papers. What was his response to those shocking charges against him? Was he a cold man who grew colder? More focused on work? Meaner still? If he were, would anybody believe Agnes's word?

As time drew near to deliver her fourth child, Agnes made her way back to Nenana, presumably to St. Mark's Episcopal mission hospital. Somehow, despite stories of deprivation, mistreatment, and malnutrition, Agnes managed to deliver a healthy baby boy on February 12, 1916. She named him James Day Sherman, not James Paul. He was not a junior to her husband. Rumors were still alive in the mid-1970s when Clara Rust shared her recollections about Agnes living loose in Nenana, when "men would wake up and find her in their beds." It sparked speculation: *Had infidelity fueled J. P's cruelty?*

With the birth of James, Irene finally had a little brother, a baby to dote upon. The Shermans continued to live apart, either by desire or convenience, with J. P. out on the creeks doing what he did best, and still providing for his family. He set up Agnes, Irene, and James in a rental cabin on Fifth Avenue near Cushman in Fairbanks, just behind Gordon's dry goods store and across from Eagle Hall. The place was a typical one-room structure with a lean-to. It was heated by a stove and lit with coal oil lamps. Like its neighbors, the cabin had been hastily built during the gold rush. It had a low roof, like others all over town, which made for cramped living, but also meant it was easier to heat. In early November 1916, Fairbanks had been bitterly cold. But that was about to change.

On November 18, the oversized thermometer outside McIntosh & Kubon's drug store on Cushman confirmed what everyone already knew. In a matter of hours, the temperature had rocketed from well below zero to forty degrees above in a meteorological whiplash. A warm wind called a "Chinook" had poured down the mountainsides and blasted across the Tanana Valley, transforming solidly frozen trails into mud bogs or ponds, and dangerously softening creek ice. Even cabin roofs began dripping as if it were spring. All of Interior Alaska was "sweltering," reported the *Alaska Citizen*, "in its first Chinook of the season." Except for the *cheechakos*, everyone knew to expect one or two Chinooks each winter. And they knew the reprieve would be temporary. As surely as the mercury rose, it would fall like a pile driver and once more the piercing cold would rob them of their breath.

True to form, within a week, McIntosh & Kubon's street-side

thermometer displayed twenty-six degrees below zero. Twelve hours later, it hadn't budged. Above each cabin, wood-stove exhaust formed a white column that flattened and joined its neighbor, blocking out the sun or stars, and lending the appearance of a fluffy ceiling over town.

Two days before Thanksgiving, on November 28, J. P. was working about thirty miles away at Fish Creek; his wife was at the Fairbanks cabin with their children. But Agnes Sherman had no intention of staying home that day. She banked the stove against the deep cold and slammed the cabin door with a *wump!*, leaving behind five-year-old Irene with baby brother, James, now nine months old. Before leaving, Agnes directed Irene to take care of James. He was her responsibility, and she took it seriously. Most of the time, James was corralled in his baby buggy, which served as a bed and playpen.

After noon that Tuesday, Agnes had been gone for hours. The sun had barely brightened the sky when a neighbor named Hannah Porter let her daughter go over to play at the Sherman place. The couples knew each other from mining in the Totatlanika. Now Irene was in charge of Mary Porter as well as James. Just two months from her sixth birthday, she was already toughened by life circumstances, while Mary was a tender age four. The Porter family lived near Agnes, Irene, and James. Yet their lives differed dramatically. Mary was a well-loved child from an intact family of two parents and three siblings ranging from fourteen to two. Her father brought his family along as he worked teamster jobs in camps from Nome to Chatanika to Fairbanks.

Little Mary was popular for her sweet vocal performances, especially at the Pioneers of Alaska gatherings. The old men of Igloo No. 4 adored her, maybe because she reminded the sourdoughs of the daughters or granddaughters they hadn't seen in years. In her seventies, Irene looked back on the events of that day and remembered Mary as a "hellion" who "more or less throws lit matches all over the place."

"Well, I'd a-done all right if the damn Porter family woulda kept their brat home!" she told me in 1988, delivering each word with the intensity of a fresh injury. "She wouldn't leave things alone! . . . All I wanted was to be left with my brother, so I could take care of him. And keep him happy! He was just a little shaver."

At the Sherman cabin, below-zero cold was soaking the logs and seeping through invisible cracks. It rolled off the frosted window panes in waves. The stove had cooled considerably, and the little girls could see their breath. Irene made up her mind to rekindle the fire. By two in the afternoon of November 28, the little girls were wearing layers of clothing under their coats and were still freezing cold. James was likewise under multiple blankets. Irene thought they should gather up some papers and lay them on nearly cold embers. She poured an inflammatory liquid over the pile—either coal oil or maybe gas—and tried to get a match to light, with one failure after another. Perhaps Mary tried, too. Irene's memory of that day said she did.

"I don't know what my mother had to leave home for, but she had to leave home," Irene told me, "and all hell broke loose. And that damn Mary Porter come over to the house, and that made me mad, and I couldn't keep watch on both of 'em. I don't know how she got ahold of them [matches] either. My mother always tried to keep the matches out of the way of all of us, but by god, I don't think she had much success with that doggone little hellion. And I didn't want that god-damn kid over there to the house anyhow. I figured I had enough to care, taking care of my brother. Mary Porter, just a damn pack of nuisance."

At last a match flared, and the effect was instantaneous. The Shermans' rented cabin was like so many others in Fairbanks, where homemakers decorated their walls by gluing cheesecloth to the logs before adding a layer of pretty wallpaper. They had what was called a "balloon ceiling." For Irene and Mary, the combination of a flash flame and a low-ceilinged room was deadly. The fire caught a piece of dangling cheesecloth, and it roared to life.

Screaming and frantic, Irene and Mary tried to escape. Baby James was still in his buggy. In a panic, one of the girls pushed the bulky carriage to the door as the other tugged at the handle. It wouldn't budge. They tried pulling together, but they weren't strong enough. An ice dam had formed at the bottom, effectively locking them in. Smoke quickly filled the room from the top down as fire streaked across walls and furnishings, and consumed the winter stores. The girls pressed their faces against the window and screamed while James shrieked from his buggy.

Now the children themselves were burning, their lungs, skin, and hair. In that moment, a passerby identified later as "a man named Taylor" saw them in the window and acted, kicking and throwing himself against the door. Ducking low and holding his breath, he grabbed the girls and pulled them to safety. But in forcing his way into the cabin, the rescuer had shoved James and his carriage behind the door and out of sight.

The baby was no longer crying.

Across the street at Eagle Hall, Jesse Rust and a few other members were convened in a routine gathering when an unidentified man, perhaps Taylor, opened the door and shouted, "Fire! There's a fire across the way!" Jesse followed him out in the rush and witnessed all that happened next. What filled his eyes as he tried to help would not allow him to sleep that night.

As she was pulled from the burning cabin, Irene was screaming, "I have set the house afire! I have set the house afire!" The skin on her face, neck, arms, and hands had melted away. Clothing hung in shreds where it hadn't burned into her flesh. Within seconds, three volunteer firemen arrived. Irene was desperately shouting, "My baby's inside! My baby! Save my baby!" Bystanders held Mary and restrained Irene as she struggled to go back inside. They worked to get the girls across the street and inside Eagle Hall for medical attention. Amid the confusion, the volunteer firemen acted decisively.

"Jack O'Conner, 'Red' Ricker, and Jack Hansen rushed in to search for the child," the *News-Miner* reported later that day. "O'Connor, going further into the blazing structure than the others, was overcome by smoke, making it necessary for the other firemen to drag him. Hansen then crawled into the building on his hands and knees. Unable to find the child, he started out again, when back of the door he felt part of the baby carriage. He stirred it and as he did the child cried out feebly. Reaching farther, he caught the child by the head and dragged it to him so that he could pick it up in his arms, and with the suffering infant, he staggered from the building."

Pioneer doctors Mahlon F. Hall and James A. Sutherland had separate medical practices, and each responded quickly.

Local papers ran special editions as their readers demanded updates on the tragedy. (*News-Miner* Archives)

Everyone in town knew that the Sherman cabin was burning. The fire hall's practice of blowing a siren with one long and several short blasts told listeners how many blocks the fire was from the river. Telephone operators kept a line open for people calling in, repeating their message: "The Sherman cabin on Fifth, the Sherman cabin on Fifth."

The fire department depended on the Northern Commercial Company boilers on First Avenue to pressurize their hoses. Less than a month earlier, the McNeil cabin on Eighth had burned to the ground because the hoses couldn't reach that far. Even though the Sherman cabin was within range, by the time they got the children out, the structure was beyond saving.

Suffering from seared lungs and extensive burns, Irene and Mary wilted, drifting in and out of consciousness as each was laid out at Eagle Hall. There Dr. Sutherland performed medical assessments. He'd been the delivery doctor when Irene was born. Surely he remembered the tiny girl.

It seemed Mary had fewer visible burns and might be able to recuperate without hospitalization, while Irene was much worse. Some said it was because she had stayed inside so long to maneuver the baby carriage.

After fireman Jack Hansen emerged with James, he was near collapse himself. Someone took the infant and hurriedly carried his frail form across the street. He was then moved to Dr. Hall's well-equipped medical office at Sixth and Cushman, just a block away.

Where was their mother? people were asking. *Where was Agnes?* Finally, she was located where she'd been for most of the day, drinking with a couple of friends. Not out and about in the saloons, but in the home of a woman who was sympathetic to Agnes's situation. According to the gossips, Agnes had been enjoying the company of a woodchopper who delivered cut wood to his customers. The scandal ran deep, breaching the social mores of their time, especially where women and minorities were concerned. Agnes was a married woman; he was a Black man. For many, this was an unacceptable friendship, let alone romance. Agnes snubbed the gossips and continued to accept his invitations to come along on his rounds. They had been seen together often. Finally, town leaders had approached the man with a threatening message to stay away from the Sherman woman. In response, the couple found a rendezvous location at the home of a mutual friend, a Black woman named Chloe, who lived on Fourth, her back door facing the end of "The Line," as the Red Light District was known. According to Clara Rust, Chloe washed "the silks" for the prostitutes and supplied them with beer for their customers. As a person in the margins of society, Chloe readily accepted others in the margins.

The trio had been drinking away the day. When Agnes learned the horrific news, the realization of what had happened and her role in it, she dissolved, screaming and slashing at anyone near her. Finally officials managed to restrain Agnes and get her across the Cushman Street bridge for medical help, just a few blocks away. *The Alaska Citizen* noted, "When she heard of what had befallen her babies, Mrs. Sherman was distracted, going immediately into hysterics. She was taken to St. Joseph's hospital, where she was placed in a straitjacket last night to keep her from doing herself harm. The father of the children, it is understood, is working on Fish creek."

That evening, the *News Miner* published a late edition for an eager readership, announcing "SHERMAN BABY IS BADLY BURNED IN AFTERNOON FIRE."

"Dr. M. F. Hall, the physician in charge of the case, said this afternoon just before the *News Miner* went to press that he doubted very much if the child could survive," the paper said in its update, "as it was burned practically to the bone around the head and face, and badly about the limbs and one side of the body.

"Should this child die, as the physicians think it will, it will be the second child of the Shermans to meet a sad end, as another one was frozen to death in the Totatlanika country a couple of years ago."

Baby James lasted until 11:00 P.M. Afterward, *The Alaska Citizen* published an update: "All of the physicians who examined the Sherman infant coincided in the opinion that it could not possibly have lived, after making an examination," the paper reported. "The head and upper part of the body were literally cooked, the ears being burned entirely off."

Out on Fish Creek, a musher approaching J. P.'s cabin in the night sent his dog team into frenzy. He was peering out when the messenger slid to a halt. The news was inconceivable. Shaken, J. P. immediately gathered what he needed and hooked up his team. He would push them to exhaustion in his thirty-mile run to Fairbanks.

Back on Fifth Avenue, embers at the smoldering cabin kicked up into fresh fires twice during the night. The fire department received two "still alarms" and sent out men to extinguish them. A victim of smoke inhalation, fireman Jack O'Connor did not have to respond. The fire hall related that he was "pretty sick."

When the *Nome Nugget* went to press on November 30, they summed up their story with, "It is thought that Irene used coal oil or gasoline to start the fire, but this cannot but learned, for the house is a ruin. The Sherman baby and Mary Porter are dead and Irene is at the point of death. Mrs. Sherman is distracted."

At age seventy-seven, Irene retold the story, again, of what happened that day—to herself, to her brother, and to Mary Porter.

"She wound up burnt, as I did. And my brother died. I think she died, too. And I was the only one that seemed to stay alive."

✳ ✳ ✳

After the Third Avenue Hotel was destroyed in winter 1914, the Pattens sold their unfinished building and discussed moving Outside. But those plans were derailed when other inviting prospects in the Tolovana mining camp northeast of Fairbanks reached John Patten, and he answered. He decided to jump back into gold-mining.

Eight months later, in October 1916, the *Alaska Citizen* reported that Patten was in town from Tolovana country, where he projected "considerable doing in a mining way there this winter." It's likely that he was there to resupply before heading back. It was early October and freeze-up was imminent, but sluicing had continued because heavy rains had raised the streams and allowed the miners to keep working. The Tolovana had had a hard start, he said, but hoped that the fall clean-ups would "see all old scores settled up."

The very next month brought with it the sickening events of the Sherman cabin fire. *Were Minnie and John both in town by then? I wondered. Did they witness the horror up close?* Just weeks after John's last trip in from the Tolovana, baby James was dead and Irene was barely living, and all fingers were pointing at Minnie's daughter, Agnes.

The Pattens were both approaching fifty. He was no longer a young man on the diggings, but he'd worked hard on the Tolovana that fall to scrape up enough for their next steps. With the hotel fire, financial setbacks, and so many personal tragedies, the couple knew they didn't have time or energy to ride out any lows on the Tolovana. It was time to leave. There were other fish to fry in Southeast Alaska.

Dr. James Sutherland, standing with his dog team leaders, was Irene's delivery doctor and one of two physicians who treated the children after the fire. His medical office and home stood at Front (First) and Cowles. He also had mining interests in the Kantishna region and on this day was about to depart. (Library of Congress, Carpenter Collection, LC-DIG-PPMSC-01599)

CHAPTER 13
BITTER GRIEF, BRUTAL COLD
November 1916

Irene was barely recognizable and speaking in whispers

The day before Thanksgiving 1916, in the wee hours of Wednesday morning, Mary and Irene were sinking. "They were in such a critical condition that it was considered advisable to remove them to the hospital," the papers reported.

When J. P. arrived, he stabled his dogs and looked for someone to give him the whole story. He knew the basics: his baby boy was dead; his daughter was near death; his wife had suffered a nervous breakdown and was now straightjacketed and sedated in the same hospital as the injured girls. Sisters of Providence nurses were seeing to their needs. The Sherman cabin and all of its contents were gone. Heartsick, J. P. rushed to St. Joseph's to find his daughter. Sitting by her bed at the hospital, he found Irene conscious and able to tell him what had happened.

Fresh headlines in the *News-Miner* that morning were lurid: *HORROR SHOCKS THE WHOLE TOWN; Seems No Doubt Irene Sherman Started the Fire In Attempting to Start Fire In the Stove.* "Dr. J. A. Sutherland, who is attending both of these children, stated that the children were practically unconscious and in a most critical condition. Both are badly burned about the body and particularly about the head and face."

Stories are liquid things, changing even when retold by the same person, let alone by competing newspapers or town gossips. Before long, conflicting stories in the press dimmed public understanding. *The Alaska Citizen* published a recap that added one more Porter child to the fire, a younger brother of Mary's who was not mentioned in other accounts. The writer also made a hero of Irene and ignored witness narratives about the rescuer named Taylor, reporting, "That the Porter children managed to escape at all is probably due to the little Sherman girl, who dragged them outside of the house, but who was unable to bring out her baby brother who sustained the burns which caused his death."

On the night of the fire, Agnes Sherman was straitjacketed and transported to St. Joseph's Hospital (right), where Irene had already been admitted. When J. P. made it to town, he hurried to his daughter's bedside. (Library of Congress, Carpenter Collection, PNP-CPH-3c2000)

In Wednesday's early hours, when J. P. finally reached his daughter's bedside, Irene was barely recognizable and speaking in whispers. What Irene told him, J. P. shared in a statement to the local papers, which relayed the details and added a few of their own making. "This afternoon J. P. Sherman, the father of the Sherman children, stated that his daughter Irene told him that the house was cold and that she attempted to start a fire in the stove and that in this way the house caught fire. The father was unable to say whether or not the child had used coal oil." In his statement, J. P. also confirmed that the girls had attempted to drag out the baby, but couldn't open the door, and that the man named Taylor, in passing, forced his way in.

Another *Alaska Citizen* article pointedly wrote of Agnes's irresponsibility: "It seems that the fire was caused by the mother's carelessness in leaving the children alone in the house all day."

On Wednesday, Eagle Hall was buzzing as members and their wives prepared for the annual Thanksgiving Ball, a cherished tradition scheduled for late that evening. The dance was *not* cancelled, despite what had happened yesterday just across the street. The smoldering cabin had been dampened by a light blanket of snow. Party volunteers from Aerie No. 1037 stared at the rubble as they came and went throughout the day. They elaborately decorated the hall, arranged seating for Victor Durand's orchestra, and set tables upstairs with linens, china, and silverware for the traditional midnight turkey dinner.

Dancing to live music, men in their dress apparel, the ladies in their finest floor-length gowns, would go on as planned that night, followed by the Thanksgiving feast with all the trimmings. No doubt, conversation at every table touched on the news that another child had died and the last one was failing. Gossip about Agnes Sherman prevailed throughout the night of dancing, dining, and toasting.

On Thanksgiving Day, November 30, *The Alaska Citizen* recapped the story that broke hearts across town: "SECOND VICTIM OF TERRIBLE ACCIDENT." Late Wednesday afternoon, Mary Porter's suffering ended at St. Joseph's hospital, the public learned, "after having sunk gradually since early morning."

"At 4:10 yesterday afternoon Mary Porter, the four-year-old daughter of F. J. Porter, passed away at St. Joseph's hospital," the *Citizen* reported. "She is the second victim of the terrible catastrophe that has already claimed the infant son of Mr. and Mrs. J. P. Sherman. The little girl was taken to the hospital early yesterday morning, and the doctors labored all day to save her life. She remained unconscious all day, nor could their efforts rouse her from that state. Finally, late in the afternoon, she died, too.

"She was playing with the Sherman children on the fatal afternoon of last Tuesday. According to the little Sherman girl's story, she, Irene Sherman, tried to light the fire, as they were getting cold. In some way the house caught fire. The two little girls were rescued from the fire by a man by the name of Taylor, according to the story told yesterday by those who were present at the scene. He is reported to have been severely burned.

"However, both of the children were terribly burned by the flames and suffocated by the dense smoke that issued from the house. Irene was reported to be better last night, but she is still in a critical condition. Mrs. Sherman was not at home at the time. She is in the hospital now, suffering from a breakdown as a result of the terrible accident. Her husband is with her, as he came in from the creeks late last night."

In the following days, errors continued to creep into stories appearing in Skagway and Valdez newspapers, from the date of the fire to the number of children who were present. Even that the Sherman children were left in the care of Mary Porter, not vice versa. But it was this hard truth that made readers of the Valdez *Prospector* shudder: "Irene is expected to recover, but will be disfigured for life."

Days later, on December 3, Alaska Engineering Commission teamster Dave Patterson left Fairbanks for Nenana with a fully loaded freight sled drawn by four draft horses. The cold was so severe that once Patterson made it to the Ohio Roadhouse, twenty-seven miles out, he stabled his horses and didn't leave for five days. A normal two-day trip had taken seven and pinned him down in fifty-below temperatures. Meanwhile, "automobilist" Tom Gibb, driving for the Sheldon Auto Line, discovered the only way to keep his machine operating meant continuous use of a blow torch to warm the gasoline feed. Often he'd had to stop and use a wire to clear ice crystals from the line. During his repeated efforts, Gibb badly froze his thumb.

That bone-chilling December 3 was also the day of Mary Porter's funeral Mass in Fairbanks, an event that would have turned out much of the town if not for the severe weather. Instead, attendance was light and travel in general was hampered. Gathered in the front pew at Immaculate Conception Church was the grieving Porter family: parents Frank and Hannah, and their children Harry, Margaret, and little Kenneth. Mary had been the third child, between Margaret and Kenneth.

The church stood next door to St. Joseph's Hospital, where the sole survivor of the fire, Irene, was in the continuous care of the Sisters of Providence. Miraculously, she was showing some improvement.

Thinking about that day and who was in attendance—and who was not—I see two families, the Porters and the Shermans, both of whom had both mined out in Totatlanika country. And both had lived as neighbors in town. Hannah Porter personally knew Agnes and trusted her enough to allow her four-year-old to go over to play with the Sherman children. No doubt, guilt poured over Hannah every time she replayed that decision. Hannah and Frank were suspended in living misery.

Surely J. P. did not attend Mary Porter's funeral. His immediate concern was seeing to Irene's needs and arranging for his baby's burial. There had been no public notification of a funeral service for James. And what about Agnes? Had she been released from her straitjacket and the hospital? If so, where did she go to recover from her overwhelming grief? Would someone declare her insane and send her off? Again, so many answers seemed unknowable.

The day after Mary's funeral, townspeople who didn't make it to the funeral Mass imagined it with fresh sorrow as they read the *Alaska Citizen* story under the headline "Porter Child Laid at Rest."

"The funeral of Mary Porter, the four-year-old daughter of Mr. and Mrs. F. J. Porter, who was so badly burned in the Sherman cabin fire of last week that she died, was held yesterday afternoon.

"The funeral was largely attended by the friends of the Porter family, but not so largely as it would have been under different weather conditions. There were numerous beautiful floral offerings. The pall bearers were six little girls." While the service was going on, Irene was right next door at St. Joseph's Hospital, still in agony, but slowly recuperating. And there she would stay for a couple of years.

The fire victims, Mary Johnson Porter and James Day Sherman, were both buried in the Clay Street Cemetery, mere blocks from the burned-out wreck of the Sherman cabin. Mary was interred in the Catholic Circle, under a wooden cross, whereas James was buried elsewhere on the grounds. Again, the winter burials in such extreme cold would have been physically demanding for the diggers.

In twenty-first-century Fairbanks, after a winter death and funeral, the remains are normally stored above ground at the cemetery or funeral home until spring, the season of burials. When the snow melts and the ground softens enough for a backhoe to do its work, one by one, interments begin around Memorial Day, with or without a second memorial service at graveside, according to the family's wishes. Some Alaskan towns prefer to estimate the number of winter deaths and will pre-dig graves in the fall. They're lined with Styrofoam to prevent the soil on the sides from caving in. The open graves are covered with plywood sheets—and insulated by several feet of snow. But in early Fairbanks history, gravediggers chopped and hacked into rock-hard soil or relied on those drift-mining steam points.

Before the first week of December 1916 had ended, there were two fresh, child-sized graves in the Clay Street Cemetery. In the weeks that followed December 4, St. Joseph's Hospital raised Irene's condition from "critical" to "guarded" to "Irene probably will live."

The lives of two families—the Porters and the Shermans—seemed to have rolled out in parallel tracks until the day of the fire. At the head of the Porter family was Frank J., or as Clara Rust recalled his nickname: "a fella by the name of 'Dirtyface Porter.'" Another pioneer said Frank Porter had gained the nickname by cutting wood after forest fires and was always dirty. "[His] little girl—she had a beautiful voice—about four years old, and they had her at the Pioneer programs and all to sing," Clara said. "She had a strong voice for a small girl like that."

When he wasn't cutting wood or mining, Dirtyface Porter was a teamster employed by a local freighter. In 1915, the family lived across the Chena River in the area known as Graehl (the neighborhood where Irene would spend most of her adult life). Next the Porters rented a cabin downtown near the Shermans.

The Porter family had grown with a new baby at each mining camp as Frank stampeded to Nome in 1900, then to Chatanika, and then Fairbanks, where little Mary was born in 1912. By 1914, while Agnes was giving birth to Frances in Nenana, the Porters' youngest, Kenneth, was born in Fairbanks. How and when did Dirtyface Porter come to know

J. P. Sherman amid all those intersections? Their place of work did overlap in 1915, when Frank formed a partnership with two other men as Porter, Heald, and Lovette. They selected several leases in the Totatlanika district, the same region where J. P. was mining. And in Fairbanks, the two families were neighbors, close enough that Mary was allowed to come and play.

Tragedy forever bound the two families after the 1916 cabin fire. How did the Porters view the Shermans after that heartbreaking day? I couldn't imagine. By the twenty-first century, the graves of Mary Porter and the Sherman babies, Jeanette and James, had all lost their markers, most likely during seasons of catastrophic flooding.

※ ※ ※

After the fire and after the burials, one of Mary Porter's old sourdough friends, Joseph Handbury, composed a memorial poem for the girl. Handbury, born in 1851, was a member of the Pioneers of Alaska Igloo No. 4, and had landed at Nome on June 22, 1900, before joining the next rush to Fairbanks. Like so many other old-timers, Handbury was among Mary's admirers when she sang at local gatherings. His poem appeared in the *Alaska Weekly Citizen*:

"Mary Porter, the little four-year-old child who died recently of burns sustained in the fire at the Sherman cabin last week, was a great favorite with everyone who had acquaintance with her. She was the idol of many old sourdoughs, and among them who feel keenly the loss of little Mary is Jos. Handbury . . . who penned these lines "In Appreciation of Mary Porter."

"Like a bud that has blossomed for only a day,
Like a sunbeam that flashes, then passes away,
Like a strain of sweet music that scarcely is heard,
Like the song of a child, or carol of bird,
Little Mary came to us with heart pure and fond
And at sunrise in life she passes beyond;
All that is mortal sleeps under the sod,
But the beautiful soul is at home with its God."

Below the poem, another update appeared: "The latest information obtainable states that Irene Sherman, the little fire sufferer, is still improving. Although she is not entirely out of danger, her chances of recovery are greatly improved."

※ ※ ※

The loss of a child can destroy a marriage, but the Porters somehow endured. Yet, constant reminders of Mary's absence touched every family member. The Porters relocated to Cordova on the Gulf of Alaska, where Frank found work, then finally they landed in Anchorage, where their children grew up. Frank was still going strong in 1940, when, at seventy-five, he was foreman of a sheep ranch on the Palmer Highway. I wondered if he ever again visited Fairbanks to stand by his daughter's grave. I wondered if he ever gave Irene a thought.

CHAPTER 14
A SHATTERED FAMILY - Nenana 1919

*Dad stomped on Momma pretty damn much and said
no more leaving that kid alone!*

One month after the cabin fire, on Christmas Eve day, Dr. James
Sutherland performed surgery on J. P. Sherman to remove as many as
two hundred small donations of skin for grafting onto his daughter's
arms. In the Christmas day edition of the *Alaska Citizen*, the operation
was declared a success and that "while somewhat painful, is not a serious
affair." J. P. was able to "be around as usual," the doctor reported.

"For several days, [Irene's] life was despaired of. Her injuries are
now not considered necessarily fatal, but they are still very serious," the
paper reported. "The skin on her arms was roasted off, and the grafting
operation was absolutely necessary. Mr. Sherman upon learning of the
facts, at once gladly volunteered to furnish the necessary skin for the new
covering. Her face is also very badly burned, and it may be necessary to
have the same operation performed on it. This, however, cannot be stated
definitely until the injuries are more nearly healed. The little girl is
gradually improving, and every day adds to her chances for recovery."

Two weeks later, the city council approved a proposal to pay
Irene's hospital bill. Ever on the edge of infection or recovering from yet
another surgery, she would spend nearly four years under intensive
medical care. The *Douglas Island News* later reported, "The child, who
was terribly burned, has never fully recovered."

Still, two years after the fire, J. P. fetched Irene from the hospital
and moved the family out of Fairbanks. "My mother had a hell of a time
taking care of me, too, because she didn't understand this hospital deal
too well," Irene remembered. "We had to take another home, and this
time, by god, Dad stomped on Momma pretty damn much and said no
more leaving that kid alone! And no more having her with kids that don't
know the word behave. Or anything else."

Irene was sixty-four and sitting on a barstool at Ken's Bar on
Third Avenue as she held forth to a *News-Miner* reporter. As Irene

remembered, her father "up and grabbed me and my mother and moved us to Nenana, because some so-called doc said he was gonna cut my hand off." I could imagine her tone of voice as she spoke.

Later, Irene was reflective about that time when she talked to me, recalling home life with Agnes and J. P. She easily switched tenses, speaking of her father as if he were still alive: "My dad had one of those freakish feelings—he wanted all of his blinkity-blank kids home, where he could get his mitts on 'em. He didn't want the damn doctors saying no, you'll contaminate the kids and this, that, and the other thing. He says, 'I'll contaminate them!' By god, he wasn't gonna stand for any nonsense.

"He's like the cat on the tin roof, he's not able to stay put in one spot for very long. He's got a lot of business to take care of."

In 1918 Nenana, J. P. registered for the WWI draft, although he was never called up. He'd written Agnes's name as next of kin, and reported that he was a contractor employed by the Alaska Engineering Commission, builders of the Alaska railroad. Following the death of baby James two years earlier, the Shermans had had no more children. Frances was still with the Burnetts, so Irene alone lived with her parents in Nenana, getting medical attention at either the mission hospital or the one that served the AEC. Or was she, given J. P.'s disdain for doctors? Her parents were under scrutiny, and not just from the town gossips. In 1919, the U.S. commissioner in Nenana decided to intervene on behalf of the Sherman children, both Irene and Frances.

Where were the Pattens? I wondered once more. Now at a new season in their life? Mining, or gone Outside? Then I learned about John's entrepreneurial brother who'd been thriving in southeastern Alaska, in that narrow strip of mountains and rainforest snugged up against Canada's British Columbia and Yukon Territory.

John H. Patten had come to Skagway in October 1897, followed by his brother Fred just a few months later. Fred was a carpenter, while John was a contractor. In 1900, Fred, his new bride, and bachelor brother John were sharing a place in Skagway. When John joined the rush to the Interior's gold fields, Fred stayed in Southeast, selling lumber, fox farming, and doing handyman work.

Twenty years later, John returned to Southeast with Minnie, moving to Petersburg to help out his brother. On March 24, 1919, the *Alaska Citizen* updated the Pattens' Fairbanks friends in a piece titled, "Former Boniface Selling Fish on the Alaska Coast."

"A late arrival from one of the coast towns reports that John Patten, at one time owner of the Third Avenue hotel property, is engaged at the present time in the herring saltery business at one of the coast towns and is doing well."

By 1920, John and Minnie had permanently resettled in Kent, Washington, where they resided until they died.

※ ※ ※

As some had anticipated, Agnes's maternal instincts for little Frances did reawaken. As yet there was no legal adoption, so Agnes repeatedly and loudly made it known that she wanted her child back from the Burnetts. Blanche managed to hold her off. Finally someone who'd witnessed Shermans' conduct made the decision to act on behalf of the children. Perhaps it was Blanche herself.

On April 11, 1919, legal proceedings began in the juvenile court of the Fourth Judicial Division: ". . . a complaint was filed herein by a reliable person alleging that the aforesaid defendants Agnes and J. P. Sherman were the mother and father respectively of Irene and Francis [sic] . . . and that said parents were improper and unfit persons to have control and custody of said children whom they did not provide suitable homes for and praying that said children be committed to the Board of Children's Guardians for the aforesaid Division."

The next day, U.S. Commissioner R. S. McDonald, judge of the juvenile court for the Nenana district, issued a citation to J. P. and Agnes, asking for an answer to the complaint. The Shermans were required to show just cause why it should not be granted.

In a letter dated April 14, Agnes and J. P. jointly answered, submitting a typewritten letter referring to "many causes of misfortune and hard times," and admitting their failures as parents before agreeing to relinquish custody. Each had signed the legal document.

I found it so odd that in their letter's introductory paragraph, J. P. and Agnes identified Irene Mary as nine years old, when she was actually eight, plus someone had handwritten "Francis Beatrice" instead of Frances Marguerite. Did they not know these things? Or perhaps Blanche herself had given her foster daughter a new middle name that didn't stick. Reading the Shermans' statement about the hard times they'd slogged through from the outset of marriage gave me pause to think about how much hardship Irene had endured in her first eight years, how much she'd missed out on life already.

The Board of Children's Guardians had been created by an act of the territorial legislature at its first session just three years earlier, establishing juvenile courts and "providing for the care of dependent children, to create guardians in Alaska and for other purposes." The governor himself appointed the board's three members. But in its early

At the present time and for several years last past our financial condition has been such, due to many causes of misfortune and hardxxixe times, that we have not been able and have not given our above mentioned children a proper home or proper attention. We have done the best we could under the circumstances or at least what at the time seemed to us to be the best but xxx we realize that the children were not done by as should be.

Having struggled along for so many years in the hope of xirxnxxix better times and the present still being hard and lean times for us and the children being of an age when they should be going to school we are now willing that our children should be taken charge of by the Board of Childrens Guardians as provided for by law.

Dated this 14th day of April 1919.

Mrs Agnes Elizabeth Sherman.

J P Sherman

In April 1919, the Shermans signed over custody of Irene and Frances to the territory's Board of Children's Guardians. (Alaska State Archives, Office of the Territorial Governor, Subject files, VS 163)

years, the board had accomplished very little. Harmon Caskey, publisher of the *Alaska Citizen*, was critical in his February 23, 1916, editorial: "There the matter has rested to the present time, evidently nothing worthy of their official notice having attracted their attention."

This complaint against the Shermans had captured the board's attention at last. The board in 1919 was comprised of U.S. Marshal Lewis T. Erwin, Mrs. Harriet Hess, and Judge Charles Bunnell.

Frances had been a member of the Burnett family since infancy and was still with them. It wasn't clear where Irene was living that April. But on the 14th, a U.S. deputy marshal took Irene into his custody and placed her with Agnes as temporary custodian until the case was settled. I saw his act as one of compassion for this mother, as negligent as she had been, knowing with certainty that soon she'd be surrendering her daughter. Irene's time with her parents was brief.

J. P. and Agnes seemed to give up the fight. The next day, they requested the hearing be moved up a day to two o'clock that very afternoon, and the court agreed. At the appointed time, only four-year-old Frances, along with Blanche Burnett, was present. Agnes, J. P., and Irene were no-shows. Frances answered a few important questions, and a new hearing date was set for the next day, again at two o'clock. Again, Agnes, J. P., and Irene did not appear.

The verdict was reported in the April 21 *Alaska Citizen* under the headline *Nenana Court Takes Action on Children*. Representing the territorial government was Harry E. Pratt, assistant district attorney. " . . . a hearing was held on matters pertaining to the welfare of the children of Mrs. Agnes Sherman, Frances, aged 4, and Irene, aged 9 [sic]. The outcome of the hearing was that the children should be turned over to the board of guardians for the territory of Alaska for their future care. . . . The consent to this action was given by both parents of the children.

"The board will hold a meeting at some near date to decide what is best for the children. At the present time the child Frances is under the care of Mrs. Burnett, who has had it since infancy and wishes to adopt it. It is more than likely that her wishes will be complied with."

When I spoke to Frances in the summer of 1988, she was seventy-four years old and living comfortably in Van Nuys, California.

All those years later, she still remembered a crystallized moment in time: the wonder and joy of taking a horse-drawn sleigh ride, literally "dashing through the snow," to the federal commissioner's station in Nenana, eager for her formal adoption ceremony.

※ ※ ※

In the winter of 1929-30, Frances was sixteen years old when Blanche accepted a job cooking for the federal government's railroad crew. The work kept Blanche away from home often and at odd hours, so Frances moved in with her big brother Searl and wife Ethel. Searl was one of her favorites, and the teenager loved to spoil her infant nephew, Jack, christened John Andrew. The Burnett home was a gathering spot.

Searl and Ethel had met at one of those famous Eagle Hall dances just four years earlier. Ethel Peterson was a sixteen-year-old deb in a lovely white dress. Searl was twenty-six and fresh in from mining and prospecting on some of the outlying creeks. On a whim, Searl decided to clean up and get over to the Eagle Hall dance. There he laid eyes on Ethel and experienced a true "love at first sight" moment, family said. They declined dances with any other partners that entire evening, and before the night was over, Searl was ready to propose.

The typewritten story of their meeting was preserved in a Burnett scrapbook. Ethel gave Searl a conditional yes. First she'd have to ask her mother. They'd known each other for mere hours when Ethel brought her new love to her mother, Thora. "Are you sure, Ethel?" Thora asked. "Do you really want to marry him?" The teenager's quick reply was: "Yes, I really do." With Thora's blessing, the couple and their friends from the dance went to the commissioner's house at midnight. After two days of honeymooning, Searl went back to the creeks, and Ethel went home to mother until her groom wrapped up his work and came for her a couple of months later.

Frances was still a teenager living with Searl and Ethel in 1931 when she fell in love, too. Nathan Wolfe Jacobs, known as "Brick," was a Brooklyn-born man who ran a menswear store on First Avenue.

Frances and Brick Jacobs, 1940s. (Courtesy Burnett Family)

In 1932, the couple married with Searl as a witness. Frances and Brick lived in rooms above First and Cushman, and together they operated "Brick's Shop." They relished the same things: offering excellent goods and service, wearing top-quality tailored clothing themselves, and going out on the town, especially to dances.

Frances had grown up along with Fairbanks itself, as the town was still pulling stumps to grade its streets, adding paid firemen to its volunteer force, expanding its boundaries, and enacting laws about taxes and dog teams in town. She'd attended Main School, finishing all twelve grades. As a married woman, Frances remained close to her big brothers, Searl and Dewey.

With his wife Ethel, big brother Searl raised a brood of kids and left a positive, service-oriented legacy to their children and grand-children. I met some of them myself as looked into Frances's life story with the few people who remembered her. In ways, she remained a mystery. The Burnett descendants told me that she was a naturally private person, never one to seek attention. So unlike her birth sister.

Even though Blanche and John F. Burnett divorced before Frances reached age six—the result, family members say, of the elder Jack "hiding" some of his gold and other assets from his wife—Frances had had a happy childhood.

The girl with the white-blonde hair had never lived with her birth parents, so by nurture, she was thoroughly Burnett, even before the 1919 judgment for custody in Nenana. And yet at the "nature" level, DNA dictated that she was an Eckert-Sherman.

Still ahead, that legacy would become apparent in several important ways.

CHAPTER 15
OUTSIDE, ALONE - Seattle 1919
*When I was a child of eight, I should have been sent
to my aunt and uncle's place*

Once the U.S. commissioner in Nenana reviewed the details of Irene's traumatic history and ongoing hardship, the burn-scarred eight-year-old became a ward of the Territory on April 14, 1919. With that, the Board of Children's Guardians lifted her out of the extreme poverty to which the Shermans confessed. And surely, they hoped to protect Irene from what the Shermans *didn't* confess on paper: verbal and perhaps physical abuse, alcoholism, and fallout of untreated mental illness.

Board members had planned to send Irene to Seattle for further medical help and residential care for an indeterminate time, assessing it was the best to put distance between Irene and Agnes. There was no other family to turn to, not even Irene's grandmother Minnie Patten, who seems to have become estranged from Agnes, or vice versa.

When Irene was in her late sixties, she remembered that transition time with deep regret at not being claimed by a family member. There was an aunt and uncle on her father's side, the Sherman side, she was certain. At some point, she'd read family letters in her father's papers. How she wished they'd have taken her in! "Boy, those letters knocked me for a 10-karat loop!" she told author Joan Koponen. "I says, 'Boy, if I could have only become one of them, you know, being in the family . . .' And what makes me so hoppin' mad, I wish to

SHERMAN CHILD GOING OUTSIDE

LOCAL FIRE VICTIM BEING SENT TO SEATTLE HOSPITAL FOR TREATMENT.

Irene Sherman, one of the little girls who was so seriously burned in a fire which destroyed the Sherman home on Fourth avenue two years ago, is being sent to an outside hospital for treatment by the Board of Children's Guardians of Alaska. She will leave on the steamer Alaska and will be accompanied by Mrs. Fern Johnson. The little girl has never fully recovered from the terrible burns she incurred and will be placed in the Orthopedic hospital at Seattle for relief.

The Weekly Alaska Citizen
June 23, 1919

gosh that when that I hadda been sent out to them. When I was a child of eight, I should have been sent to my aunt and uncle's place. And to Grandpa Sherman. Because if I would have been kept in the Sherman side of the family, I wouldn't have run into so much damn difficulty."

I had deeply researched the Sherman family tree. J. P. had only one sibling back in the Midwest, a sister born in 1879. Perhaps the letters Irene was referring to had been written by that aunt. And as for Grandpa James Paul Sherman Sr., he couldn't have taken in Irene. He'd been chronically ill for years and had separated from his wife Jennie before his death in 1919—the year Irene became a ward of the Territory and was shipped away. The senior Sherman's instructions for his estate's disbursement left no clue whether J. P.'s sister was still alive. The only mention was his son in Fairbanks.

As for Minnie and John Patten, Irene had nothing good to say about her grandmother and the only grandfather she'd ever known: "But here, my mother's side of the family, her mother and her stepfather, those sidewinders were up to adopt me off to people I didn't want no part of. And I wasn't about to change my name for nobody."

Through the actions of the court at Nenana, Irene and Frances were legally protected from their birth parents. Frances would grow up among relatives who incorporated service to family and community in their code of ethics. Irene would not, and yet she would one day be recognized as a valuable member, indeed The Queen, of that same community.

※ ※ ※

Irene was not yet nine years old when Board of Children's Guardians sent her Outside. She and a paid matron boarded the "big boat," as locals called the steamer *Alaska*, on the bright Solstice midnight of June 22, 1919, leaving Fairbanks with mail and passengers bound for points along the Tanana and Yukon Rivers. Eventually they would connect with a ship bound for Seattle.

"The steamer will also make connections at Dawson with upriver boats," the *Alaska Daily Citizen* reported the next day. "Captain Adams will take the *Alaska* to Dawson this trip only, and will transfer to his old command, the *Julia B.* on her return trip to Tanana, where the latter ship will be met."

The list of fourteen outbound passengers from Fairbanks included Irene Sherman, Mrs. Ferne Johnson (Irene's paid chaperone), and five other people destined for Seattle. Eight more were headed for points on the Tanana River: Nenana, [Manley] Hot Springs, and the town of Tanana at the confluence of the Tanana and Yukon Rivers.

After Irene left, as always, the folks back home stayed vitally interested in her future, and occasional updates appeared in territorial newspapers. The August 19 issue of the *Alaska Daily Citizen* offered: "The little girl was recently sent Outside by the Territorial Board of Guardians to the Seattle Orthopedic hospital. Mrs. Ferne Johnson accompanied the girl and placed her in the hospital July 16. The Seattle physicians believe that they will be able to aid her considerably and that she will show much improvement after the operation."

When Irene was admitted, the Orthopedic Hospital was a forty-bed facility housed in a large brick building on Seattle's Queen Anne Hill. Within the month, little Irene was scheduled for yet another surgery. She would undergo multiple follow-up procedures over one year that spilled into another. She was sick often, battling pneumonia and other contagious sicknesses while healing from surgeries.

"Did you ever come close to dying?" I asked her decades later.

"I don't know," Irene said without drama. "It was nip and tuck."

The hospital was unique in many ways. It was founded by Anna Herr Clise, an affluent woman who gathered twenty-three of her wealthy friends to address a gap in medical care for "crippled and malnourished children." With each woman's donation of $20, in 1907 they created the eight-bed Children's Orthopedic Hospital with an all-female Board of Trustees. When Irene arrived twelve years later, the hospital had grown and was already in its third location.

Fundraising was a constant yet successful effort to ensure patients' families would not have to pay for care. Doctors and other professionals had volunteered their skills; King County and Alaska

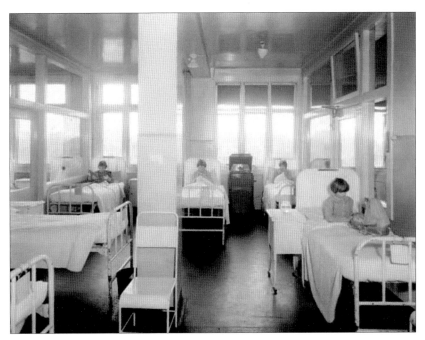

The Girls' Ward of the Children's Orthopedic Hospital as pictured in 1929. (Courtesy MOHAI 983.10.194.2)

Territory contributed to the care of the indigent and Alaska Native children. Meanwhile, Alaska's Board of Children's Guardians covered the costs of Irene's transportation and meals, and received reports on her and other hospitalized wards. In time, the Orthopedic Hospital would emerge as the renowned Seattle Children's Hospital.

Irene was just a child, but her name was already well known to Alaskan judges and politicians who were charged with her safety and health. Her long-term recovery continued to make news back home.

In early 1920, the *Cordova Daily Times* wrote: "Judge Charles E. Bunnell states that he has been advised that Irene Sherman . . . is getting along very well. He is informed that several minor surgical operations have already been performed to correct disfigurement, and the Seattle surgeons hope to make such permanent improvement that she will be able to associate with other children on even terms without feeling the disfiguring marks left by the flames."

What Bunnell said about Irene "getting along very well" just wasn't true. Irene's bad memories of her hospital stays were still vivid in June 1978, when Joan Koponen recorded her saying, "So anyway, they got me down there in the States, and woe betide me, they no more get me there at the Orthopedic Hospital, but what the deuce do they do, they slam me in a room by myself and lock me in. I could see out the windows but that's all the good that did me. And I was used to being free. Goin' where I wanted to, within reason. You know."

Besides undergoing multiple surgeries, while hospitalized, Irene suffered a painful double ear infection affecting the both mastoid bones. Next, she survived an epidemic of diphtheria that swept through. Later still, she was transferred to a sanitarium, where she picked up another contagious disease and developed spots from head to toe—perhaps chicken pox. "And God, I couldn't even hardly walk," she remembered. "Well, I was there for a good three or four months, and for some reason or another, I couldn't seem to shake those things right off the bat."

But little girl Irene somehow gathered a handful of good memories from her time in Seattle. She fondly recalled the playmate and his family who were kind to her: "There was a little youngster and his parents used to come to see him, and then not only that, but his sister. Well, by gosh, they'd bring toys to me, and I used to play with this little boy, Richard Sole, and he was a nice kid, brought up real nice, and his parents were lovely people. I often wondered what happened to the whole family. I thought the world of them. That was the only good thing I ever run into out of that thing."

But there was more. In her next breath, she mentioned the joy of watching a parade that she never forgot. My thoughts flew ahead to all those years of starring in Fairbanks parades, waving to her fans.

After release from the hospital, Irene next entered a series of Seattle-area foster care homes. Following house rules was near impossible for such a lonely, defiant child. By the time she was a preteen, she was able to finally complete the fourth grade. And there her formal education ended.

"They kept transferrin' me into different homes, you know, and one thing and another, and I wasn't wantin' that," she remembered. "I said, 'Dang it, I want to go back to Alaska, where I belong.' I says, 'This place isn't doin' me no good. I ain't getting my hands and face fixed. I ain't getting a school education, and I can't get any school education because I'm dissatisfied with the whole setup.'" In each of the foster homes, the troubled child was disruptive, mistrusting, and angry. Of course.

"By that time I seen I wasn't getting anywhere. I got fed up with the place. I was horsewhipped if I didn't do just what she thought right. And my parents were up here . . ." Irene paused to take a breath. "Then just before I hit fifteen, I run away from the damn place . . ."

CHAPTER 16
ANOTHER BABY, and ANOTHER, and ANOTHER
Nenana 1920

[Sherman] was hunting game for his 'more or less demented wife and three children'. . .

Considering Jeanette's death in 1914 and James's death in 1916, along with Irene's near-death on both occasions, why wasn't Agnes herself arrested, declared insane, and housed in an institution before the dawn of 1917? I'd asked myself that many times. It seemed like a sure thing given the circumstances, especially when jurors of so many insanity suspects were quick to sentence others with lesser issues. But in 1920 Agnes was still freely moving around Nenana and up in Fairbanks.

Within two years of the cabin fire, while Irene was receiving treatment at St. Joseph's, the city ceased paying her hospital bill, and the Board of Children's Guardians picked it up. After Irene's parents surrendered her custody to the board in 1919, chairman Judge Charles Bunnell's indigent fund had seen to her expenses. Through J. P.'s lean and fat years, even when he was earning plenty from trapping and mining, he wasn't financially responsible because his daughter was a ward of the territory.

About a year after Irene left Alaska, in March 1920, J. P. and Agnes were living in the Nenana River "scattered population area," as census takers described the region. It was just the two of them, but Agnes was young, only thirty-one, and still fertile. Indeed, she may have been pregnant again. While Irene was living in Seattle, the Shermans experienced a baby boom as Agnes carried three more children to term.

Years later, counting kids and looking back over seven decades with me, Irene remembered Frances, but had no idea where any others might be. Yet she believed there were others. A decade earlier, when her memory was more acute as she talked with Joan Koponen, Irene was pining for connection: ". . . the funny part of it is my daggone family of sisters and brothers and all the rest of us, has gone to the four winds, scattered to the four winds, and don't want to seem to unite at all.

Of course with me, I'd give the world if my two sisters and my nieces and nephews, and even my brother-in-law, would get up here, so that I could administer to them and tell them where they been goin' wrong . . ."

How many brothers and sisters did she actually have, and what had happened to each? If they'd been looking for Irene, she'd be easy to find—still at her home base in Fairbanks. Did they not even know about her? Maybe they hadn't tried. Or maybe the rest were all dead.

In 1920, Nenana, Alaska, wasn't a safe place to live, despite its burgeoning wealth from railroad jobs, growing local businesses, and its role as a commerce hub for outlying mining camps. While the rest of the U.S. was encountering its second wave of the Spanish flu in fall 1918, the epidemic was landing for the first time in Southeast Alaska. Reports said about 51 percent of all deaths in Alaska were the result of the flu. And 82 percent of those deaths were Alaska Natives.

When the flu finally reached Nenana in April 1920, the town lost nearly 10 percent of its population, most of them Alaska Natives, despite a month-long quarantine. Some villages in Alaska's northwest and southwest had been nearly wiped out; communities were abandoned by the living, too weak to even bury their dead.

On June 16 of that year, a former Nenana pastor living in Albany, Oregon, sent his local paper, the *Albany Daily Democrat,* a letter he'd received from his friend back in Nenana, C. M. Grigsby. Titling the piece "Whole Town has Flu in Alaska," Grigsby gave a grim report: "There were nearly five hundred cases in town, which is more people than we thought we had here—almost every soul in town had it. Sixty odd died. Over two hundred were down at the same. We had great difficulty to keep the dead moving to the cemetery fast enough, for warm weather had set and the ground was thawer [sic] only a little below the surface. The graves took much work, even much blasting.

"We were short of help to nurse, and that is why some died, perhaps. It was pneumonia in each case that killed the folks. People exposed themselves to the air while sweating. They went quickly.

We had a very malignant type of flu here. Fairbanks, with about twelve hundred people had over eight hundred cases and only twenty-some died. They had a very mild form and had all the advantages for handling a lot of people. That is an old-town, a hometown. Our town is a new town and more of a camp than a really truly town. It is NOT a hometown."

Nenana had ridden out the first waves by obstructing entrance into their town. Guards were placed on the Tanana and Nenana Rivers and along trails to prevent outsiders from bringing in the virus. Then when the worldwide numbers had fallen significantly, just when they thought it was safe, they relaxed their regulations and the fourth wave took Nenana down.

In 1921, the Presbyterian Church's Board of Home Missions reported "the scourge of influenza, which had seemingly passed by the Interior while the coast lands of Alaska were in places almost depopulated in 1919, visited Fairbanks and Nenana with accumulated violence in 1920."

The next child born to the Shermans may have arrived during that wave and died young, but without formal records, I had no proof, just a strong hunch based on the calendar. After the territory took Irene and Frances in 1919, there was an extraordinary gap in the line of seemingly continuous pregnancies for Agnes. The last two Sherman children were easy to trace: Pauline Agnes Sherman, born June 26, 1922, at St. Mark's Mission hospital in Nenana, with Dr. William Kirby attending. And then, finally, a boy named Richard DeWitt Sherman, born at St. Mark's on September 12, 1923. But that would total six siblings, not seven. I suspected another, an earlier birth, between spring 1919 and early 1921.

Finally, I found proof of that child in a 2009 regional history written by Alaskan Tom Walker and titled *McKinley Station: The People of the Pioneer Park that Became Denali*. J. P. Sherman was a neighbor of the park, and I found his name in the index. Some of what Walker had written was familiar to me, but some was fresh from Walker's dive into the national park archives. His book included details of J. P.'s prospecting, from the Little Delta River to the upper Susitna country. Walker wrote, "In 1908, [Sherman] pushed for the construction of a winter trail from the Wood River, across to the Nenana River and upstream to Broad Pass." I'd followed the road through Broad Pass—now the Parks Highway—uncountable times, but now I made the drive with fresh eyes. What might it have looked like back then? The stark beauty of the mountains was unchanged.

To me, most fascinating in Walker's book was J. P.'s appearance in a chapter touching on illegal hunting inside the national park. From the start, J. P. had provided for his family by living off the land in what contemporary Alaskans refer to as a "subsistence lifestyle." It remains everyday life for rural Natives and others who live off-road. Even urban Alaskans seasonally fill their freezers or smokers with fish and game.

In the early 1920s, J. P. was invested in a Nenana River fish wheel, a Native-engineered, water-powered invention that made subsistence fishing as simple as possible. He was an able big-game hunter, too, bringing home sheep, caribou, or moose on good days. Ptarmigan, grouse, and hare were also fair game in season. But what set J. P. apart from many others was his passion for protecting the food resource from hunters who misused it—in particular, "market hunters," who were paid to hunt for commercial interests. Walker wrote that J. P. even helped form a group of miners to protest overhunting of fowl and game meat. In that sense he was aligned with the mission of Superintendent Harry Karstens—protecting the park's resources.

In 1922, Mount McKinley National Park's boundaries were changed when the federal government expanded the eastern edge, making a broad swath unavailable to many like J. P., who were accustomed to hunting on that land. In fall 1923, not long after the Shermans' last child, Richard, was born, Karstens got a tip about some illegal hunters. He sent rangers Fritz Nyberg and Robert H. Degen to look into it. They were questioning another man at his cabin when they heard shots and left to investigate. Walker recounted what happened next: "The rangers soon located a cabin two miles inside the park near Dry Creek and saw a dead sheep on the roof and a man dragging another down off the mountain. After dark the rangers returned to Healy with the two sheep and James Paul Sherman in custody.

"Unlike other local residents, Sherman did not claim the

prospectors' hunting exemption," Walker wrote. As superintendent, Karstens reported the outcome of the encounter this way: "Mr. Sherman admitted having killed the two sheep in the park. Sherman produced an old map, professed ignorance of the 1922 park expansion, and said that he was hunting for his *'more or less demented wife and three children,'* who were wintering in Nenana." In summary, Walker wrote, "Karstens, though not an admirer of Sherman's, congratulated him for not claiming to be a prospector but rather hunting in the park accidentally. In lieu of charges, Karstens required Sherman to sign a notarized and witnessed statement admitting his act."

I had made a hard stop and U-turn to the previous paragraph. *What's that J. P. said?* He'd referred to his "more or less demented wife and three children," including a newborn son, who were overwintering in Nenana in 1923-24. *Three* children. That newborn son was baby Richard. So J. P.'s explanation was proof in his own words of yet another child born before the two youngest Shermans.

Somehow, the family had managed to survive the severe Spanish influenza pandemic in 1920 Nenana. But had they all? Or, given Agnes's reports of neglect and malnutrition out on the Totatlanika years earlier, could that child have succumbed before age three in some other way? There was a dearth of information on the eldest of the last three children —its gender, its birth date, and ultimately, its death date. The child was no longer present in 1924, when the territory once more stepped in to protect the Sherman children.

That October, Agnes was closely examined by a newly-appointed and zealous Red Cross nurse named Dorothy Sleichter, who was based in Fairbanks. Pauline was two and Richard was one when the nurse was authorized to ensure the health and wellbeing of Alaska's children. Immediately she visited Main School in Fairbanks, where every child was weighed, measured, and tested for defective teeth, eyesight, tonsils, and posture. Next Sleichter traveled to outlying towns.

In Nenana, the nurse found Agnes's home situation untenable. I wondered what she knew of the child born before Pauline. Had Agnes confessed her troubling circumstances during the visit, as she'd done years earlier when the Totatlanika neighbors came by? With the public health nurse pressing through official lines, Agnes was again in a crisis. The nurse had a solution in mind for the Sherman problem, and she reached out to Agnes's family in the Pacific Northwest. Two months later, the nurse's action plan was in place. J. P. himself was not mentioned in the solution.

"Several social service cases have been taken care of by Mrs. Sleichter," reported the *News-Miner* on December 2, 1924. "She leaves this Friday to accompany Mrs. Agnes Sherman and two children of Nenana to Seward, where they will board the outgoing steamer for Seattle." Again, I considered the missing third child . . . and J. P. What was his role in all of this? In future court documents, only Agnes was named as the parent of Pauline and Richard. The question of fatherhood arose once more.

In decades to come, although Agnes and J. P. remained apart, they remained married until Agnes's death parted them.

CHAPTER 17
AGNES SAILS SOUTH - Nenana 1924

She left this morning for Seward, having in her care
Mrs. Sherman and two children

The long-awaited government railroad was officially completed in 1923, and Alaskans were celebrating. The rail line between Seward and Fairbanks now extended four hundred and seventy miles through forests and boggy tundra, over mountain passes, and across numerous streams and rivers. Now a new railroad bridge finally spanned the Tanana River at Nenana, eliminating passengers' need to cross the river via ferry or launch in summer months, whether on foot, with horses, or vehicles. Temporary railroad tracks that were once laid on the river ice were no longer necessary in winter.

That July 15, President Warren G. Harding arrived to do the ceremonial honors by driving the "Golden Spike" at Nenana, surrounded by an entourage that accompanied him on this leg of his international "Journey of Understanding." The president and First Lady Florence Harding had sailed from Washington state to Seward on the USS *Henderson*. They'd next boarded a special train car to Mount McKinley National Park, then onward to Nenana, drawing crowds wherever they went. I wondered if the Shermans were moved to join the locals at the Nenana platform, curious enough to get a glimpse of the President.

On a hot and sunny July 15, at a spot just north of Nenana's new railroad bridge, the Golden Spike ceremony signified the joining of the last northernmost section with the main line. An enthusiastic audience cheered as the president swung the maul, missed, swung again, missed again, and finally nailed home the ceremonial spike into its pre-drilled hole.

Harding's Alaska trip was significant in American history. His whirlwind tour and speaking schedule had left him depleted. At the President's next stop in Fairbanks, temperatures would soar to ninety-four degrees Fahrenheit as he addressed fifteen hundred people at the baseball park. Turning south again, he would travel to Talkeetna and

It took President Harding three tries to hit the spike, but his entourage and onlookers warmly applauded his final, successful effort. (Courtesy Fairview Inn, Talkeetna)

lunch at the historic Fairview Inn before continuing to Seward and his homebound sailing. Though he felt unwell, Harding paused to speak at Vancouver, British Columbia, on July 26, as the first American president to visit Canada. His Portland, Oregon, events were cancelled due to illness. And then, following a hurried train journey to San Francisco, the U.S. President died there of cerebral hemorrhage on August 2, 1923.

If you stepped into the century-old Fairview Inn in the little town of Talkeetna, where Harding stopped for a meal on his way out of Alaska, and where a wall is covered with photos and ephemera about the former president, they'd tell you that Alaska killed Harding. About a month after the president's death in California, Agnes Sherman delivered baby Richard at St. Mark's mission hospital, where Jeanette had been born eleven years earlier, just a stone's throw from where Harding had driven the Golden Spike.

At age one, Richard was so young that he wouldn't remember the day that he, his mother, and two-year-old sister boarded the train at

Nenana in the dead of winter. The Shermans were embarking on a life-changing journey of their own, destined for the end of steel at Seward on Resurrection Bay. The trip Outside began on a snowy, cold Friday, December 5, 1924. *Fairbanks Daily News-Miner* readers watched the paper for news such as this. They knew the family, their hardships. The Shermans had long been fodder for gossip, which ook fire following the afternoon edition report:

On December 5, 1924, Dorothy Sleichter, Agnes, and the children waited here for their train to Seward and points Outside. Now a museum, the restored depot at Nenana looks much as it did that day. (Tricia Brown)

"Mrs. Sleichter left this morning for Seward, having in her care Mrs. Sherman and two children of Nenana, whom she will put aboard the *Northwestern*, bound for Seattle. Upon their arrival in Seattle, they will be met by Mrs. Sherman's father, in whose care the Red Cross is placing them." Fred Eckert, now living in Portland, Oregon, with his second wife Harriet, was back in the picture. At age sixty-seven, he was employed as a carpenter in a Portland shipyard.

Seward, Alaska, was a deep-water port, ice-free year-round, the perfect location for Alaska rails to meet oceangoing vessels, both in- and outbound. For decades, tons of mail, freight, gold, and passengers had moved through Seward. Even before the rail line existed, dog teams and horse-drawn freight wagons and sleds, and later automobile stages, had met ships at Seward, Valdez, Cordova, and other ports marking the end of a trail.

When Agnes disembarked the government train at the Seward depot, stunning beauty surrounded her. Surely she was awestruck, even in her anxious state. Snowy mountain peaks reflected in the dark waters of Resurrection Bay, unlike anything she'd seen in the Interior. Waterfalls burst over the edges of rocky cliffs. Towering spruce trees marched up the mountains behind the town. Finally the little family joined the queue to board the Alaska Steamship Company's *Northwestern*, an elegant 336-foot liner that had been connecting Seattle with Alaska's coastal towns since 1906.

Nurse Sleichter introduced Agnes to a different traveling matron who'd be making the crossing with her. As the Shermans settled in on board the SS *Northwestern*, Sleichter hastened to leave. She'd planned additional checks on families and schools on her return trip.

Spectacular landscapes slid by as the *Northwestern* made stops at southcentral coastal towns of Cordova and Valdez, before finishing

The SS *Northwestern*, of the Alaska Steamship Company's fleet, transported the Shermans to Seattle. (Archives, University of Alaska Fairbanks, UAF-1975-84-1509)

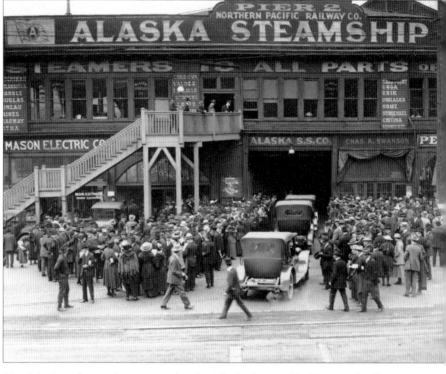

Pier 2 in Seattle was home port for the Alaska Steamship line. Fred Eckert traveled here to meet his daughter and her two children arriving from Alaska. (Alaska State Library, Skinner Foundation Photo Collection, P44-03-180)

at Seattle's Pier 2, home port for all Alaska Steamship vessels. Agnes had grown up in Seattle, and she'd spent happy times among her mother's extended Jenott family. Maybe she sensed glimmers of hope in this relocation, especially after those harsh years with J. P. on the Totatlanika and in Nenana. With change, maybe her unreliable thinking, her difficulties in steadying her mental health, would improve. Others seemed to be making all the decisions for her now. What would become of the three of them?

In Nurse Sleichter's tidy final report covering her December service, she wrote, "Mrs. Sherman and two children accompanied to Seward, from where she was put on board the outgoing steamer for

Seattle. She is going to Portland to make her future home with her father, at his request." Reading that, I had a distinct sense that Fred Eckert hadn't volunteered for the role. More likely, Dorothy Sleichter had drafted him.

※ ※ ※

As agreed, Fred Eckert was waiting at Seattle's Pier 2 when the three Shermans disembarked from the *Northwestern*. Minnie and John Patten were living nearby, much closer to Seattle than Fred was, having permanently relocated to John's old stomping ground in Kent, Washington. Their proximity made me wonder if Minnie was there, too, to greet her daughter and these two grandchildren she'd never met.

Many questions swirled around this trip to Seattle. To me, the level of Minnie's involvement was paramount to understanding Agnes's future. It felt like Minnie was as much responsible for the outcome as was the indomitable Dorothy Sleichter. Conceivably, Minnie, unable to help her daughter anymore, was instead orchestrating how to save her grandchildren.

I speculated that after landing, the children went into Minnie's care in Washington while Agnes went to Fred's in Oregon. Possibly. Still, the ultimate outcome of their relocation to Washington was verifiable: Pauline and Richard were separated from their mother . . . and each other. The toddlers became wards of King County in Washington state, overseen by Marion Southard, chief probation officer of Washington's Superior Court. She would seek safe foster homes for the littlest Shermans until they might be adopted. As with most family law cases, foster care among family members held preference before placement in the homes of strangers. And two women did step forward from within the family. To my pleasure and surprise, the identities of the two foster mothers were familiar.

What of Agnes? Fred Eckert was there in Seattle as agreed and took Agnes home to Portland. However, shortly afterward, she moved north to Tacoma, Washington, where she was living in 1925. A year later, she reported that her home was Kent, Washington (where Minnie and John Patten were living). Was it the Pattens' tough love that determined her next steps? In 1927-28, Agnes had a different address, although back in Tacoma, and she was working as a Montgomery Ward clerk. And then, in 1929, the year that Irene was allowed to leave Seattle and return to Alaska, Agnes dropped out of sight.

How or exactly who was involved in Agnes Sherman's next chapter is not part of the public record, nor has it been passed down in what remains of the Sherman or Eckert families. Stories are scant or non-existent. A descendant of Agnes's brother had only this to say: "My grandfather said he'd had a sister who went crazy after her baby froze to death, but he didn't know anything else."

Sometime in 1929, Agnes entered Western Washington Hospital in Steilacoom, near Tacoma, beginning residential mental health treatment that would span decades. Even her descendants would require a court order to gain certain details, like exactly what event tipped the scales and sent her into an institution? What was her formal medical diagnosis? And who signed the admittance papers?

The Eckert-Jenott family tree that I'd constructed held clues. The data revealed that 1929 was a critical year in the family's story. Minnie Patten died on July 26, 1929. Agnes was institutionalized at Western Washington Hospital in 1929. Irene was released from the Home of the Good Shepherd and returned to Alaska in 1929. And Irene's youngest brother, Richard, found a home in southern California in 1929. His sister, Pauline Agnes, already had been adopted away.

CHAPTER 18
CARRIAGE OF JUSTICE - Juneau 1926
*To my shock, it was Irene who was under arrest
and facing trial . . . for insanity*

Irene was in her late sixties when she spilled a burdensome memory to author Joan Koponen in a taped interview. Listening to her voice, I noted how she was seemingly emotionless, talking fast as the details of her life unspooled in a series of Seattle-area foster homes as a young teenager. At one of them, she said matter-of-factly, she was sexually assaulted by an Army man. Somehow, fifteen-year-old Irene had managed to fight him off. I listened without prejudice, but soon I was confused by her account as she dissolved into speculative details about her attacker's arrest and jail time. It was particularly frustrating to listen to the tape, hearing her skipping around essential information and landing on old familiar clichés and pronouncements. What had actually happened? Had anyone ever helped this poor girl, victimized yet again?

My thoughts grew heavier as I considered the attack may not have been the first. The encounter surely scarred Irene further still, destroying what semblance of trust she may have held for people who were supposed to take care of her.

※ ※ ※

I was studying Irene's name in a July 1926 ship's manifest of passengers arriving at Juneau. Back in Alaska? It made no sense. Irene was fifteen years old, still a ward of the territory, and lodged in a Seattle foster home by the Board of Children's Guardians. There's no way she'd have been released to Alaska for even a quick visit.

And there was the matter of her father's whereabouts. I tried to shoehorn in the possibility of a rendezvous with J. P., but it didn't work. Irene landed in Juneau on July 3; newspapers told me that on July 27, J. P. was among a traveling party of miners who'd just spent nine days far out in roadless southwestern Alaska, in the Kuskokwim River region.

They were headed home from the remote mining camp of Ophir on the launch *Bonzilla*. Ophir to Juneau was an impossible distance for that timeline. *So how and why was Irene in Juneau in July 1926 when, as a ward of the Territory, she wouldn't have been allowed to leave Washington state?*

As yet, I was unaware of the taped interviews Joan Koponen had made decades earlier. Writing a book in 1978, she intended to merely question Irene about her unusual home place and how she'd built it. The quotes would be part of Koponen's self-published essay collection about unique Alaskan homes. But when Irene began talking, she free-ranged into other parts of her life story. I was well into my own research when I finally traced Joan's daughter, Chena, and then Joan herself, aged ninety and still living on the family's Fairbanks homestead. I gained permission to review her valuable recordings and hear Irene's voice floating through time. The tape was a gold mine.

But I was still scratching my head over *why* Irene landed at Juneau in 1926. Then a friendly email arrived from Roger Brunner, the friend of a friend, who'd been studying legal documents surrounding charges of insanity in Alaska's history. He had stumbled across Irene's name. He'd photographed the documents. Did I want the images?

"Please tell me what you found is from July 1926," I emailed back. *Bingo!* Yes, it is, Roger said. The forwarded documents showed that on July 3, 1926, territorial officials with charging documents in hand were waiting for Irene to disembark at Juneau. The charges had nothing to do with a sexual assault case against Irene's attacker in Washington. To my shock, it was *Irene herself* who was under arrest and facing trial . . . for insanity. There was no mention of the sexual assault or her attacker's arrest in Seattle. Of course, had there been an arrest, the U.S. Army or Washington state would have filed charges, not the Territory of Alaska. Timewise, Irene's story of the attack and legal action that followed fit, but how had she gotten this memory so turned around?

Without acknowledging the insanity probe against her, Irene told Koponen in detail about how she'd been treated: "So, anyhow, they kept bombin' me around, and then they got me into one home that by gosh, a court case come up with a damned G.I. that attacked me, out the water a ways away from Seattle. They [had] sent me to a place there across from the Army base, and this farm was right across from it. And this guy built rowboats and stuff like that.

"Well, the G.I. situation come up from that, and there was an old lady that lived nearby this home I was put in, and she told me what to do if any guy ever touched me. So I fought that damned guy. Of course, I was fifteen at the time. I fought him to a standstill and finally got away from him. And got home."

Irene's traumatic story was hers alone—the account she carried through life and had lodged in memory—even if her memory didn't always match reality.

What *did* the Juneau paper trail show? The complaint from U.S. Attorney A. G. Shoup named Irene as "an insane person at large in Juneau." Probate Judge and U.S. Commissioner V.A. Paine commanded Irene's arrest and transport to court to examine her mental condition.

On July 6, U.S. Marshal Albert White and Deputy W. M. Eddy arrested Irene and delivered her to the federal jail for commitment pending trial, where they would "inquire as to her sanity."

"And so then the case come up," said Irene, referring to the assault in Seattle. "And being I was Alaskan, they had to bring the case up to Juneau. . . . and what made me mad at Juneau right now is the dirty son-of-a-guns, they put me in jail with the rest of those felons! You know, the underworld, the jailbirds.

"They tried to claim that they didn't have any place for me. They should have slammed me in a private room there at the hospital. Our capital of Alaska. That was during territory time, see? So what they did, they had me at this damn jail. . . . *That was no way for one of us Alaskan kids to be taken care of.* And if my father would have known I was in Juneau, he would have turned the damn world upside down and gone down there and demanded my return to him. Right then and there. But he didn't know anything about it."

Subpoenas went out to so-called witnesses: Mrs. T. J. White, Mrs. P. O. Herriman and her husband P. O. Herriman, Harry Watson, John E. Pegues, and Dr. L. P. Dawes, who were instructed to appear before the territory's Probate Court in Juneau at 10:00 A.M. on Tuesday, July 20. (Irene had been jailed since July 6.) On the related court documents, someone had noted that Irene's father was "somewhere about Fairbanks"; the same person wrote that Irene's mother, unnamed, had mental health issues.

For the trial, Dr. L. P. Dawes filed his medical certificate following an exam. In the field for "Previous peculiarity of patient as to temper, conduct, etc.," the doctor wrote "Perverted mind (sexually)" and for that reason, "Patient has to be kept under close surveillance." He added that she "always has been weak; never has grown up mentally," and that her issues have been evident for "several years past." Dr. Dawes was asked to describe as fully as possible Irene's present symptoms of insanity, as well as class and character of mental derangement, and duration. He wrote: "Chiefly that of undevelopment of mind. Also has a perverted mind (sexually), which is undoubtedly inherited."

For nearly two weeks, teen-aged Irene was jailed with the hardened criminals of Juneau. On July 20, the jury panel thoroughly questioned her and considered the medical advice of Dr. Dawes before they conferred alone, then Judge Paine read their verdict, "*We, the Jury, empaneled and sworn in the above entitled matter to diligently inquire, justly try to determine whether the above named Irene Sherman is really and truly insane, after hearing the evidence, find that the above named person is NOT really and truly insane and that she ought not to be committed to the sanitarium or asylum for the care and custody of the insane of the Territory of Alaska. Dated at Juneau, Alaska, this 20th day of July, 1926.*

"*IT IS THEREFORE ORDERED, ADJUDGED AND DECREED, That the said Irene Sherman is not insane, and that she be released from custody.*" The clerk had typed the release order above the form's ominous, preprinted directive, which was obliterated by a line of x's. But the form's text beneath the long row of xxxxxx was still readable: "*. . . and that she be conveyed at once to, and properly and safely kept in the*

If Irene were found guilty of insanity at the Juneau trial, she would have been automatically remanded to Morningside Hospital in Portland. The sentence was preprinted on the judgment form.

Morningside Hospital at Portland, Oregon, until (s)he be discharged therefrom according to law."

Irene had dodged Morningside, but she wasn't completely cleared. The jurors put their signatures to the page, and someone had penciled a postscript: "We recommend Irene Sherman be confined in some institution for the feeble-minded, preferably Medico Lake, Wash., or some similar institution." (*Medico Lake*, as they called it, was actually Medical Lake, near Spokane, the site of today's Eastern Washington Hospital.)

Judge V. A. Paine signed off on the order, and while Irene was not free, Paine did not follow the jury's suggestion. She was not forced to enter Morningside, nor Eastern Washington, but instead was sent to the Home of the Good Shepherd, St. Anthony's School, in Seattle, the place she would forever refer to as "the convent."

Irene had resolved one of my questions. She had eventually learned where her father was while she was stuck in that Juneau jail.

"[My dad] was off on a goose chase over in a gold mine chase, and he didn't know anything about it 'til they railroaded me back to the States again," she said. "I don't know how the devil he ever heard about it, but he did . . ."

Yet, Irene left a more important question unresolved: What became of her attacker? Decades later, in her mind, the assault was still entangled with the insanity trial: "The case comes up and this guy that attacked me was slammed in jail for ten years for his conduct." Had he? I hoped so. There was usually a kernel of truth in most of her tales that went sideways. Maybe she'd manufactured that ending and repeated it enough times to view it as truth. Maybe there was a separate case in which the U.S. Army put away the man for ten years.

But as for the insanity trial, thanks to an open-minded jury, it seemed that finally—at least this time—justice had been served for Irene. I saw her amplified sense of independence in a new light.

※ ※ ※

Back in Seattle, Irene went to live at the Home of the Good Shepherd, where she dwelt among nuns, orphans, and other girls in need, a place where she remembered days of chores and learning the word "obey." Although she was treated harshly, Irene recalled "when I was with the Catholics" as the best years of her life. When I talked with her at age seventy-seven, she claimed that they turned her in the "right direction."

"I wanted to be a hell-raiser. And somehow or another, they wanted to SNAP me out of that," she said. In her usual way, Irene put great emphasis on certain words in her narratives.

"Snap you out of what?" I asked. "What did you do?"

"Oh, just tried to be opposite to what they wanted me to do. And I says, 'To hell with you guys,' and I tried to BLOCK 'em. But HA! As soon as I'd pull anything offbeat, I'd wind up sitting in a chair and not allowed to leave the place."

The Seattle facility was operated by the Sisters of the Good Shepherd. With support of many local benefactors, the nuns' stated mission was to provide a loving, stable environment for orphans and girls who had survived difficult life circumstances. Set on an eleven-acre site at 4649 Sunnyside Avenue, the majestic brick building was designed and built by noted architect C. Alfred Breitung, and surrounded by acres of fruit trees and vegetable gardens. When the original home opened in 1907, it welcomed one hundred and seventy-one girls from all over Washington, plus a few from Alaska. Their families brought them here or, as with Irene, they'd been referred by the courts. Tuition costs varied according to what families could afford or what county government would pay. Irene's monthly expenses were paid with territorial dollars.

Teachers and administrators wore white habits with a black veil, as prescribed by their order. There was no mistaking a nun for a civilian. On the list of virtuous subjects the girls studied was "character education, voice, piano and other instrumental music, needlework, dressmaking, public expression, catechism, vocational training, basic academics, and physical education." An on-site commercial laundry also helped defray the costs of running the home as well as training the girls for future employment. And though it was founded and operated by a Catholic order, the home accepted children from all religions, asking only that residents respect the customs of their faith.

Children were not permitted to leave the grounds, so Irene's home, school, and church were self-contained in north and south wings. An online history explained, "The south wing of the building housed the 'penitent' girls, those whom society considered 'wayward,' and rooms for those nuns who worked with them. The Good Shepherd Sisters maintained an orphanage in the north wing along with their own rooms. The two populations were separated." Interviewed as a senior citizen, Betty Mayes, who had been placed in the orphanage wing in 1924, remembered: "There was a good side and a bad side—the Angel Guardian side, on the right as you go in, and Sacred Heart side on the left. On the left side . . . they did the laundry and that sort of thing. There could be some real hard girls over there."

Irene was an orphan as far as the law was concerned, a ward of the territory. While I wanted to imagine that she might have lived in the same wing as Betty Mayes, given Irene's disposition, more likely she was problematic, resisting correction and, as she confessed herself, a hell-raiser. She was probably funneled toward the "bad side," the Sacred Heart side. I imagined that she did lots of laundry.

I remembered that Irene once told me how she'd helped the nuns with the flowers as a "chapel girl." Beyond that, she hadn't said much more, just that she wanted "to get the heck home." Sitting nearby and hearing Irene reminisce in 1988, her friend Wally Burnett had injected, "She didn't like it there at all . . . they mistreated her."

Irene was ready with a counterpoint: "That was a very good experience anyhow, because they curtailed me from a lot of my shenanigans. I think back on lots of things, and I think back, and by gosh, *You must not do this, you must not do that, for God's sake, don't do anything that'll displease God.* And when you do things that displease God, he's gonna take a sideswipe at ya, and you'll wonder where it came from. And boy, he can sure sideswipe ya, and you'll darn well know when you're doing something wrong!"

From feisty to introspective in a flash, Irene said, "When I was a young girl, I was close to the Lord then. And I had to learn how to react toward the Father and master of the church, and the nuns, and what have you. And I worked with one nun that had been a Protestant before she became a Catholic nun, and by God, she was all right."

In 1973, the student population in "Irene's convent" had dwindled dramatically, and it was forced to close. When developers wanted to turn the eleven-acre site into a shopping center, neighbors fought back. After purchase by the city, the property eventually was transferred to Historic Seattle, and landed on the National Register of Historic Places in 1984. In this century, Irene's convent houses non-profit arts organizations as the Good Shepherd Center.

CHAPTER 19
YOU'VE GOT A VISITOR
Steilacoom, Washington, 1929

*A surgical procedure called the frontal lobotomy
was used for a period of time*

Agnes worked a job in Tacoma for a few years before she or someone
else finally concluded that she required residential care. In 1929, she
entered Western State Hospital, an inpatient psychiatric institution on the
site of historic Fort Steilacoom, just ten miles south of town. What had
tipped her house of cards? Who had signed her in? I sent a medical
records link to John and Michelle Moore in Idaho. As Agnes's grandson
and his wife, maybe they could begin inquiries. That's when they learned
that unsealing files, even for them, takes a court order.

When Western Washington first opened in 1871, it was called the
Insane Asylum of Washington Territory, housing fifteen males and six
female patients; later, its care was framed as an inpatient psychiatric
hospital, and it expanded as one of the largest west of the Mississippi.
Under the auspices of the state's Department of Health and Social
Services, Western Washington became one of two state-run hospitals for
mental health care with eight hundred beds for adult patients. Its sister
hospital, Eastern Washington, had been the facility suggested for Irene by
the Juneau jury at the close of her insanity trial, but she was sent to the
Good Shepherd nuns.

The grounds that Agnes once walked and worked at Western
Washington are now a park. The old hospital's derelict buildings were
tagged by skilled spray-paint artists through the early 2000s. Twenty
years later, the remnants had been torn down, and a memorial marked the
cemetery for the thousands of patients who'd died at the facility.
Elsewhere on Western State's acreage, the contemporary, working
hospital is contained in classic, multistory brick buildings sprawling in a
complex that has known much controversy.

In 1930, Agnes was living in Dwelling No. 12 with twenty-three
other women, taking direction for what would happen in every day,

The entrance to Western State Hospital in Steilacoom, Washington, was the subject of a 1907 postcard by Artvue Publishing.

accepting treatment or sleeping off the effects of treatment. Daily life for female patients, if they were able, meant working in sewing rooms and kitchens, and helping with farm chores. The men usually labored in the orchards and fields, building furniture, or handling livestock. There were dances, Christmas parties, and visiting theater troupes. And there were dark stories of mistreatment and death. During three consecutive federal census years—1930, 1940, and finally 1950, when Agnes was sixty-one—she experienced firsthand the changes in medical and mental health treatment, some of which was experimental for its time.

"Hydrotherapy was the early treatment of choice," wrote one historian for the state institution. "Wet packs, hot tubs and showers were used for nearly fifty years to create a calming effect for the patients. Insulin therapy was started in the mid-1930s, followed by electric shock therapy. A surgical procedure called the frontal lobotomy was used for a period of time. It was later replaced with psychotropic drugs, counseling, and behavior modification therapies, practices that remain in use today."

Those electroshock therapies or insulin injections actually induced coma, which staff psychiatrists believed would help "reset" the brain. Starting as early as the mid-1930s, lobotomy was growing in popularity across the country, promoted by Dr. Walter Freeman, a Yale graduate who was a neurologist, but not a trained neurosurgeon. Yet he could legally perform lobotomies because his "ice pick" method did not require actually drilling holes in the skull, but rather accessing the brain through the thin bone of the eye socket.

Crossing the country to promote his work, the cavalier Freeman used an actual ice pick from his kitchen drawer as a medical tool, demonstrating in mental health hospitals how the slim metal rod was hammered into the prefrontal lobe, then manipulated to sever neural pathways connecting the thalamus. Altogether, the operation took only minutes and could alter the patient's personality from dangerously aggressive to tranquil and harmless, or it might make no change at all, or it might lead to death. Freeman was the subject of a 2008 *American Experience* documentary titled "The Lobotomist." Filmmakers noted that in the 1940s, his lobotomy method was "hailed as a miracle cure for the severely mentally ill. But within a few years, lobotomy was labeled one of the most barbaric mistakes of modern medicine."

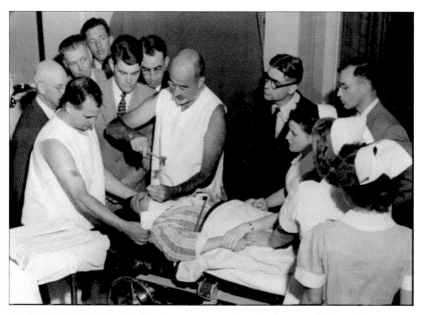

On July 11, 1949, Dr. Walter Freeman, center, Professor of Neurology at George Washington University, demonstrated his new surgical technique called "trans orbital lobotomy" at Western Washington State Hospital. At left, staff psychiatrist Dr. James G. Shanklin had first administered electric shock and anesthesia. (NIH *Record*, Vol LXXI, No. 22)

When the famous doctor visited Western Washington State in 1949, he was photographed performing a lobotomy on a female patient. In the photo, hospital psychiatrist Dr. James G. Shanklin assists Dr. Freeman. The two doctors huddle over their patient, while surrounding them, nearly a dozen others angle for a clear view. Not one person, including the doctors, is wearing gloves or a surgical mask.

If Agnes had had a lobotomy, voluntarily or otherwise, it might have been at the hand of Freeman, Shanklin, or any other staff who were trained during that 1949 trip. She may have even benefitted from it, considering her release just a few short years later. Something seemed to be working.

While some patients did see improvement—converting from belligerent or violent to more settled—sometimes they were reduced to the level of "pets," as Freeman wrote in one published paper. He did not view that as a bad outcome, offering before-and-after photos of disturbed patients who were now clean and smiling. Famously, in the "after" comments for a patient named Rose, Freeman observed that she continuously "pours and pours from an empty coffee pot" and noted that she had "the personality of an oyster." To him, that was an improvement over what could have been her "before": depressed, violent, manic, or suicidal.

CHAPTER 20
IRENE SAILS NORTH - Seattle 1929

She'd missed an entire decade of the territory's childhood.
And her own

When "the little burn victim" left Alaska for Seattle in the summer of 1919, there were 55,000 people living in the Territory. The old Valdez Trail to Fairbanks recently had been renamed the Richardson Road with intermittent roadhouses along its length, welcoming travelers with food, rest, and stables for dogs or horses. The trail was bustling with traffic from horse-drawn stages or wagons, freight sleds pulled by dog teams, and the occasional automobile. Even travelers in boots or snowshoes. The government railway linking Fairbanks to the coast at Seward was four years from finished.

Upon Irene's return a decade later, the population of Alaska had increased to more than 59,000, motorized vehicles routinely traversed the Richardson, and the Alaska Railroad had become something of a superhighway for passengers and freight, a boon for the economy. She'd missed an entire decade of the territory's childhood. And her own.

History has a way of casting a romantic light on early Fairbanks characters. Even the most scandalous behaviors found forgiveness in the herd mentality of male leadership. In that place and time, men in power did not sully their reputations if they remained discreet. Tomorrow was another day.

One of the most respected men in town was early pioneer Mahlon F. Hall, a widower doctor who had helped treat Irene, Mary Porter, and James after the fire. Hall Street in downtown Fairbanks is named for him. Hall was a civic leader, running the gun club, organizing Pioneers of Alaska events, volunteering with perennial fundraisers. And yet there was the other side of Dr. Hall. He was charged and convicted of assaulting a nine-year-old girl in his office, and raping another. Hall's sentence in 1915 included a fine and mere months of confinement. Afterward, as if nothing had happened, he continued to lead local organizations and arrange children's activities at the annual summer community picnic. Pedophiles rarely change, I remembered. What other children had he assaulted without conviction? I lost some useful hours tracing Hall's life story and those of his known victims.

Mrs. Harriet Hess was energetic and ambitious, and when the Shermans were in need, she was the only female on the three-person Board of Children's Guardians. A college-educated former teacher, Harriet had married Luther Hess in 1911, the year Irene was born. But just a few years earlier, Luther was financially backing the career of a woman in the local Red Light District, a working girl named Georgia Anna Eldredge who hailed from the same Illinois hometown as Luther. She was dabbling in the trade there when Luther, back home on a visit, took note of her beauty and suggested she could make some real money in Fairbanks. He also advised that she should first work in St. Louis to gain some polish, and he escorted her there himself.

In 1905, Hess brought "Georgia Lee" to Fairbanks, where, as author Lael Morgan wrote in *Good Time Girls of the Alaska-Yukon Gold Rush*, "he quietly backed her business." This, even as he was leaving his position as assistant district attorney to help organize the First National Bank of Fairbanks and invest in his mining interests. Morgan wrote, "Georgia Lee proved one of his most useful early assets." How long he banked on his asset is not known.

After marriage to Luther Hess, Harriet devoted herself to her church and community work, and served on the Board of Children's Guardians for many years. Once she'd seen to the affairs of Frances and Irene Sherman in 1919, she chose to linger in Seattle during the winter of 1919-20. By the rules, she was required to temporarily resign, but soon returned to Alaska and her work on the board. In her August 11, 1919, resignation telegram to Governor Thomas Riggs Jr., Mrs. Hess had one last question: "Irene Sherman entered Orthopedic Hospital July 16. Do you pay her expenses of board at Fairbanks?"

I had investigated who was covering Irene's health care expenses since that first horrific day at St. Joseph's in Fairbanks, and later at the Orthopedic Hospital, the sanitarium, various foster homes, and finally, in the Home of the Good Shepherd. Costs were covered by various sources, mostly the Territory; no money came from her family.

The reply to Mrs. Hess's query arrived three days later through the governor's secretary: ". . . I have to state that it was the impression of this office that the expenses of this child, while in Fairbanks, would be paid for from the Judge's Indigent Fund, and that the Territory would pay her expenses and transportation from Fairbanks to Seattle, and also her board at the Orthopedic Hospital."

The Board of Children's Guardians' annual budget also included payments to destitute mothers with children in the territory. At first, only white mothers received a monthly stipend. In the 7th Territorial Legislature during spring 1925, a bill written by Alaska's first Native legislator, a Tlingit attorney named William L. Paul, requested the word "white" be stripped from the requirements. Yet in that same session, Alaska lawmakers decided that voters had to be able to read and write English to vote in an election. If necessary, the individual had to read aloud a portion of the U.S. Constitution to prove he was literate.

Irene had spent nearly four years in and out of focused medical care in Alaska, then nearly ten years in Seattle among hospitals, foster homes, and the Catholic home for children. As tough as it had been to follow the sisters' rules, Irene would remember the Home of the Good Shepherd with some fondness, ever the "chapel girl." She was not yet nine years old when she left Alaska, and was now nineteen. She may have been Alaska-born, but essentially she'd grown up in Washington.

Not until 1929, when Irene was finally released to go home to Healy Forks, Alaska, did J. P. offer any financial assistance. For reasons that could only suggest warm anticipation of his daughter's return, that winter J. P. sent money to the Board of Children's Guardians for her return trip. He was still living on his Healy Forks homestead, among what the census taker referred to as the "Scattered Population of the Nenana River District." Forwarding Sherman's contribution onward to Juneau, the writer of an unsigned note expressed great surprise at J. P.'s unnecessary gift. Perhaps he'd misjudged him, he wrote.

Coming home, Irene again traveled with a paid matron hired by the Board of Children's Guardians. Ann Buckley and Irene boarded an Alaska Steamship Company vessel at Seattle, bound for Seward.

Asked to recall that trip, even six decades later, Irene's voice colored with disgust as her ire rose. "The jane I was with kept me in a room on the boat, and if she took me up on deck at all, she put a gol-darned black veil over my face," Irene said in the Koponen tapes. "She was ashamed to be with me on account of my bein' burnt. Now what the heck, don't she realize that if the Lord wanted it, she could have got into somethin' like that herself? If you know what I mean."

At Seward they boarded the train that would deposit Irene back into her father's arms. The plan was to rendezvous with him at a diner in Healy Forks, a hundred miles south of Fairbanks. ". . . they had a hash house there at Healy," Irene remembered, "and this jane [Ann Buckley] and my father got together, and I was to be turned over to him. She made me understand that, by the gods, I wasn't in his custody until she turned me over with papers and all. She was that snotty about the whole thing. She made my life miserable." When the paperwork was signed off, Ann Buckley at last relinquished her charge to J. P. and went on her way, with no thanks from Irene.

In early February 1929, Fourth Judicial District Judge Cecil H. Clegg, who was then also serving as chairman of the Board of Children's Guardians, cited the cost of getting Irene back home in a report to Governor George A. Parks. The Territory paid seventy dollars for her passage from Seattle to Seward on an Alaska Steamship Company vessel; the train from Seward to Healy was twenty-one dollars and forty cents. Matron Buckley received fifty dollars—ten dollars a day—for watching that Irene didn't leave her room without a veil.

For the first time since 1919, Irene was no longer a ward of the Territory. Her poor body was far from fully healed, and the burned areas would never be pain-free. Yet after all the years of yearning to be an Alaskan again, she jumped right in.

"Hitting the winter up here which I had been away from so long, I'm telling you I was just as unprepared as anything ever was," she recalled. "And then Dad would take me out on the trapline with him and leave me in the different cabins while he went out on the trapline and picked up the furs and reset the traps and this, that, and the other thing."

Scars discolored her face. Spidery lines crossed her cheeks, chin, and neck. She was used to working with fingers that were stunted, but strong. Her dad's skin graft donations on her arms were forever cloaked by layers of clothing.

Clara Rust recalled how hard re-entry was for Irene: "When she first came back, it was such a pitiful thing to see her around, and nobody hardly talk to her. People used to shun her."

Back at Healy Forks, Irene joined her father in all his ventures. (Candy Waugaman Collection; *News-Miner* Archives)

Given Irene's vast experience at seeing horror or rejection on the faces of so many, she learned to respond with an aggressive friendliness that was impossible to ignore. It would become her trademark. Nothing could overcome Irene's joy at being back in Healy, her favorite place. After so many years, at last she was home. "I didn't hanker for being with people any more than I had to," Irene told me. "It was through Mother that I was thrown in with people . . . she didn't want me a hermit." How she could have influenced Irene was a mystery. By the time Irene made it back home, her mother was long gone.

While Irene Sherman vowed she would never again leave Alaska, Agnes Sherman would never come back.

CHAPTER 21
FIRST COMES LOVE - Healy Forks, Alaska, 1930
*I tried to keep it right up to snuff, so that
there'd be no friction between Dad and I*

"I've got no use for the States, to tell the truth," Irene spoke with power in her voice, "after I was stuck there ten years, more or less." Remembering what that long absence was like, she recalled thinking to herself, "Dammit, I don't belong out here. I belong in Alaska where my own people are. The bunch of critters out there, I says, 'The less I see of you guys, the better off I am.'"

Now she was back along the river with neighbors she fondly remembered as her "railroad gang." In November 1929, Irene was nineteen and J. P. was fifty-one when they were counted in the federal census. Most of the locals had jobs related to the government railroad. J. P. was prospecting, and trapping and selling furs, plus collecting ten-dollar bounties for each wolf hide, while Irene was looking after their household. In reality, they worked shoulder-to-shoulder mining, trapping, hunting, cutting wood, whatever was needed. Agnes was living in Washington, but was a lingering presence in Irene's stories from Nenana and Healy.

"With me, I was down on the railroad tracks, living with my father in a cabin. And Mother was like a roaming deal. She always had to be out with the gang. And I had to trail along with him. And wherever we landed, I stayed there and played. And had to keep up with her. We never stayed in Fairbanks very long. We lived down there along the railroad belt and had a home there and . . . *Good Lord, Wally! How'd you hurt yourself?*"

Suddenly we were jolted into to the present. It was July 1988, and we were back Fairbanks, having breakfast in the Black Angus Restaurant on the ground floor of the Polaris Hotel. Wally Burnett had arranged my first "real" interview with Irene, and she was sitting across the table in a cozy booth. Now a scrape on Wally's arm had halted her stream of consciousness.

It was no big deal, he told her. He'd hurt it on a piece of wood yesterday.

"What in the hell! Did you have your mind on me too damn much?" she wheezed.

"I was thinking about how I was going to gather you up today!"

Irene laughed hard and her lungs rattled. "Oh, hell, ain't that something!" she coughed, and I flashed on how charming she could be when she was flirting.

Wally took the conversation back to 1930: "They moved down in the Healy area and they homesteaded and they lived on the river. He was trapping down there, and that's where she and her father lived most of the time."

J. P. had long been rooted in the Healy River Valley, and would make a home with Irene near the railroad tracks and the confluence of the Healy and Nenana Rivers, called Healy Forks. For a time, Irene lived in her own nearby cabin. During his daughter's first summer back, J. P. introduced Irene to Robert P. Hartman, a fellow miner-trapper from further west in the Kantishna area, a neighbor of the famous-in-Alaska pioneers, Joe and Fannie Quigley. He also ran an extensive trapline in the Lake Minchumina region to the west, beyond the national park. The couple first met in Nenana, where J. P. and Irene were fishing. Hartman had come into town to trade when he and Irene found each other. Within months, he proposed marriage.

Hartman was a brown-eyed, dark-haired man of medium build and height, born in 1892 in Tacoma, Washington. At age eighteen, he'd entered the plumbing trade in Tacoma, and by 1917, he was in Anchorage working as a butcher in the Alaska Engineering Commission mess hall. The government railroad camp at Anchorage was new and bursting its seams, optimally located on Cook Inlet. Hartman next made his way north to Kantishna, likely through his AEC connections. He'd remained single until July 27, 1930, when at age thirty-seven, he married nineteen-year-old Irene in Nenana.

"A pretty little romance culminated in a wedding on Saturday afternoon," the *Fairbanks News-Miner* reported in its society columns, "when Miss Irene Sherman and Robert P. Hartman were quietly united in marriage . . . The bride wore a rose crepe de chine dress and carried a bouquet of pink poppies and small white flowers . . .

"After a brief courtship, the two young people blissfully launched forth upon the sea of matrimony and the good wishes of all follow them. Mr. and Mrs. Hartman will soon return to the Kantishna, where they will make their future home."

When I asked Irene about her marriage almost fifty years later, she didn't have much to say about the bliss part. Or where Hartman ended up. Just that it was how "Dad and I got split up."

"How'd that happen?" I asked.

"Well, because I went and married this Hartman, and he turned out to be a flop at the tail end of it. I couldn't seem to get ends meeting the way I wanted it, and I had been schooled by my own father. I knew pretty damn well what Dad wanted and boy, I tell you, I tried to keep it right up to snuff, so that there'd be no friction between Dad and I."

I found more about those years in the Koponen recordings: "He had a trapline at Lake Minchumina ... and that thing was danged near fifty to a hundred miles long," Irene said. "Over all kinds of lakes and all kinds of trees and brush area. Seven dogs. We were there for two and a half years; that's how long our marriage lasted. But he hated the kid we had, and he hated me.

"What my ex-husband did . . . he railroads me back to my father with the kid. And deserts me. He was supposed to pay $50 for alimony for that kid when I got the divorce, but he wouldn't do it. And I never seen a red cent." In the recording, Irene also angrily implied that Hartman had tried to pimp her out to other men. She would have none of that. I hadn't yet heard that appalling story when I'd innocently asked why the marriage had failed. She'd answered brusquely, "We didn't fit together too good!" They'd been married, she said, "just long enough to give me the common sense that I didn't want no more of it."

Irene's self-survival and independent streak was in full bloom. The nuns couldn't break her will; how could a man?

The knot was officially *untied* in the Fairbanks District court on April 11, 1933, after not quite three years, leaving Irene a single mother. Robert P. Hartman Jr., had come along on October 29, 1931.

Little Robert's life would unfold on the primitive Sherman homestead in the heart of the rivers, mountains, and railbelt. He'd learn from his mother and grandfather how to take care of himself in the wilderness, and he gained some territorial schooling. While Irene was extremely vigilant about the dangers of the mining life, she was also distracted, watching her son while working all-in with her father on his claims and trapline. And she liked her drink.

"My son, Robert Hartman, Jr.," she fondly reminisced in 1978, "I loved that kid. He's one grand and glorious and wonderful lad. And of course he's in his forties now, but what the dickens, we all get some age somewhere. And he's well-loved and well-liked by everybody."

J. P.'s homestead spread near the confluence of the Healy and Nenana rivers. Decades later, Golden Valley Electric Association built a power plant fueled by Healy coal on that site. I'd seen the plant myself during a float trip on the Nenana River. Our raft had emerged from a fast-paced, roiling current through the canyon with nothing but craggy walls all around, and suddenly there it was, a blocky industrial facility popped up above us, a foreign body in the stark wilderness surrounding it. When the Shermans lived there, from their windows they could see the black-striped cliffs of Healy coal in one direction; in the other, the northern foothills of the imposing Alaska Range, crowned by North America's tallest peak. Nearby the Alaska Railroad tracks carried passengers and freight, while the rivers coursed. Humanity's highways. He'd picked a perfect spot.

J. P. made the Mount McKinley National Park reports again in 1936 and 1937, as a bounty hunter for wolves. Rangers monitored and reported on local trapping. The 1937 report said, "Ranger Houston has made several patrols from headquarters . . . He contacted trappers along the boundary and witnessed Mr. Sherman taking four wolves from traps near the head of Dry Creek. Those brought his total to eleven wolves for

The Golden Valley Electric Association power plant in Healy, pictured in 1985 along the Nenana River, was built on the site of the old Sherman homestead. (Tricia Brown)

the season. With the price per hide averaging $30.00 and a bounty of $20.00, this is a good return for a wolf. If the Alaska Game Commission is desirous of continuing the hunting of wolves, some trappers should be well paid for the efforts."

No one could accuse J. P. Sherman of being lazy, but his "git 'er done" methods often landed him outside the bounds of the law. In nearly every decade, J. P. had faced legal opposition, with charges ranging from unpaid debt, illegal hunting, selling improperly sealed pelts, shooting at a man, or insufficiently providing for his family. Yet somehow he managed to stay out of jail.

Further, for all the effort J. P. put into trapping and mining, he lived like a pauper. You had to wonder, just what did he do with the fur, the gold, and the greenbacks?

CHAPTER 22
FATHER-DAUGHTER DANCE
Washington and Oregon, 1935
Father, daughter, and granddaughter,
all lingering in residential facilities

When Agnes's father, Fred Eckert, first heard from Alaska Red Cross nurse Dorothy Sleichter in 1924, he and his second wife were living comfortably in the big city of Portland, Oregon. He was a ship's carpenter, settled only blocks from the Columbia River. Fred was the first to remarry after he and Minnie divorced, exchanging vows in 1907 with New York native Harriet F. "Hattie" Farnham. Hattie was five years older than her groom when she married—her first time—at age fifty. By 1920, the couple left Seattle for Portland, renting a place at Sixth and Pine. That's where Fred was when Nurse Sleichter reached out, requesting he meet the *Northwestern* at Pier 2 in Seattle.

In puzzling out what became of Agnes and the children after they left Alaska, I doubted that Fred and Hattie had room for long-term visitors. Space was likely an issue given the Eckerts' house number was 416½, indicating a shared house. If Agnes alone went home with her father, then who took care of the children? Was it grand-mère Minnie, who lived just outside Seattle in Kent, Washington? What about Agnes's little sister, Bessie, who also lived in Washington and was now going by "Betty"? There were still some Jenotts and Eckerts around Seattle, too.

I knew that the toddlers had been declared wards of King County, but not exactly when. City directories showed that Agnes was living in Tacoma within a year. Were her children there with her?

I had hit a wall in my research. I could make some assumptions, but couldn't state facts about where Pauline and Richard spent the eighteen months after leaving Alaska. Agnes would have had little chance of providing for her children while working. I could guess that Minnie was an essential player during those months. Had she pointed her daughter toward residential mental health treatment? Someone had signed her in, if not Agnes herself.

※ ※ ※

Agnes Eckert Sherman was not the only one in her family with mental health challenges requiring residential care. Just three years earlier, Irene had been on trial in Juneau, defending her sanity and dodging the directive to be institutionalized at Eastern Washington State Hospital. Instead she was sent to the convent in Seattle, not a mental hospital, but nonetheless, an involuntary stay.

Now, in April 1935, there was yet a third family member who needed a high level of care. About six years after Agnes went into Western Washington State, her father Fred was similarly housed, entering a Salem, Oregon, psychiatric institution that was a former "insane asylum." Later it was relabeled as the Oregon State Hospital.

Father, daughter, and granddaughter were all lingering in residential facilities in neighboring northwestern states. By that time, the Eckert family was so scattered that it was entirely possible none of them knew what was happening to the others. When Fred was admitted in 1935, his youngest daughter Bessie, the girl who'd eloped with the Canadian customs agent at seventeen, was living just twenty miles away in Olympia, Washington, preparing to marry for the third out of ultimately four times. She was going by the name "Betty" now. Did she have a clue that her father was so nearby, or if the answer was yes, did she care?

And what had become of Fred? I wondered if he'd ever been released. The answer was chilling. Just thirteen months and one day after his admission to the Oregon "insane asylum," Fred Eckert died within its walls at age seventy-seven. According to his death certificate, he passed away on May 31, 1936, from the effects of cerebral arteriosclerosis, either by stroke or aneurysm. Fred's doctor noted that he'd been treating his patient since April 22, 1935. That may have been his admittance date.

In spring 1935, both Fred and Hattie were elderly, raising pertinent questions about why Fred was admitted. The institution was specifically for treatment of people with mental health problems. But was it possible that he was incapacitated by an earlier stroke or in some other way? Was it beyond Hattie's ability to care for him at their

The Oregon State Hospital as pictured in 1900. Makers of the 1975 movie, *One Flew Over the Cuckoo's Nest*, primarily filmed here. (Courtesy Oregon State Library)

advanced ages? Just two weeks after Fred was admitted, Hattie died in Portland on May 7, 1935. Her remains were returned to her native New York for burial in Skaneateles. By then, the Eckerts had been married for twenty-eight years. I felt nothing but sympathy for them both.

Back in Alaska, in July 1938, Irene was enjoying the company of her seven-year-old son Robert Jr. as they joined a dozen other Healy locals at a dance hosted by the Healy River Coal Company. The party was held at Suntrana, a tiny coal community near Healy that was accessible only by train at the end of a railroad spur. Folks came in from throughout the area to first watch a film in the store that also served as the community's hall. Afterward, everybody pulled back the chairs to create a dance floor and play records.

"Kids had their candy and soda pop and enjoyed the antics of the grown-ups who couldn't down the 'play impulse' that makes us all human once in a while," reported the *Alaska Miner*.

A few weeks later, reporter Jim Scott had more to say about Irene in his column, "Healyites": "We've heard of strange burial services, and seen some too. What, with reading the 'Cremation of S. McGee' and soldiering two years in China, we are well prepared for the unique angle in anything. But, when Irene Sherman recently buried a 300-pound rock. in her front yard, all we could do was stand on the train platform, hands in pockets, eyes out of sockets . . . '"What the heck?' Then our nose-for-news got the scent of a story and down the bank we strolled.

"'What's up Irene? Why gouge the ground this way?'

"'Well these darn railroad sharpshooters are always pegging rocks at this big one, because it is such a good target,' she answered. 'The stones they throw ricochet into my bedroom through the window, and it was cheaper to bury this rock than somebody else.'"

A month later, Irene accepted a marriage proposal from one George Richardson, who'd been working at Happy, a government railroad camp. Most recently he'd been laboring closer to Fairbanks, in Ester. In mid-September Irene and George told the *Alaska Miner* newspaper that they would marry "in the near future."

"George is that popular fellow who makes merry whenever it's gloom," reporter Scott wrote. "Last year we met him in the California Bar at Fairbanks. He was using a chair for a drum and with a pair of table knives he accompanied Thelma, the accordion queen of Fairbanks. Throughout the three days' celebration over the Fourth of July we wandered back to the scene many times to absorb the music, color, and gayety provided by two real artists."

The writer went on to describe Irene as a long-time Healyite and that her father had settled there in 1904. "He was probably the first white man to set eyes on the Healy coal veins that stand out, huge black ribbons in the sandstone cliffs, visible from passing trains."

Scott's column continued with his personal take on Irene's scars, "She fell in a fire and was cruelly burned. It robbed her of a woman's greatest asset, facial beauty. But that never got the plucky girl down. She can trap with the best of the male trappers and is as independent as they make 'em. Has a handsome little son, Robert, by a previous marriage."

George and Irene applied for a license, yet they didn't follow through with marriage. One day Irene came around the paper asking if the engagement announcement had been printed. It was too late, she was told. So she placed a public notice for the next edition: "Mrs. Irene Mary Sherman of Healy Forks, Alaska . . . My engagement to Mr. George Earl Richardson is annulled because of false promises and drunkenness at the time of need."

By November 1939, Robert Jr. had just turned eight and completed first grade through the territorial school. With his mother and grandfather, little Robert was roughing it in the Nenana census area eight miles outside of Healy Village. They were river and railroad people, living in a three-room cabin. J. P. was now sixty, and Irene was twenty-seven. As always, she had reclaimed her birth surname of Sherman.

CHAPTER 23
THE BIRTH OF PACKSACK ANNIE
Fairbanks, mid-1940s
'Packsack Annie,' they called her, for the ever-present,
very full rucksack she carried

Fred J. Potter was a Juneau-born railroad cook and widower who next stepped forward and proposed marriage to Irene Sherman. She said yes. In October 1942, the couple was married by the Reverend Arthur Rowe Wright at St. Mark's Episcopal Church in Nenana. They took the train in to Fairbanks to honeymoon at the Crystal Bath House. However, this was another brief union for Irene. Soon, the couple separated, and Irene again reclaimed her maiden name. It wasn't clear whether they'd divorced. When Fred passed away in 1949, Irene started calling herself a widow. Reflecting back on her two husbands, she'd say, "One disappeared and one died." Truth was, Robert Hartman Sr. hadn't disappeared, but merely relocated to California and remarried, dying at age eighty-nine in San Luis Obispo in 1982.

In the late forties, Irene made a permanent move to Fairbanks, where the war years had transformed her birthplace. *Where was her darling boy, Robert?* I had to wonder. She'd spoken of the various boyfriends she used to have, and how she'd stay with them or at her own place. I also knew that territorial officials had questioned her mothering and guessed this was it. Robert seemed absent from her life; later, I'd learn that he'd become a ward of the territory, just as she had.

Now in her early thirties, Irene was still hardy, and for a time, she lived year-round in a sturdy wall-tent across the Chena from downtown on the Graehl side. Camping among the birch and cottonwoods, it wasn't half-bad by her standards.

"I had a big double bed and then a table with all my stuff on top of it and under it," she told Koponen. "The tent wasn't insulated, but it had a tarp over the top and two stoves. . . . I lived in that tent for a good five years." She became a popular figure among her soldier friends, sharing food and drink and companionship.

"Packsack Annie," they called her, for the ever-present, very full rucksack she carried. Irene had begun to collect and keep things that were valuable in her eyes. She filled up the rucksack, and she filled up the tent—and the space around it—with her treasures.

The federal government had established Ladd Field on the outskirts of Fairbanks in 1940 as a Cold Weather Test Station for the military. Throughout the war years, the town was overrun by servicemen as well as occasional "Lend-Lease" pilots pausing at this strategic point while ferrying war planes from the Lower 48 states and across Canada on the Alaska-Siberia route. At Fairbanks, Russian pilots took over and flew American planes across the Bering Strait and further west. Soldiers from Ladd, as well as Russian and U.S. pilots, were often about town, looking for recreation. Always open to a free beer, Irene was welcoming. They made friends with her, drank with her, kidded with her. She found companionship among them, and wasn't tied to her tent.

"Of course, I had a few boyfriends elsewhere and I'd stay with one for maybe a night or two or some gol-darned thing," she remembered later. "But I'd always gravitate back here when I got fed up with him. Sooner or later, I'd have to bomb the son-of-a-gun and tell him to scram out of my life. Cause if he got to disbehavin', that'd end that situation."

Of course, Irene was already known for doing her share of disbehavin'. In time, she would discard the nickname "Packsack Annie" and create a new title for herself: the "Queen of Fairbanks."

While Irene was living large in Fairbanks, her mother was still housed against her will down south in Steilacoom, Washington. In the 1940 census, inpatient Agnes Sherman was among ninety-nine other women as Western Washington Hospital's population grew to a level that was considered overcrowded. A decade later, the federal census reported that she was still confined there and had worked three hours during the previous week. And then, sometime in the early 1950s, Agnes was free. But to what? Could she ever live on her own again?

※ ※ ※

On April 27, 1950, in Fairbanks, a census-taker noted that Irene Sherman was a resident of 302 Clay Street, an address she shared with two roommates. Irene and each of the men, both Native Alaskans, were heads of their own households. One man named Shirley Phillips reported he was Eskimo, fifty-one years old, widowed, and had completed fifth grade. He worked for the U.S. government as a "stationery [sic] fireman" at nearby Ladd Field. The third roommate was a forty-one-year-old Athabascan man named Jake Butter, who oversaw a kennel on the premises and stated his occupation was "dog keeper."

As for Alaska-born Irene M. Sherman, her tongue must have been firmly in cheek when she reported her race as "Indian." By then, she was thirty-nine, divorced, and working as a maid, whether it was at their shared abode, or elsewhere, you couldn't say. As for her industry, she listed: "Housekeeping and trapping." I doubted that Irene was a permanent resident when the census-taker came around, because by then she was settled across the river in Graehl, squatting on land that belonged to someone else. That someone, a pioneer known for his generosity, was Arthur Leslie "Les" Nerland.

Irene wasn't homeless, ever, even counting the years of tent camping in Graehl. She made a home for herself thanks to the oversight of people like Nerland and his wife, Mildred, who tried to meet Irene's needs without removing her freedoms. She went from tent to tarpaper shack.

In the late 1960s, there was even a little house there for her, next to the shack. But you could barely see the frame structures for all of her collectibles around them. The lot in Graehl was across the Chena from downtown in a forested area once considered out of town. By the time I first interviewed Irene in 1988, she'd already been living there for more than forty years.

In the early 1970s, the pipeline construction boom was cranking up, and downtown's Two Street was overrun with partying pipeline workers, prostitutes, and hard-drinking locals. This was once the familiar Second Avenue, where parents used to drop off their kids for ice cream and a matinee at the Empress Theatre. The Mayberry-like qualities of pre-WWII Fairbanks, where everybody knew everybody, had vanished. No longer was it safe to let your children freely roam around downtown.

Irene already was known throughout the Interior as "local color," enough so that when a reporter from the *Los Angeles Times* came up to write about construction of the remarkable engineering feat called the Trans-Alaska Pipeline, he wrote a sidebar on Irene.

Packsack Annie crowed, "I'm queen of the whole damn bunch up here." In those rowdy days, she was partying with the best of them and known for her open-carry policy. Her handgun even had a name: "Gunsmoke." It was all irresistible to *Times* reporter Charles Hillinger. He wrote, "Townspeople recall times when a situation has gotten out of hand in a local bar. That's when 'Packsack Annie' pulls out her pistol and threatens to shoot 'the blue blazing pants off all the loudmouth SOBs if they don't split, but quick.'" A conductor for the Alaska Railroad chimed in that he'd personally witnessed a time when Irene waved

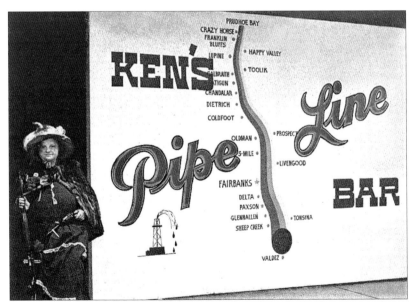

Irene was packing "Gunsmoke" in this photo taken outside one of her regular stops. (Courtesy B. J. "Butch" Hardy)

Gunsmoke around and cleared out a bar. The legendary stories shored up the image of Irene as a northern version of Yosemite Sam. And she delighted in it.

Once oil started running through the pipeline in 1977, most of the jobs for Outsiders drained away, fulfilling the heart's desires of many locals. As a favorite bumper sticker of the day read, "Happiness is a Texan leaving Alaska with an Okie under each arm." But Fairbanks was never quite the same.

※ ※ ※

When I met up with Irene in 1988, she'd been building onto her place for forty-plus years, hauling heavy things home to fortify her place, so her safety zone was tucked behind an orderly, yet jumbled fence of discarded wood, rock, metal, cardboard, and large appliances.

"Over there in Graehl there, you can see my effort," she told me. "I've barricaded my whole place."

Scanning your eyes over the place begged the question "How?" How in the world could she have created this, and stayed alive behind its borders year-round?

"Did you build all that yourself?" I asked. "How in the world did you do that?"

"More or less," Irene began, and chuckled. "Well, you'd be surprised what a little Shenanigan Sherman can do when I want to do something. Course sometimes I get someone to give me a hand here and there and elsewhere, but damn seldom. Because I've always wanted everything up for safety's sake, so the thing would stay there."

Her place appeared impenetrable, the distant, dark windows of the house protected with tough plastic, its flanks guarded by that high wall of building scraps, ancient refrigerators girdled with chains, and collected refuse. Paths of approach dead-ended against false entrances. Inside the fortress, narrow tunnels and debris-filled walkways connected two structures: Irene's old shack, and a newer building that was absorbed into the complex in the late sixties. It was a ten-year-old's dream fort created by a chronic hoarder. "I like to have stuff stored so I can dive into it if I need it," she explained, scanning her treasures. Irene said she liked the location because it was out of the way, across the Chena and at the dead-end of Front Street and a bend of Hamilton Avenue near Noyes Slough. "I could build up around it if I wanted to. And I fixed the thing so they couldn't crowd me." That worked for a while. A decade earlier, Irene had spoken about the demands of her lifestyle choices and how she managed without running water or central heat. The house was wired for electricity; her wood/coal stove provided heat. Sometimes Usibelli Coal delivered a load for free, a gift from the Usibelli family; occasionally, from another friend.

"For a while, I didn't have to light the fire in the stove, I had some hot pads inside the bed," she said. "I don't like a hot house, anyway. I just like a place where I can sleep comfortable. In the wintertime I buy a sack of ice at the store and melt that for cookin' and drinkin' and what have you."

The logistics of living as she'd chosen would have challenged even a young, healthy individual. For Irene, pushing through those difficulties and enduring physical pain was an everyday affair, made harder as the years passed. Still she fought to live independently.

"I'm not completely all intact," she said, "like across my hips and in my back I got these aches. And then of course, what the heck you call it, charley horses in my feet and legs and my upper part. And then I have a hell of a time with the flu bugs."

As Irene aged, she remained a favorite subject in the local press, photographed while picking up construction garbage with her own wheelbarrow, cutting her birthday cake donated by Gavora's, posing with Gunsmoke in front of Ken's Pipeline Bar. One spring day, Tom Snapp, editor of the *Pioneer All-Alaska Weekly*, posed Irene for a photo checking her mailbox at 740 Front Street. The image ran a second time during extreme below-zero stretch in late December 1980, alongside a front-page story of how Irene had suffered frostbite on her hands and feet.

After a hospital stay, Snapp assured his readers, the feisty woman was back at home.

Yet more scars, I thought.

Along the property's south-facing side, the gable of the house that Les Nerland had built for Irene was visible in 1988. (Tricia Brown)

In many ways, Irene reminded me of my sister, Lynette, who'd lost her pet cat to the Yukon Territory wilderness during her 1975 drive up the Alaska Highway from the Midwest. Staking her claim on and in Fairbanks, the bartender, pipeline camp maid, and eventually gold miner later became chairman of Alaska's third official political group: the Alaska Independence Party. The group advocated for another statehood vote because they believed members of the military stationed here were transients and should not have been counted.

My extremely Alaskan sister became known as "Yukon Yonda" or just "Yukon" out in Fox or the Circle Mining District, where she and her husband successfully labored to uncover "little yellow rocks." Their unique home on a mining claim in Fox lay along a road that eventually dead-ended at the Yukon River. While her house was much more orderly than Irene's, it was also filled with rare treasures. Look around and you'd see mammoth tusk fragments unearthed while mining for gold. A whale rib was lashed to an overhead beam. A twisted propeller leaned against the wall, testifying to the remote-site plane crash that they'd survived. They'd strapped on their skis and came down the mountain that way.

But it was the gold that hung from Yukon's neck and wrists, and nuggets that decorated nearly every finger, that told of back-breaking labor at their mom-and-pop operation, using heavy equipment, yes, but still sluicing and panning, sorting soil, sand, and rocks to find the gold in the same way J. P. had back in 1904.

Inside my sister's funky house was a framed poster that I loved and coveted for decades, even though I felt it was best suited to this place and this couple, not me. Splashed across the poster were the words, "Alaska: Land of the Individual and Other Endangered Species."

Naturally, the sentiment suited Irene perfectly.

CHAPTER 24
TRACKING FRANCES
Fairbanks to California, 1950

Actually, she has something more like an addiction
than a habit, I guess . . .

Frances Burnett grew up in Fairbanks with scant knowledge of Irene. Her birth sister was just a sad story of a distant stranger, either hospitalized, in a foster home, or in residential care around Seattle. So as teenagers, while they knew about each other, and that they were related, the sisters remained disconnected. After Irene's return to Alaska in 1929, she lived well south of Fairbanks, at Healy Forks, near Lake Minchumina, or even Talkeetna for a while. Frances remained in the city. That distance was a preference for Frances, whose personality bore little resemblance to the wild-and-wooly Irene.

Yet there was a stretch in the mid- to late 1940s when the incompatible birth sisters were adults and sharing the streets of town, although clearly moving in different circles. Not everyone in Fairbanks knew they were related, and that's how Frances preferred it. Irene was a loose cannon, a runaround, a heavy drinker who'd approach Frances for money or rides. Frances didn't want to be drawn into Irene's tumultuous world. She determined to set boundaries protecting her private life and mental health. Frances would return a wave on the street and sometimes lend a few dollars, but that was about it. Her Burnett relatives described the relationship as "cordial, but not close."

By the end of the 1940s, Frances's marriage to Brick Jacobs was over after nearly two decades, and she was looking forward to a fresh start in southern California. The breakup and move were traumatic, but that hard interlude was followed by yet another with the 1950 death of Blanche Burnett, the dear mother who had rescued her from growing up Sherman.

When I sat down with Wally Burnett and Irene in 1988, Frances had been a Californian for nearly four decades. She was twice married, twice divorced, and maintaining a friendly distance from her birth sister.

Frances Burnett Jacobs in 1940s Fairbanks. (Burnett Family Collection)

However, there was the occasional phone call if Wally set it up. He gave me Frances's number, and later, I reached out. Speaking from Van Nuys, Frances described herself as a "white-haired kid" and talked about how once she'd discovered an old Bible in a cabin, whose cabin she couldn't remember. *Was it a Sherman home?* I asked. Frances suggested yes. It was so long ago. It was water-stained and hard-backed.

"Inside, all the pages were written with all the kids' births," she said, "and when some of the kids died, it stopped." That intriguing loose end would never be tied. In the next breath, Frances told me how she still vividly remembered that sleigh ride to the Nenana courthouse for her formal adoption.

"The judge asked who I wanted to live with," she recalled. "Blanche E. Burnett."

"What's your relationship with Irene like?" I asked.

"She kind of has a one-track mind," she answered, demurring. "I really don't have too much to say." But on the subject of coming back to Alaska, Frances's voice warmed. "I've been wanting to ever so much. I'd love to."

Frances had another surprise for me, something about a nephew whom she loved dearly. As a boy, he'd grown up in a foster home and become a miner like his grandfather, J. P. Sherman. *Well, well,* I thought. *This is Irene's son, Robert!* He had worked for operations in Goodnews Bay and Nome, Frances told me, digging for platinum and gold; sometimes he vacationed Outside. Occasionally, he sent his Aunt Frances platinum nuggets, right in the U.S. mail! She'd expected him for Christmas in California one year, but he didn't show. The following spring, he died. "He had diabetes on both sides," Frances explained. Robert had never married nor started a family. So his death marked the end of another Sherman branch, like her own, that was childless.

I knew there was so much more to this woman than what little I'd managed to piece together. What about her happy occasions, her interactions among her Burnett siblings, the other dimensions of her personality? I knew she'd loved to dress nicely. To go dancing with her man. But she remained almost two-dimensional. Unlike her birth sister, she was not loud, rarely in the paper, merely a name on her Burnett brothers' draft cards as a person who would always know where to find them. Finally, I talked to a great-niece, Jen Walker-Mang of Fairbanks, a mother, grandmother, and a gifted quilter with a passion for local history. In February 2018, Jen cleared up misinformation about how the Sherman and Burnett families were connected, writing on Facebook, "In 1914 [Irene's] mother also had another daughter, Frances, that my family adopted because she asked them to. Her mother wasn't right in the head."

Months later Jen and I talked by phone and exchanged emails. She suggested I reach back a generation to the aging daughter-in-law of Searl and Ethel Burnett, her Aunt Connie Burnett.

"Just take it easy," Jen said. "She's getting up in years, so don't bombard her with questions, but if you get her warmed up, she loves to talk about the old days." Indeed, when I phoned Connie in January 2019, she could nimbly recall the Frances years. Connie confirmed stories from when Frances lived in Fairbanks, how Irene expected better treatment from her birth sister, but Frances kept her lines intact. According to Connie, over the years, Irene's tangled perceptions of

Frances's adoption events had turned Irene's bitterness and anger toward Blanche Burnett instead of her own culpable parents.

"Irene always blamed Blanche. She'd say, 'If they hadn't taken the baby, [my dad] would have been home, and I wouldn't have been burned.'"

Of course, baby Frances had not been taken from Agnes, but relinquished by her birth mother. Whether Irene knew or remembered that didn't seem to matter. As always, her truths were immutable.

※ ※ ※

In January 2022, I flew up to Fairbanks to meet Connie Burnett and two of her adult children in person. I'd been advised that Connie had suffered considerable memory loss in the three years since our phone talk. Still, she'd been the family historian, and I hoped her daughters might help fill in some blanks—maybe unearth any adoption records? Once I arrived, it was clear that the woman who'd conversed with me so comfortably in 2019 could no longer reach back to yesterday, or even this morning.

"What year is it?" she softly called out to her daughters as nearby I turned the pages of her photo albums with Jeannine and Celeste. These women were granddaughters of Searl and Ethel Burnett, with whom Frances had lived as a teenager. Neatly dressed and made up, Connie moved slowly and seated herself at the kitchen counter, enjoying the pound cake I'd brought. Her daughters smiled, knowing that their mom had a sweet tooth. For now, Connie pleasantly lived in the moment, in the midst of loving family and familiar things, like her teapot collection, and these immediate pleasures were rewarding. Here before me, the Burnett family was carrying on its unfailing duty to take care of its elders.

※ ※ ※

Frances and Irene, these two eldest daughters of Agnes, may not have had much in common on the surface, but they shared a trait that inexplicably bound them: both women had become chronic hoarders.

I recalled a sentence fragment that Frances had uttered in our phone call thirty years earlier, when I was first researching Irene. With my shoulder wedging the rotary phone receiver against my ear, I'd penciled notes all over the green-and-white stripes of a dot-matrix printout. Nudging Frances's memories, I brought up Irene's home place and her habit of "collecting" things.

I took a moment to correct myself: "Actually, she has something more like an addiction than a habit, I guess . . ."

Frances's response was immediate and frank. "I think I do, too," she said quietly. "The thing is, we have that in common . . ." At the time, I had no idea how important those words were. And now, decades later, I considered the real possibility that either or both of Frances's two marriages may have ended because of her chronic hoarding. Another puzzle piece seemed to fall into place.

Frances's disorder may have been snowballing in Fairbanks when she was married to Jacobs, but it seemed to drastically increase after they divorced. In our 2019 talk, Connie told me that divorce left Frances in good straits financially, that is until her second marriage a few years later to Walter Bilowas, a New York native who was a tailor in California when they met. To my ears, it sounded like Walter was trying to keep Frances's "collecting" at bay, selling items when he could. But Connie was loyal to Frances as she spoke.

"She married this other guy who ripped her off big time," Connie said. "She became very sour. She became, 'I got to hang on to this, I got to hang onto that.' She had two houses, one very old, but very beautiful. He even took off the glass doorknobs and sold them! She got more and more disgruntled and said 'I gotta hang onto everything.'"

Frances freed herself from Bilowas, or vice versa, but the lasting effects of her hoarding would take a toll on her extended Burnett family. It was harder as Frances aged in California and couldn't live alone anymore. In 2018, Connie had said that moving Frances into assisted living required that the extended family rent large containers for valuables and collectibles, some of which were nothing more than refuse that ended up at the dump.

"They needed three or four of those great big things that cart away stuff," Connie said. "Beautiful clothes that were totally ruined."

A great-niece of Frances's, Sharron Johnson Wasser, came to the rescue. Sharron had grown up in a mining family on the creeks outside Fairbanks. She and her husband had operated several successful businesses in town, raised their kids, and happily retired to Tempe, Arizona, in 1999. By then, Great-Aunt Frances was eighty-five.

"Sharron was the one that came and kind of took care of Frances when it was getting really bad," Connie explained. "She found a place in California for her. But Sharron was going from Arizona to California all the time."

Knowing she couldn't keep up the pace of traveling that distance several times a month, Sharron secured a small residential facility for Frances about a mile away from her own home in Tempe. "Nice, nice place," Connie said. "Little place—just a few people. They took wonderful care." Sharron got the calls when Frances struggled with dementia in the years that followed, as her personality changed in radical ways, as happens to many afflicted with the disease.

True to the Burnett tradition of caring for family, Sharron would look after Frances until the day her aunt passed on August 17, 2011, at age ninety-six. The last survivor among the children born to Agnes Sherman, Frances died a long, long way from Nenana, Alaska.

CHAPTER 25
CALIFORNIA 'COUSINS' – Los Angeles, 1950s
This is how Irene might have looked if she hadn't been burned

The first time I talked with Michelle Moore by phone, I had to ask about her late mother-in-law's name. Why had her new adoptive parents in California discarded "Pauline" for "Georgerene"? *Seriously? That's not a typo?* Indeed, it was not, she explained. The little blonde preschooler had become the only child of George and Irene Coover of Glendale. They merged their first names to create "Georgerene Irene."

Following a rough start as Pauline in Nenana, Georgerene had landed in a solid home with well-to-do parents who doted on her. High school friends called the fresh-faced girl "Georgie." Then in later adulthood, she preferred to be called "Irene." How could the Moores and I keep the two women straight in conversation? For a while, I used "your Irene" and "my Irene." Then we stuck with "Georgerene."

John and Michelle sent me a black-and-white Hollywood-style beauty shot of John's mother. She was a classic beauty, a knockout. Later, I found an online yearbook picture from when she was a cute teenager with fluffy curls. During a pause one day, I opened three digital photos on my screen and studied them side-by-side. The Sherman sisters: Irene with her impish, scarred face beneath the wide brim of a ragged Easter bonnet, a matronly Frances posing for a formal portrait in cat's-eyes glasses, and Georgerene, with her flawless skin, lipsticked smile, and Jane Wyatt hairdo. In all three, their eyes and widow's peak hairline were so very similar. Looking at Georgerene's beauty shot, the resemblance was an echo of her eldest sister.

"This is how Irene might have looked if she hadn't been burned," I whispered to no one.

Working with John and Michelle, I gained more insight into Georgerene as we dug, me through electronic means, and the Moores through memories and the boxes and papers left at his mom's passing. They were hoping to find adoption paperwork or clues as to how long she had lived as "Pauline Agnes" with her birth parents. They were also

Georgerene looked like a starlet in this formal image made in the early 1950s. (Moore Family Collection)

curious about the youngest brother, Richard DeWitt Sherman. When was he adopted, or had he remained a foster child? I sent a fat printout of the Eckert-Jenott-Sherman family tree to John's older sister, who preferred snail mail to email. And John and Michelle shared a copy with his younger sister. Every so often, someone would comment, "This is amazing, but why are you doing this for us?" I had no short answer, other than curiosity fueled by mother-hen passion, a desire to protect the accuracy of Irene's story. So much hearsay and bias had been attached to her. I wanted details as complete as possible. Now there was Georgerene to consider, to make things right for her, too.

As any enthusiastic genealogist will tell you, there's nothing like the shockwave that passes through you when an essential kernel of knowledge comes to light. It happened to me as I worked back in time outlining the ancestors shared by Irene, Frances, Georgerene, and Richard, and extending to Georgerene's three children and two grandsons. The living were eager to learn more about the dead.

That shockwave occurred on the day it dawned that Georgerene's adoptive mother, Irene Coover, was a member of her family. She was actually grandma Minnie's sister, a French Canadian great-aunt, christened Irene LaChappelle Jenott in Quebec. Indeed, this sister was the Irene for whom Irene Mary Sherman was named in 1911.

"Hoooo," I breathed out as I typed that detail into their family tree. I couldn't wait to tell John and Michelle. Hand to heart, I shook my head. Within the hour of more searching, another revelation: yet *another* of Minnie's sisters, Elizabeth Jenott Goreska, had taken in Georgerene's little brother, Richard, and raised him in California.

Suddenly I flashed back to my talks with Irene in 1988, when I'd asked her the name of the baby brother who died in the fire. "I think it was Richard or something or other," Irene had said brightly. "He was a cute little dickens!" And I wrote that down.

Now I realized that she'd remembered incorrectly. It was not Richard, but baby brother James Day Sherman who'd died in the 1916 fire. Perhaps she was aware of this youngest Sherman, baby Richard DeWitt, who came along in September 1923, even though she never got to hold him. Richard had been born, swept out of Alaska a year later, made a ward of King County, Washington, then eventually placed in his great-aunt's California home . . . all while Irene was Outside, lingering in the hospital, foster care, or among the nuns in Seattle. The same had happened with Pauline, aka Georgerene. What did Irene know of her?

The pieces were fitting, but the picture was only slightly clearer. Minnie's two childless sisters, Irene and Elizabeth, then in their fifties, had lifted the youngest Sherman children out of poverty and chaos into orderly, loving homes in southern California, close enough to occasionally see each other. There was just one more detail: by agreement among the adults, Georgerene and Richard grew up believing they were cousins, not brother and sister.

※ ※ ※

In 2022, Michelle was looking for receipts at tax time, when I got a text that began with "OMG!" and was full of exclamation points. Georgerene's lost adoption papers had surfaced. We could confirm some dates. Pauline Agnes had left Alaska at age two, but she was nearly four at the court adoption proceedings. So she'd spent her first two years with Agnes and J. P. in Nenana, most likely in dire home conditions. The newly found papers had specified her adoptive name was "Georgia Irene Coover." Somehow it had been changed in everyday use to its awkward form.

Although Pauline was a ward of King County, Washington, her

adoption case was heard before a California Superior Court judge in Los Angeles on April 22, 1926. According to the decree, Agnes was present and consented to surrender this daughter to her aunt and uncle without dispute. Mysteriously, no mention was made of J. P. in the legal documents. It did record that Agnes lived in Kent, Washington, which rang a bell. Ah, I realized, that's where Minnie and John Patten were living in retirement. What role had they played on behalf of Minnie's granddaughter?

With the judge's signature, Pauline held all the rights and privileges of a child born to the Coovers. The little girl would grow up in Glendale, California, at a single address where she'd spend the rest of her childhood and many years as an adult.

Georgerene bore a family resemblance to her adoptive mother, and no wonder, because they were blood relatives, but as yet she didn't know it. When she was a teen, "Georgie" was a pretty and petite five foot, four and a half inches tall, blonde with medium brown eyes. Everything in her world was good. But her stability was undermined on the day the only parents she'd ever known told her she was adopted.

In a time when nearly all adoptions were closed, George and Irene Coover had waited until Georgerene was out of high school before breaking the news. The Coovers must have anxiously anticipated that conversation from the day they signed the adoption papers. It's hard to imagine the disbelief Georgerene must have experienced when they produced her birth certificate from Nenana, Alaska. However, in time, Georgerene went "Alaskan," taking on a frontier persona of her own: rough and wild, relishing her roots and learning more about gold mining, old-school camping, and the arts of survival. Her kids remembered that she'd routinely say, "I was raised by Indians," with some measure of pride, harkening back to her earliest years in Nenana. But what did she really know or mean by that? Did Agnes rely on Native friends to help her? There was usually a nugget of truth in every muddy story.

After Georgerene married Frank Moore in 1951, she received a letter from William Frederick Eckert, Agnes's older brother. It was a typed copy of her genealogy showing many generations above her, including grandmother Mina "Minnie" LaChappelle Jenott Eckert.

Her own name was there, too. There in print, Georgerene could see her place in a birth family that went back centuries to France.

The paper was dated November 7, 1941, and titled "Genealogy of Janot Family." To personalize it for Georgerene, her uncle had typed in "Pauline Agnes Sherman, born June 26th, 1922," and underlined it. Above, in cursive, he'd written: "P.A.S. aka Georgerine [sic] Irene Coover Moore." The interruption of her adoption made no matter, this uncle was saying. She carried Jenott blood, Eckert blood, Sherman blood.

I imagined the young mother tracing her finger down the page of names, following the levels to her own name and that of her cousin in the eleventh generation. None of the other Sherman children had been included, however. So who had gathered all this information? At the bottom, a note informed that Minnie's late brother, Joseph L. Jenott, the gold miner who made riches in the Klondike, had gathered it up. Translated from French to English, the tree reached back to June 17, 1513, during the reign of Louis XII, and an ancestor named Sire de Pienne, governor of the province of Picardy, France.

For Georgerene, the tangible document, an indelible record, was a mooring as well as a motivator. She wanted to learn more about her birth family.

※ ※ ※

Agnes Sherman's brother, William Frederick Eckert, was a master mariner known simply as "Captain." Now an older man, he seemed to be rethinking his place in the family, too. He was the one who'd run away from home at age fourteen and basically divorced himself from Fred and Minnie. William Frederick had pursued life on the high seas, eventually marrying happily and earning his Master Mariner's license at age twenty-eight. His ships took him to exotic places, sometimes with his wife Elizabeth along and listed as "crew." In 1926, the couple welcomed their only child, a son named Richard Frederick Eckert.

In Washington state, Captain and "Bumma," as Elizabeth is remembered, filled their Puyallup home with treasures gathered in their worldwide travels. And while their grandchildren grew up hearing plenty of adventure stories, they had little to draw on for family stories. Captain had mentioned a sister who "went crazy" after her baby died in Alaska. That would be Agnes. And there was another sister who married several times. That would be Bessie. Not much else about his family.

"I think he knew more than he told us," said one of Captain's granddaughters. "We really didn't have any relatives that we were aware of or familiar with. . . . We heard later on about ornery Uncle Clarence." I remembered that this was the Clarence who'd come to Fairbanks with Agnes and Minnie in 1905. He'd also signed as a witness to J. P. and Agnes's wedding in 1910. Now this great-niece remembered meeting him in her childhood. The visit went poorly. The old man was "kind of a cold fish," she said.

In another evil parallel to earlier generations, the Puyallup, Washington, home of Captain and Elizabeth Eckert burned to the ground when their son was five. Captain had hired painters for the interior, and he planned to stay during the painting while his wife and son left for a while. In preparation, some of their precious collectibles from decades of travel were transferred into the garage for safe-keeping. Much more was still in the house when some oily rags near a heat source caught fire. Captain was home alone.

"He called the fire department and was told, 'Sorry, Mr. Eckert, your house is just outside the fire district,'" his granddaughter told me. "The only things that we have from China that survived were put in that garage." Gone was the rosewood grand piano, the mahogany pieces, the ebony dining room set with inlaid mother-of-pearl, the boxes, jewelry, jade, and brass treasures collected during a lifetime.

"Everything he had acquired in his life . . . ," she said. "Captain was trying to put [the fire] out with a garden hose. Desperately trying to put it out. My dad talked about coming up to the house and seeing nothing but a black pit. It was shattering."

Looking into this family, I was amazed at the improbable intersections among generations of Eckerts. Even though Captain had intentionally cut himself off from the Eckerts at fourteen, as an adult, he'd moved to Tacoma, where his sister Agnes had lived for a few years after leaving Alaska. It's where his teen-aged sister was buried before his parents divorced, and Minnie moved to Alaska. And it occurred to me that both Agnes and Captain had a son named Richard.

There was another crossing: Captain's son Richard grew up in Tacoma, then married and moved to Portland, Oregon, where the couple raised six children starting in the 1950s. Was Richard Frederick Eckert aware that his namesake grandfather had once lived there, too? It's highly unlikely. Captain's only son knew nothing about his grandfather Fred, and Captain's six grandchildren grew up knowing nothing about him either. What could have created a rift that deep?

Questions about old Fred Eckert were lingering in my mind. Back in 1924, he had dutifully appeared in Seattle when he was asked (or was it ordered?) to meet Agnes, her Richard, and Pauline at the Alaska Steamship Company pier.

I had learned about Fred's sad last months as an inpatient at Oregon State Hospital, but I didn't know where he was buried. In 2021, during a cursory online search, Fred's name popped up, leading to the astonishing image of a metal identifying tag that marked his cremains at the Oregon State Hospital Patient Memorial. I discovered that Fred was among three thousand, six hundred patients who'd died there, but whose cremains had never been claimed. Instead they were memorialized in what was once known as the Asylum Cemetery.

Eighty-five years after his death and still unclaimed?

I realized that, scattered as they were, most likely, Fred's family wasn't even aware that he'd died. This branch had collapsed, while Minnie's side, the Jenotts, somehow remained strong and supportive of each other.

A couple of weeks passed before I was again at my desk, ready to download the photo of Fred's marker. To my surprise, I found a fresh note on his locator file: "Cremains claimed by family member in 2021."

My thoughts leaped from *What?* to *Who* and *When?* I was just here two weeks ago! The timing seemed impossible. "Family member," it said, but what were the options? I emailed Michelle and John Moore in Idaho. The response: *My great-grandfather's urn is at the Oregon State*

In 2021, Fred's cremains were part of a vast memorial for patients who went unclaimed after death. (Oregon State Hospital)

Hospital?! Now they were lit with curiosity, too.

"I don't think they'll tell me who claimed his ashes," I emailed back, "but you guys, as family, you can ask them, "Who has Fred?""

They started the chase. At my end, I stumbled across yet another Oregon state website that shed light on the mystery. For years, starting back in November 2013, a volunteer genealogist named Phyllis Zegers had been leading a group dedicated to matching descendants with long-dead Oregon State Hospital patients, all of whom were cremated and interred there between 1914 and 1973. To date, they'd made eight hundred and ninety-four family matches, now among them Frederick Eckert. Often the families they contacted were flummoxed by news of an ancestor who was merely a name in memory.

So who was that family match? Who had claimed Fred? Michelle and John Moore's inquiries finally led them to John's "new" cousin, Barbara Eckert Tripp, one of Captain's grandchildren. I gave her a call and we explored her memories. Barbara said she and a couple of siblings had each received a shocking letter outlining the story of Fred's ashes and his relationship to them. They had grown up in Portland, unaware that their great-grandfather Fred had once lived there. After conferring with the others, Barbara accepted the urn. They'd heard only snippets about how Captain had run away from home in boyhood. But were the stories true? All Barbara knew for sure was that despite a hard start, her grandfather had had a long and fulfilling career, loving one wife and raising one son before his death on Christmas Eve 1952. He was buried in Tacoma. Now, seven decades later, Barbara was pondering a serious question of personal ethics.

"I was wondering what to do with Fred's ashes," she said. "I was thinking about interring them with Captain. Then I thought, "What if

Captain really did run away? He must have had his reasons." For now, the question of where to bury Fred would remain undecided.

※ ※ ※

While Fred's release from Oregon State Hospital had come through merciful death in 1936, his daughter Agnes's release from Western State Hospital did not occur until sometime in the early 1950s, when she was finally deemed well enough to live independently. At her discharge, Agnes transitioned into a rental apartment in Centralia, Washington, and began a final, more peaceful chapter in which she devoted herself to friendship, the local Catholic church, and volunteerism. But she was still feisty, according to the scraps of memories that have lasted.

Within a few years, Agnes would reunite with at least two of the children who were removed from her decades earlier. In the 1950s, the daughters who'd been raised in separate adoptive homes, Frances and Georgerene, would separately call on their birth mother at Centralia. They also arranged to meet each other.

※ ※ ※

There remained the matter of the last Sherman child, the youngest, just thirteen months old in 1924 when he was carried aboard the train at Nenana with Agnes and sister Pauline. How had life turned out for Richard DeWitt Sherman after Elizabeth, another of Minnie's sisters, took him home? She was a single woman and had no other children.

While Pauline's adoptive mom Irene Coover had one husband for life, Elizabeth had gone to the altar three times. In 1911 Seattle, she'd married a barman named Frank Goreska and divorced in short order. After joining her sister Minnie in Fairbanks, she married and divorced two more times until finally coming to two conclusions: one, she wasn't cut out for Alaska, and two, maybe she wasn't cut out for marriage. She went back to Seattle and unpacked her maiden name.

By 1920, "Mrs. Elizabeth Jenott" was living on 13th Avenue South and employed as a domestic. Still, she wasn't done moving, next fleeing to the sunny warmth of southern California. Two other sisters, Irene Jenott Coover and Margaret Jenott Lance, plus their husbands, were sharing a house in Los Angeles. No doubt had they invited Elizabeth to come join the family rush to the Sunshine State.

Where Richard landed after Pauline was adopted, I did not know. But the little blond boy with the brown eyes finally appeared in the records with his great-aunt Elizabeth when she was fifty-six and he was six. He may or may not have been formally adopted through the courts, but he belonged to her. Elizabeth and Richard settled into a multifamily bungalow with a separate entrance on West 59th in Los Angeles.

Raising Richard to adulthood gave Elizabeth purpose and erased her loneliness. The little bungalow became his refuge, the place where he'd grow up, go to school, leave for the Marines and return after WWII, the place where he came home at the end of every workday, and where he coped with bouts of deep depression.

Elizabeth never remarried, and Richard never married. At five-feet-nine inches, he was slender, but fit and strong, especially after his time in the military. In 1941, when Elizabeth decided to finally apply for naturalization, she was described as slightly over five-foot-six inches and 165 pounds, with gray hair and a scar on her face. She signed with her legal surname, Elizabeth Saguin, from her third marriage in Alaska. But in daily life, Elizabeth had long ago reclaimed her first husband's surname of Goreska, even reporting it to U.S. census-takers. Therefore, Goreska was the name she bestowed on her beloved boy.

Census and military records show that Richard signed legal documents as "Richard DeWitt Sherman Goreska." I wondered if he knew that Sherman had once been his last name, or did he see Sherman as a middle name?

From 1949 to 1959, Richard drove for a trucking and transport business. He looked after the aging Elizabeth and wrestled with a daily reality that had been especially difficult while serving as a Marine: he was a gay man living in mid-century America.

Growing up, one of Georgerene's kids had opportunity to meet Richard Goreska. Decades later, she still remembered his seemingly constitutional sadness. It was here in this familiar house, when Elizabeth was eighty-six and Richard was thirty-five, that he placed a gun barrel under his chin, angled it toward his brain, and pulled the trigger.

The coroner said his death had occurred somewhere before two in the morning of March 3, 1959. I considered whether Elizabeth was home at the time, asleep in her room. Where else would she have been?

A close examination of Richard's death certificate delivers another jolt. The family informant, the person who was questioned for

Frances wanted to help, but knew little about her birth sibling's family history. (Burnett Family Collection)

essential details about the deceased, was Frances Burnett Bilowas. She'd left Alaska for California nearly a decade earlier and was living in nearby Tarzana. While Frances knew Richard, her birth brother, well enough to serve as the coroner's family contact, she couldn't offer many solid facts. Under the field for Father's Name, first and last, they'd written "Unknown Unknown" For Mother's name: "Elizabeth," his adoptive mother's first name. In the box for her maiden name: "Unknown." So many questions: When had Frances learned about and met her Aunt Elizabeth and Richard? Did she know Richard was a sibling, or was she told they were cousins?

Picturing the aftermath of that horrific death is hard and doubly hard when you see an eighty-six-year-old in the midst of it. I consider if Frances stayed to comfort her Aunt Elizabeth, to help with the funeral arrangements, clean the place, and sort through Richard's things. No one alive knows.

Elizabeth Jenott Goreska lived yet another year, suffering kidney failure in the last six months of her life. Her home address had not changed in decades when she died in Los Angeles's View Park Hospital at age eighty-seven.

When officials were filling out Elizabeth's death certificate, it was not Frances who served as family informant, but another great-niece from her Jenott side: Winnifred "Robin" Carmien, a grand-daughter of Elizabeth's big brother, Joseph L. Jenott, the man who'd made his fortune in the Klondike Gold Rush. Robin was yet another Alaska-born Jenott descendent living in California.

Elizabeth had lived a meaningful, sacrificial life, pouring herself into the little lost boy whom she'd rescued and loved so dearly. By law, she was no longer a Goreska; however, that's the name on Elizabeth's grave at Holy Cross Cemetery in Los Angeles, where she was laid to rest on November 26, 1960.

CHAPTER 26
THE KINDNESS OF PIONEERS - Summer 1988
Well-considered assistance was calculated to do much good

"I always seem to have a godfather or godmother or something that resurrects me and grabs me and takes me off someplace else—to keep me out of harm's way." Irene was contemplative on this bright summer day in Fairbanks, knowing full well that the life she'd lived had been equal parts tragedy and luck . . . with a heavy dose of grace.

Irene's longtime protector was Arthur Leslie "Les" Nerland, born in Dawson, Yukon, in 1902, making him nine years older than she. It was Les who owned the property where Irene's castle was growing with each passing year. Long before I lived in Nerland Hall on the university campus, long before my boyfriend delivered couches for Nerland Home Furnishings, I saw and knew about Les, but never chanced to personally interview the Fairbanks icon. How I wished I could have asked the essential question: "Why? Why did you take on the job of looking out for Irene Sherman?"

Les's father, Andrew, had been a Klondike stampeder who'd recognized there was more money in selling wallpaper, window sashes, and home décor than mining the muck for gold dust—and besides, most of the claims had been taken by the time he arrived in Dawson. So Andrew Nerland partnered with the Anderson Brothers and set up shop in the Yukon. With the boom in Fairbanks, they opened there, too, and then expanded to the Iditarod camp, following one gold rush after another. Andrew was among the old-timers who would help write the constitution of a brand-new state in the 1950s.

Son Les stepped into the business and eventually ran a retail furniture chain with elegant stores in Fairbanks and Anchorage, even Seattle. Likewise, he'd served as a delegate during Alaska's Constitutional Convention and was a university regent for many years. And bank president. And mayor.

When I was asked to write a profile of Les Nerland for inclusion in a book about Fairbanks, he'd already passed away, but those closest to me spoke in union to the question of why he helped Irene—and others.

Invoking Les Nerland's name was Irene's trump card whenever she sensed a threat to the security of her home place. Nerland's legal measures allowed her to live on Front Street for life. (Stu Rothman photo/Courtesy Nerland Family Collection)

Simply put, Nerland was a true humanitarian, a quiet, yet intentional servant. After all that he'd done for his town and state through the years, he didn't stop in retirement. For eighteen years, he worked on the Pioneers Home Board, overseeing the management of care facilities for Alaska's seniors. He was named Outstanding Alaskan of the Year by the Alaska State Chamber of Commerce, and in 1980, the University of Alaska conferred an honorary doctorate in public service. It wasn't because he was good at selling home décor.

I thought of Les again when I stumbled across the code of the Pioneers of Alaska, a society that newspapers called the most meritorious since the local Igloo's founding on November 22, 1909.

Three years later, when pioneers from "all over the creeks" flooded into Fairbanks for the 1912 Pioneers Ball honoring Lincoln's birthday, the order's membership numbered six hundred men. By then, Igloo No. 4 had already distributed about $6,000 among the needy, whenever "well-considered assistance was calculated to do much good." The *Alaska Citizen* reported, "It is this real old sourdough style of helping out the unfortunate without ostentation that has endeared the order to those who are acquainted with its great work."

Les Nerland and others like him carried the torch for doing much good. They did it because they cared, because it was right, and because they could. Just like so many others along Irene's lifeline. Was that level of helping now a bygone era here? I didn't think so.

When seeing to Irene's increasing needs got too burdensome for the aging Les, he turned to Wally Burnett, who'd grown up in a family that honored the same pioneer code. Wally's grandmother, Blanche Burnett, had been a charter member of the Pioneers of Alaska Women's Igloo No. 8. Other old friends were around when Irene needed help, too. When her health was going "too doggone haywire" with frostbite injuries or pneumonia, they'd usher her into the hospital or a local nursing home. After a few months of regular food, a warm bed, and skilled nursing, she'd migrate back to her place along the slough. Irene still claimed her independent lifestyle, but always had a safety net. She was never destitute, said Frank P. Young, that pioneer who'd crossed the Chilkoot Pass as a boy. There were fewer people in their ranks, but they were still there, telling their stories to anyone who would listen and still lending a hand.

There wasn't much to see in the Graehl neighborhood of Fairbanks when Irene first settled there in the mid-1940s—a few little houses, but mostly birch and cottonwood trees. The "skookum" woman set up a wall tent among the trees and there she lived, summer and winter, for five years. She slept over at a friend's when it was desperately cold. Irene next took over a small shack near the slough on Nerland land.

But the catastrophic flood of August 1967 swept through, destroying her place and so many others on both sides of the Chena.

"We had four feet in the flood," remembered Gloria Corey, who was ninety in 2023. She'd been Irene's neighbor in Graehl and they'd been neighbors long before, back in the Nenana coal district. That's when Irene was in Healy Forks and Gloria lived between Healy and Suntrana, "just down from Old Goat Mary," she told me. The description made me smile.

When the August 1967 floodwaters receded, Irene returned to Graehl with Les Nerland's permission and assistance. He even went so far as to build a little frame house for Irene to enjoy, even though eventually it would be filled up then disappear behind her collectibles, with only the gable still visible. Gloria remembered that Les also bought Irene a new, expensive mattress after the flood. She described the day she saw Irene dragging home a supply of creosoted railroad ties, and then watched in horror as Irene wrangled her new mattress atop a stack of sticky black ties.

"Irene says, 'I'm never gonna get wet again!'" Gloria joked. "We'd have her out to dinner sometimes. Irene was panhandling downtown, and if she got some money, she'd buy something like grapes —they were more rare then, but she'd bring them over. She wanted to do for you, but she had so little to give."

In time many homes surrounded Irene's junkyard castle at the edge of Noyes Slough. The city was filling up across the slough on the Garden Island side, too.

In the early 1980s, city officials acknowledged that Irene's raggedy home place was standing in the path of a proposed bridge over the slough to Island Homes. There was only one road to access the subdivision, and for public safety's sake, another was required. What if there was a devastating earthquake or a sizeable fire? There'd only be one route of escape, and only one way in for emergency vehicles.

The Fairbanks City Council approved funding for the bridge and connecting roads, and the city began surveying. To complete the project, Irene's abode—a primitive, technically illegal structure—would have to be razed. And there the project stalled. No one was willing to move the Queen off.

In September 1988, City Manager Brian C. Phillips restated the city's stance in a *News-Miner* letter to the editor: "As long as Irene lives at her home on the edge of Noyes Slough, the project will not proceed." The city council was in complete agreement, Phillips said.

For years, a mere finger of blacktop dead-ended on the Island Homes side of Noyes Slough. Standing there at the bridge approach that lacked an actual bridge, you could make out Irene's fortress through a veil of small birches across the narrow waterway. I knew it well, because that was the view from my father and stepmother's picture window on the Island Homes side. A bridge that wasn't.

"Are you ever going to run out of space?" I asked Irene.

"I can only go so far and that's that. That's when the damn road commission will put the foot down. You always got to think two ways to the middle. If you're displeasing anybody, as long as they don't say anything to me, I ain't gonna say anything to them."

"What about that bridge the city wants to build?"

At the mere suggestion of moving, Irene's reply was quick and guttural: "They can go piss up a rope!" She wasn't going anywhere. "They can't move me off, cause I'm gonna be there until the Old Man Upstairs takes a notion to . . ." Her sentence hung in the air. Distracted by a passerby, Irene's mood lightened instantly. "Hi there, baby! Say, that's some beautiful hair you got there!"

Despite all the talk of tearing down Irene's home, her address remained secure because of Les Nerland's benevolent planning. In the aftermath of the 1967 flood that ravaged Fairbanks, when people were paddling canoes over city streets and sheltering up on College Hill, Nerland created a licensing agreement to protect Irene's future.

Working through a corporation called "Interior Alaska, Incorporated," for the consideration of one dollar, Nerland granted Irene the privilege to "reside on said lands during the remainder of her natural life." The license was to automatically terminate upon her death. All parties signed the agreement on August 9, 1967, with Irene present and Les Nerland's interests represented by Interior Alaska's president and secretary. She'd always have her house. And although she often preferred sleeping outside, behind her security wall, it was her choice to make.

Four years later, on March 31, 1971, Les Nerland went a step further, conveying the warranty deed for the property to the Fairbanks North Star Borough for $56,000. "Subject however," the document asserted, "to the life interest vested in Irene Mary Sherman by virtue of that certain license executed and delivered by Grantor, dated August 9, 1967." The conveyance was signed by A. Leslie Nerland, vice president of Interior Alaska, Incorporated, and the corporation's treasurer, Ray Kohler. Irene's house was hers for the rest of her life, but the land was not. When we talked in 1988, twenty-one years after the flood, the house was barely visible, the lot unrecognizable, and she was still kickin'.

"As long as she's alive, her existence is holding up the road," shrugged the city surveyor that year. Dave McNary spoke with affection as yet another longtime resident and Irene supporter. "I don't want to see her be moved if she doesn't want to be moved."

What was inside? Anyone who'd seen it shared those thoughts. I could make out the gable of the tiny house Nerland built, high above the appliances and debris, but there was no visible doorway. How did she come and go? In 1978, Irene had given a tour of her wigwam to Joan Koponen, narrating how she'd customized it over the years.

"I've got it so the kids can't break my windows," Irene said. "Even taking a hatchet and hittin' that pane, it's about impossible to break it. It's a new kind of glass deal. And I've got them covered all the time. For light I have seven fifteen-watt lights, and some of them are always on.

"Of course, if I didn't have drapes over the windows, I'd have more light. Jiminy Christmas, since the lights stopped workin' this week, I'm tellin' you, I have to have a flashlight right handy. You know, I got lights strung all over this damn place. Inside, outside, along the trails through that stuff. But gosh darn, I'm in a quandary to know why they're not workin' now. I don't want no damn electrician in there because he wouldn't get it done the way I want it."

It had taken years and years of collecting and building, dragging home lumber and pallets, shoring up and chaining refrigerators, and aligning piles of newspapers and cardboard, but Irene finally had her home just right. What appeared to be a hellhole to you or me was, for Irene, a place of rest.

In an early February 1971 trip to the Gavora Mall, Irene was dressed for the deep cold. (*News-Miner* Archives)

CHAPTER 27
GROWING UP GEORGERENE
We called her the Queen of Stainless Steel

The count of full-term babies born to Agnes Sherman may have come to seven, but none stayed in her care past age five. They either died in infancy or were removed by authorities. Other women, others with mothering instincts, would see the need and fill it. Even so, among the children who made it through childhood, only one would live long enough to carry the Sherman family line into the twenty-first century: Georgerene.

Georgerene's adoptive parents were not young in 1911 when they married in Seattle. Both were in their mid-thirties. The couple made Seattle their home until heading to Los Angeles by 1920. A decade later, George Coover was making a good living as an accountant for the Sante Fe Railroad, and the family home at 416½ Piedmont in Glendale was full, with three Coovers, plus George's widowed mother, and Irene Coover's sister and brother-in-law, Margaret (Jenott) and Edward Lance. Through the years, the makeup of occupants would change, but effectively, the Piedmont place was their little "Tara," their permanent family home.

In December 1943, Georgerene enlisted in the U.S. Naval Reserve Women's branch called the WAVES (Women Accepted for Volunteer Emergency Service), taking up needful positions on shore to free male personnel for military action. She helped build airplanes in California and later worked as a telephone operator. In all, she served for just over a year, discharging honorably from San Diego in March 1945.

That fall, Georgerene married a Navy man in Long Beach, California. She'd kept her Piedmont address with her parents in Glendale, and brought home her new husband, Elvin Choppin, who was originally from New Orleans, Louisiana. Choppin was ever mobile, and the union only lasted a few years. After her divorce, Georgerene soon fell in love again with another sailor, a Chicago Irishman and ship's oiler named Patrick Donovan. He was red-headed, fair-skinned, and six feet tall. Georgerene and Patrick took their vows on January 13, 1951, but again, he spent most of their early marriage on a ship somewhere else in the world. Hardly a good start. They divorced within months. Before the year ended, on November 9, 1951,

Georgerene married a third and final time following a whirlwind romance and a pass through Reverend Coleman's Drive-In Chapel in Yuma, Arizona. Not surprisingly, Francis T. Moore of Long Beach, California, was a career Navy man. He was a risk-taker, an Explosive Ordnance Navy diver. Both possessed strong personalities. And while the couple suffered the deep grief of multiple miscarriages, she and Frank eventually welcomed their two daughters and a son.

Frank and Georgerene would stay married "til death us do part," but truthfully, for most of the marriage they didn't live under the same roof, understanding that divorce would not benefit their children's futures, especially financially. Each parent wanted their kids to gain advantage from his military benefits.

Frank and Georgerene Moore, attending the wedding of friends in 1964 . (Moore Family Collection)

Georgerene already had experienced ample loss and heartache by the mid-1950s. But perhaps the most difficult challenge in the series of personal blows was the death of the mom she cherished, Irene Jenott Coover, who passed away in 1953, when Georgerene was thirty-one and the mother of a toddler. After forty-two years of marriage, George Coover was a widower.

When Georgerene was growing up, her mother Irene had fingered her expensive jewelry or pointed to the lovely collectibles in the Coover home. Routinely, she'd tell her daughter, "This will be yours someday." But all that would change in a traumatic "overthrow," as far as Georgerene was concerned. Her father chose a new bride and remarried within a year of his wife's death, bringing his second wife into Georgerene's beloved childhood home in Glendale.

With the arrival of a new stepmother named Claire, Georgerene's sense of slight was in high gear. She was still talking about it to her children decades later. Gone were the promises that one day this or that collectible or sentimental piece would be hers. George Coover was not supportive of those long-time promises. All of the expensive jewelry and other elegant décor and furniture that had once belonged to her mother now belonged to Claire. Georgerene's bitterness grew.

"She was used to nice things," daughter-in-law Michelle remembered, "and she'd buy them herself if she had to. She used to say, 'I'll just get more.' And she did."

※ ※ ※

In September 2022, I flew to Lewiston, Idaho, rented a car, and drove north to meet John and Michelle Moore in person. The transition from emails, phone calls, and texts to a face-to-face conversation is always an exploration for both sides, kind of like a blind date. We'd arranged our first meeting at a local Mexican restaurant, and in the moment of my enthusiastic greeting, I feared that I was perhaps too enthusiastic. I found two happily married grandparents who were still in the workforce, strong and energetic, and youthful in their outlook.

Michelle's fine features were framed by long blonde hair touched with gray. John's face was strongly Sherman—the classic widow's peak hairline and broad face, like his mother's in the family photos. He was well known in this region for his work in heating and air conditioning, and for his skill as a mechanic, but he was trying to do less of that.

The Moores lived above town at 3,500 feet on the mountain, where dense fog could surround their house while below, people along the Clearwater River were feeling the warmth of the sun. John was a middle child with a sister on each side, all three Boomers. His sisters still lived in California, the state where they'd all grown up. They talked by phone, especially when a stranger from Alaska was about to arrive and ask a lot of questions about their family history. There was great caution, of course, in a time when personal privacy seems constantly at risk. One sister decided no, she'd rather not participate. Another was open to a phone call or two. But it was John and Michelle's curiosity, and that of one of their sons, that spurred contact.

John was the only one of Georgerene's kids who married and had children. Sons Daniel and Jay were grown and married, too. Also each had a son and a daughter, the latest generation in the Sherman-Eckert line that I'd traced back to Canada and further to France, Scotland, and Germany. Remembering Georgerene, her kids recalled her adventurous spirit, how sometimes she took them along on her trips, exploring other countries and cultures.

"She had a beautiful singing voice and was a good swimmer," Michelle said. She lived "clean"—as in no smoking, no drinking, no illegal drugs, and no junk food, instead buying organic products at Trader Joe's. She was always keen to learn more about living healthy. She couldn't resist picking up stray dogs. And she was focused on learning, teaching Montessori and urging her kids to do the same. Many boxes of Montessori materials were added to her storage. John's mother also used to live above this Idaho town, having moved several times, from southern to northern California, then on over to Idaho. The last two moves were especially hard and required the help of many friends and family who loved her, but were weary of the ordeal.

Georgerene's similarities to Irene became clear as I compared notes with the Moores. Both had strong personalities, loud voices, and great endurance. Both women loved a challenge. (Moore Family Collection)

I was hearing echoes of Frances, of Irene. Impossible, but real. The "collecting" patterns of Georgerene's two birth sisters had emerged in this woman's lifeline, too, although all three had grown up in vastly different households. Like Irene and Frances, Georgerene had long ago developed a habit of buying, trading, or finding treasures and holding onto them. She needed more storage for her things, so she started filling up old busses and trailers on her southern California property. The things she owned, her excellent finds, would be nice to put in a resale store or sell online, she thought. But not everything was ready to sell. Some items were seriously broken; others needed a quick fix. And parting with certain things became more difficult over time.

She found a shopping partner in her daughter-in-law. Georgerene often told Michelle that she loved her like a daughter, and the love was mutual. To Michelle, she really was like a mother. If Georgerene bought a special gift for her own girls, Michelle got one, too. She began teaching Michelle how to shop, how to look for quality items, solid old-style furniture, stainless steel cookware, and wool, especially wool, because it would not burn. Georgerene had favorite pieces in her extensive wardrobe of wool articles of clothing, especially a certain heavy wool coat in green.

"We called her the Queen of Stainless Steel," Michelle recalled with a smile. Georgerene had showed her how to use a magnet to test a piece. "If the magnet doesn't stick, it's really good stainless steel," she said. And if it passed the test, Georgerene likely bought it, even if it was missing a part. She'd have a plan for fixing it later, replacing a handle, a knob, whatever was needed. And yet, the truth was, she rarely did.

There was another aspect of this complicated woman that aligned with her personal faith journey—to be ready for the future, to be prepared for what the Bible calls the last days, when civilization as we know it would no longer exist and owning survival skills would serve a primary purpose. Sometime in the mid-1990s (for vast numbers of Americans, still pre-internet), Georgerene had heard Colonel James Gordon "Bo" Gritz speak, perhaps on American Voice Radio. "She liked short-wave radio," Michelle explained. After contact, Gritz, who described himself as the model for the "Rambo" franchise, invited Georgerene to join his survival skills training camp, and she was game.

The most decorated veteran of the Vietnam conflict was already a controversial figure for his outspokenness against government actions or inactions. He engaged in non-sanctioned gung-ho tactics, like dropping into foreign countries to retrieve lost Americans. To the U.S. government, he was dangerously unpredictable.

In workshops and outdoor training, Georgerene learned from Gritz about first aid, survival foods, canning, hunting, and tanning hides. Even in her early seventies, Georgerene attempted the hard stuff, like rappelling and traversing, courses that a forty-year-old might find daunting. A year later, Georgerene introduced John and Michelle to the Bo Gritz camps and workshops. They joined her and soaked it up. Michelle wanted me to know that despite what I may have read about the controversial leader, the camps were "*not* about opposing government intervention," she said, but rather "preparedness for the last days." That focus aligned with their mother's biblical ideals of living in the world, but not of the world. She took seriously the admonition of 2 Corinthians 6:17: "Therefore, 'Come out from among them and be separate,' says the Lord. 'Do not touch what is unclean and I will receive you.'"

Gritz's reputation as a decorated Green Beret carried him into real estate development, selling lots in "Almost Heaven," a community of like-minded preppers and patriots in northern Idaho. In the late 1990s, many of those who settled there were largely concerned about fallout from Y2K, wondering what would happen worldwide when the calendar and computers clicked into the new century. The chaos that some anticipated did not happen. In 1999, Gritz no longer lived among them, having moved to southwest U.S. after a devastating divorce and a suicide attempt.

Back in Idaho, local government had been briefly troubled by an increase of far-right separatists in their midst—some newcomers even calling for Idaho's sovereignty—but most longtime locals were logging and farm people who were already used to carrying guns and filling their pantries.

Georgerene may have gotten her mail in Idaho, but she was living like an Alaskan.

CHAPTER 28
WHAT THEY HAD IN COMMON
You had to walk pathways to get from one room to another

The more I studied Irene, Frances, and Georgerene, the more obvious their behavioral similarities became. What emerged was that singular fact: *All three* women, born to the same mother but raised separately, had become chronic hoarders. How the disorder shaped and likely destroyed multiple marriages among the three—seven broken marriages in all—I could only guess, but as I discovered, left untreated, the affliction often destroys relationships.

All of Fairbanks already knew about Irene's addiction to "collecting." And Frances had already timidly confessed her own "packrat" tendencies, as she put it, in our long-ago phone conversation. Later, a great-niece confirmed that it was all-out hoarding for Frances: "They couldn't even walk into the hall because of the papers and magazines. You could hardly squeeze through. You had to walk pathways to get from one room to another."

Specifics from Georgerene's children illuminated how their mother's hoarding dramatically affected home life from their youth into adulthood, all while they sincerely loved their mother. Understanding waxed and waned as they tried to maintain balance, enjoying her quirkiness while taking the brunt when she died and it was time to deal with all she'd left behind.

Now I was meeting Georgerene through the loving eyes of adult children and her daughter-in-law, who spoke honestly of the frustration, along with a dose of suppressed anger, at dealing with all of "Mom's crap or, excuse my language, shit." Michelle then jokingly hinted that they, too, might have a touch of the same thing.

Not long after I had written the Moores about Frances's hoarding confession all those years ago, Michelle responded by email, "OH MY GOSH to the Frances hoarding similarities. Traits? Or 'Depression-era babies' traits? Wow! I warn our daughter-in-laws . . . about the potential hoarding disease that we can inherit, just for marrying into the Moore family. It really comes from the Sherman side, I see now! I think all of us Moore wives have already inherited it!"

What does science have to say about hoarding? I looked into reports from Mayo Clinic that identified differences between hoarders and non-hoarders on the 14th chromosome. Hoarding is associated with Obsessive-Compulsive Disorder, and some cases are worse than others. Research shows that while onset often occurs in the late teens and into

On May 27, 1970, the *Fairbanks Daily News-Miner* ran a photo of Irene captioned "She Means It." Her neighborhood project that spring was cleaning up Hamilton Street south of Farewell. Thanks to Irene, it was clear of paper, wood, and pieces of glass. (*News-Miner* Archives)

the twenties, it increasingly worsens as individuals approach late midlife and their senior years. Worsens, as in there's so much more coming in than going out, or the person develops an inability to stop buying at all. Attachments to things can send sufferers into hysterics if a broken item in their collection is discarded, or even if it's moved from where it was usually kept. Relationships can unravel when the hoarder is blind to the effect of his or her collecting. I supposed that several ex-husbands of these women could attest to that.

What I found most illuminating in the case of the three sisters was this: Most hoarders have a first-degree relative who suffers from the same thing. However, for each individual, a unique trauma can trigger the need to collect inanimate things. The things themselves need not be valuable. It's only the effect they have on the person. Like Michelle had said, it feels good. Genetics plays a role, as do traumatic life events. All three women had ticked both boxes.

Was Irene squirreling everything away when she was sharing that remote Healy Forks cabin with J. P. and her son Robert? It's common for Bush-dwellers, or even those in Alaska's cities, to hang onto objects that might be useful in the future. You may see bizarre lumps covered by blue tarps in their yards. But Irene's hoarding had gone beyond that, enlarging and accelerating after she resettled in Fairbanks in the 1940s. As time went by, her collection at 740 Front Street was like water adapting to the shape of its container. She did not intrude on the street, but behind that edge, it was anything goes.

As for possible triggers, Irene had had a laundry list, from her painful childhood of violence, poverty, and death, to separation from her family, two failed marriages and a reneged engagement. She had graduated from "Packsack Annie," hauling around a full backpack, to filling a tent, to occupying an abode on a city lot that was overflowing with mostly no-longer-useful items. From mid-century into the sixties, seventies, and eighties, she continued to bring home more discoveries from garage and yard sales all over Fairbanks.

I remembered the Saturday she pulled her Radio Flyer wagon into my father's driveway, where I was helping my stepmother run her garage sale. Irene shopped for a half-hour, handling many of the knick-

A 1976 painting by Janet Kruskamp of California was purchased and shipped to Fairbanks by Ken and Ida Ryfogel, who owned Goldmine Jewelers. Their print sales of "Miss Irene" generated $10,000 in donations to the Fairbanks Memorial Hospital's new burn center in Irene's name and that of her friend, Eva McGown, who'd perished in a 1972 fire. (Courtesy Ryfogel Collection)

knacks, chatting all the while, and then paid for her purchase from an invisible pocket. She slipped the items—I can't even remember what she bought—into her wagon before heading back down Slater Drive. It was like a visit from a celebrity. Irene came to *our* garage sale!

The OCD aspect, how Irene expressed that subset of Obsessive-Compulsive Disorder, was evident. She was also known as a meticulous picker-upper of trash on city streets and sidewalks. Whether "cleaning" meant picking up or collecting, for her, it was compulsive. In a *News-Miner* photo she was pictured with a wheelbarrow full of construction debris left behind at a worksite and lauded for helping clean it up.

In another piece in the *Pioneer All-Alaska Weekly*, a columnist listened in on a conversation between Irene and two other longtime locals as they stood outside the Mecca Bar on Second Avenue. The topic turned to ways to increase local tourism. One man suggested some of the historic cabins at Alaskaland be moved back into town to fill the vast empty space between First and Second. Tourists would love that, he said. The other man believed that same space should be used for a massive downtown hotel, maybe with a luxury restaurant circling 360 degrees at the top, like the Space Needle, so diners could see Mount McKinley. The columnist watched and listened and noted that Irene said nothing. She gazed in the direction of the empty lot as the men spoke. Then she bent and picked up a wrapper she'd noticed on the sidewalk. To the writer, Irene, more than the progressive thinkers, silently conveyed volumes about what was most important to her: the city she loved, just as it was, but without that wrapper.

※ ※ ※

As for the youngest Sherman sister, unlike some reality show folks who suffer from a hoarding disorder, Georgerene did not walk over garbage and feces to reach her front door. She tended toward high-class purchases. Quality mattered. And she loved to dicker at the swap meets that sprawled across parking lots and old drive-in theaters in southern California. She dreamed of having her own high-end resale shop. While Georgerene did occasionally resell items at one of the event booths, her dream of running a high-end resale shop never developed. Things came in, but most didn't go out again.

Growing up in the Hollywood area, Georgerene was privileged to buy some of the studios' backlot stores. Decades after Georgerene bought one piece in particular, it still stood out in the minds of her son and daughter-in-law. It was rare and beautiful: a wooden bedstead that supposedly was used in the filming of *Gone with the Wind*. Georgerene didn't have space for it in her house, and clearly had plans for its future, but it ended up inside one of the long containers that she kept outside her home, ready for when she needed it. There it stayed; there it decayed from leaks in the container. John said his mom had once put a hot water heater in a storage trailer, but had neglected to drain it first. As it rusted,

With John's marriage to Michelle, Georgerene acquired another daughter, a shopping partner she trained to find good deals. (Moore Family Collection)

everything stored with it was ruined. The longer she stored her quality wool and fine furniture, other seam leaks in the trailers degraded the contents. In time, nobody had the heart to sort through it.

When Georgerene planned to move north from southern California, John and Michelle were among the gang of family and friends who helped her organize (well, that's just not a useful word) and load up several shipping containers, along with broken down busses, trucks, and other containers. At that time, she'd been living in a "CalTrans house," owned by the highway commission.

"It was off the side of Highway 5," Michelle remembered, "and they rented it cheap to her because they knew that someday they'd tear down all these houses."

Georgerene had enjoyed the low rent for many years with the understanding that when the highway went from two lanes to four, she'd have to vacate. The rambling house had more than a dozen rooms, and every one was chock full. Narrow walkways through main living areas connected the rooms.

I asked Michelle why she thought people like Georgerene became hoarders. Her reply: "I think it makes them feel comfortable."

But moving Georgerene was beyond uncomfortable. For all. "She lived there alone and she had it filled up. When she moved up to northern California, both my husband John and I, and his sister, everybody took turns with the moving van and helping her," Michelle said. "It was quite a thing." She remembered how the house had a five-car garage and fourteen rooms. "And they were stuffed . . ."

Michelle laughed at the memory, but she wasn't laughing on those days when drivers were tag-teaming and muscles were tired. Georgerene's big move required transporting seven shipping containers measuring forty-by-eight, along with a semi-trailer and three or four school busses that she'd acquired. All had been used for storage. Along with them were some classic cars she wanted to keep: a couple of Ford Falcons and a Chevy Biscayne.

"She wanted the old stuff," Michelle said, "because she knew the old stuff was 'better,' and *she could fix it up someday!*" I heard the note of exasperation in Michelle's normally level voice. "To Georgerene," she said, "the good ol' days were better days."

※ ※ ※

The next move would take Georgerene from northern California to northern Idaho in 1995, again an extreme effort by all who loved her. She had begun to buy land as investments, and yet some of the deals flopped. I reminded myself to ask John what he knew about the Bo Gritz real estate development in northern Idaho. *Did his mom buy into those land sales?* Later he told me no, she did not. While Georgerene had great respect for Bo Gritz, her independent spirit wouldn't allow her to join the crowd. Instead, she bought land *next to* his development. Michelle and John said they then decided to follow her, moving to this community. But they chose a spot in Almost Heaven.

In August 2015, following a series of dry lightning storms, fire would touch another generation of the extended Sherman family. That month John and Michelle lost their new home in the Clearwater Complex fire that scorched nearly fifty thousand acres, destroying at least fifty homes and other structures, not to mention cattle and wildlife losses. Just six years earlier, they'd signed on as volunteer firefighters in their little community.

"We just finished putting the roof on it when it burned," Michelle said matter-of-factly.

CHAPTER 29
THE CURIOUS AND THE PERSISTENT
Tarzana, California, 1957

She wanted her children to know who they were,
who their family was

On the surface, the Sherman siblings—the remaining three sisters and their youngest brother Richard—seemed wholly disconnected from each other, either by circumstance or design. But I'd find my assumptions blown apart. They may not have had annual family reunions, but somewhat tenuous connections overrode the distances of geography and disruptions of adoption. I'd discover that surprise while visiting northern Idaho in the fall of 2022.

I reserved a room at a Kamiah lodge, a newer place that John recommended because he'd done the HVAC work and knew the owner. Good guy. While the Moores lived miles away, up a draw at a higher elevation, I wouldn't get the chance to visit their home. Michelle had hinted that they'd acquired the bulk of Georgerene's "collection," the semi-trailers and busses that held the things she had purchased or acquired for so many years. I sensed some embarrassment at having a stranger view it all, including some of their own collecting, so I didn't press it. But I really wanted to see it.

Instead, we arranged to meet in the lodge's great room, and when John strode in, he was carrying a load of boxes, with Michelle hurrying behind him. They'd been married long enough to declare them "a cute couple," wearing matching fleece jackets in a bold black-and-white plaid. We spread out the materials on a broad conference table, pulled up chairs, and I clicked on my recorder.

Gently I cracked open one of Georgerene's photo albums that Michelle had pulled from a box. Here was Georgerene, posing in black-and-white vacation photos from May 16, 1957, with her six-year-old daughter and infant son, John. She is radiant in a white sleeveless blouse and a full skirt splashed with pattern. Her chubby baby boy, nearly seven months old, is in his mother's arms; his sister nearby. In another photo,

Georgerene had written "Aunty Frances home in Tarzana, Calif." above the scrapbook photo. The porch and yard appeared in the photos, but whatever hoarding Frances did remained behind the front door during picture time. (Moore Family Collection)

big sister Renette proudly stands next to them showing a gap where her front teeth used to be. In another snapshot, I saw an unfamiliar woman with them. My eyes drifted upward to find a caption holding a surprise. It read, "Aunty Frances."

Georgerene met her birth sister, Frances!? John nodded yes. His mother had driven down from Washington state to see Frances Burnett Bilowas at her home in Tarzana, California. The image dissolved my assumption that there was no interaction between them. Later in life, tenuous relationships *had* developed among Agnes Sherman's scattered children. The reunions were likely due to Georgerene's persistence. She seemed so intent on finding family.

That evening, I called John's sister, Renette Moore, the one in the pictures with the gap in her shy smile. Renette still remembered that spring 1957 trip. At the time, Tarzana was an upscale community of about nine square miles near Hollywood built on ranchland that had belonged to Edgar Rice Burroughs, author of the popular Tarzan books. Frances and Walter Bilowas may have already divorced by 1957, maybe over her collecting. In Georgerene's photos, Frances was stylish and pretty, and the images were all taken outside. Remembering what an Alaskan great-niece had said about Frances, it dawned on me that there were probably clogged hallways behind that front door. Not unlike Georgerene's place.

"My mother would wrap up her beautiful things and stack them inside," Renette remembered. "You would walk from one room to the other, and that was the pathway."

Was there a moment of shock when Georgerene and Frances realized that both were hoarders, or had they revealed that important detail to each other before Georgerene arrived?

The Tarzana visit wasn't the last of Georgerene's forays into family discovery. She brought Renette along once to meet great-aunt Elizabeth Goreska and Georgerene's "cousin" Richard in Los Angeles.

Renette most remembers her mother as "traveling, traveling, and collecting, collecting, always looking for adventure." Mother and daughter were both forged with strong personalities, and when they clashed, they clashed hard. That had led to Renette leaving home early. As much as she butted heads and disdained her mother's hoarding habits, now Renette wasn't overtly critical, just matter-of-fact.

"After she stopped doing her traveling, she'd buy things. My mother liked to hoard big things: bathtubs with three legs, stoves with three legs . . ."

Renette strongly affirmed she herself had not acquired the "collecting bug," making a clear distinction between her mother and herself. "I can't stand clutter!" she said, with emphasis on the "I."

I looked for the similarities between Georgerene's kids and their cousin Barbara Eckert Tripp, whom they'd never met, the descendent in charge of her great-grandfather's ashes. Each line of cousins had been unaware that the other existed. And now here they were, exchanging phone numbers and emails. What they had in common was the lack of knowledge about extended family. It was fragmentary, if anything.

Georgerene's scrapbook showed that the trip to meet Frances in California was fun and meaningful. Did the sisters stay in touch afterward? It didn't seem so. (Moore Family Collection)

But in Georgerene, I saw a woman intent on making up for those relationship losses. She wanted her children to know who they were, who their family was. And she wanted to know more about herself.

In 1968, Georgerene brought her children to San Antonio, Texas, to meet a cousin at the World's Fair. Afterward, the newfound relative sent John Moore a gift that John still remembers distinctly: a pink buoy from a commercial fishing net—mailed all the way from Alaska. That cousin was Robert P. Hartman, Jr., Irene's beloved and only son.

CHAPTER 30
A NEW LIFE IN CENTRALIA
Washington, early 1950s
My mother never really talked about her mother

By the time Agnes Sherman was discharged from Western Washington Hospital, sometime in the early 1950s, she was part of the history of the institution, having witnessed (and experienced) changes in evolving treatment methods for nearly twenty-five years. The patient population had grown to 2,600. She'd even survived a major fire there on March 25, 1947, when an entire wing that housed more than two hundred "chronic and incurable patients," burned down despite twelve fire trucks responding from Tacoma and neighboring towns. One man perished and two were injured. Some escaped and were recaptured; the less dangerous, like Agnes, were shuffled around. I wondered how she had responded to the crisis. I wondered how she viewed the radical life changes that release would bring.

By early 1954, Agnes was reorienting to "civilian" life in Centralia, a town of about 8,500 people located forty miles south of the hospital. As Agnes was finding her place socially within her new community, on July 14, 1954, she even received mention in the Centralia newspaper. Meeting at the Oddfellows Hall, Mrs. Alfred Harper led the initiation rites for Agnes to join the Veterans of Foreign Wars auxiliary.

"Welcomed were Mrs. Harold C. Seiter and Mrs. Agnes Sherman, who reported that General Sherman was her cousin." (*Okay!* I thought. *Now, that's something new.* Was J. P. or his father a cousin of General William Tecumseh Sherman? Despite Agnes's assertion, I could find no proof.) Also at the meeting, a Mrs. Ronald gave a report, having recently returned from the state "encampment" attended by more than four hundred delegates. Auxiliaries from throughout Washington had spent $75,000 for hospital work, she announced. Then the ladies broke for refreshments and scheduled their next meeting.

Before then, though, the "circle club" would gather for a potluck at a local park.

Clearly, Agnes was all in with this group of women focused on volunteerism, community, and friendship. Mingling with her new friends was the perfect antidote for a woman in need of healthy relationships. I considered the healing that was going on . . . and if she ever thought about looking for her estranged children.

I should have been used to this sensation by now, but the July 6, 1955, issue of the *Centralia Chronicle* delivered a surprise in their "Twin City Locals" briefs. I learned that indeed, Agnes had enjoyed a visit from one of her children, and it was Frances. I was bowled over that such a mundane item had actually made the papers, suggesting that Agnes herself must have called in the news. It reminded me of those frontier Fairbanks papers reporting who was in town. The brief was titled *Daughter Visits*.

"Welcome visitors over July Fourth at the home of Mrs. Agnes E. Sherman, 1111½ North Washington Avenue, Centralia, were her daughter and son-in-law, Mr. and Mrs. Walter Bilowas of Tarzana, Calif. Mrs. Sherman had not seen her daughter since she was a small child. The California pair continued on to Seattle and are to visit in Centralia later."

More questions than answers arose as I considered how the mother and daughter had reconnected. When and how had she and Frances begun corresponding and planning this visit? And what in the world did they have to talk about?

Agnes continued to receive mentions in the local paper for her volunteer work. In all likelihood, she'd submitted the brief news items herself. In December 1955, before the ladies of the VFW auxiliary enjoyed their cake and coffee, Mrs. Agnes Sherman had "acted as Santa Claus" in the Christmas gift exchange. The following year, Agnes made the paper for embroidering "His" and "Hers" on a pair of pillowcases that she mailed to President Dwight D. Eisenhower and First Lady Mamie. Agnes was thrilled to receive a letter of appreciation from Mrs. Eisenhower's secretary in return.

In the midst of all the volunteerism and friendship, sometime in the late 1950s, Georgerene learned that Agnes was living only eighty miles from where her military family was based in Bremerton, Washington. She decided to make a visit. It had been three decades since they left Alaska together, and after growing up in California while Agnes was institutionalized, it seemed incredible that both were in Washington state, that Agnes could finally have visitors. Georgerene had already been to Tarzana with Renette and baby John, introducing her little family to Frances. Now she was on a roll, bravely ready for a face-to-face with her birth mother. The anticipation of that meeting, whether it would go well or badly, had to be stressful. John and Michelle told me Georgerene had brought along her eldest girl, Renette, who was then five or six years old.

"Does Renette have good memories of that?" I asked.

"For some reason, I was thinking it didn't go too well or something?" Michelle was chuckling at the thought. A long-ago letter from Agnes to Georgerene outlined the "didn't go well" part, she said.

I wondered that Renette would have to say about that first meeting with her grandmother. I leaned back against the headboard in my hotel room, my notepad in my lap, and made the call.

After introductions, I asked, "What did you already know about Agnes Sherman? Or did you know anything?"

"My mother never really talked about her mother," she answered. "I really didn't know any of my grandparents. She just said she was going up to see her mom."

Despite my probing, Renette didn't have much to say about that meeting with Agnes. In fact, she had no memory of even going along with Georgerene. Yet from what John and Michelle heard, the visit had soured when little Renette behaved poorly and even threw something that hit Agnes in the head. Whether or not it was deliberate, Agnes was not amused. She spoke unkindly to Georgerene for not disciplining her daughter very well. Agnes went even further, later mailing a critical letter to Georgerene, reminding her of the need to correct her daughter.

John and Michelle said they'd seen the letter, but couldn't find it again; Renette had no memory of it.

Agnes may have appeared often in the local newspaper's community notices, but in 1957, she left the social columns for the Letters to the Editor. It was the first piece of her writing I'd seen since 1919, when she and J. P. submitted their one-page response to the

Nenana court on relinquishing their children. I had always viewed her as a meek, broken woman in the marriage. But she had found her voice. For the Centralia paper, she was sharply critical, writing, "GONE TOO FAR. [From] Mrs. Agnes E. Sherman, Centralia. [To] Editor *Chronicle*: I think that the people down south have gone too far with their bombing of Negro homes and churches, and also the Ku Klux Klan has gone too far and my advice is that they take off their regalia and quit burning the cross. That is a sacrilege as Jesus died on it. I hope James D. York and Harry Alexander get all that comes, too, and I would like to go down there to help put them in their places."

In February 1958, the local fire department was called to put out a blaze at Agnes's apartment at 1111½ N. Washington Avenue. That *Chronicle* offered a brief report. Again, I wondered if she had flashed back to that "other" fire. How could she not?

Since her release from Western Washington, Agnes had been seeing her doctor for various ailments. After all, she was now in her early seventies. By 1960, she moved to another Centralia apartment at 701 H Street. She began suffering from headaches, dizziness, and nausea. In early December 1963, her doctor diagnosed her condition as "cerebral embolic syndrome," with symptoms similar to stroke, and moved her to a nursing home. After only five weeks from onset, Agnes died that winter, on January 11, 1964. A Centralia friend, perhaps a fellow member of the VFW Auxiliary, Mrs. C. G. Carpenter was on hand as official informant for Agnes's death certificate. She knew little, and no family was available to consult. Agnes seemed alone. There were several "unknowns" on the document.

Agnes died at age seventy-four in a Centralia nursing home after what was described as a long illness. Her obituary appeared in the January 11 edition of the *Chronicle*, where she was remembered as a resident for the last ten years and a former resident of Tacoma, without mention of her decades at Western Washington Hospital. Besides her membership at the Centralia VFW Auxiliary, Agnes belonged to St. Mary's Catholic Church in town. Details of her service followed.

Although Irene's mother had several surviving family members in 1964, only one was mentioned in her obituary: brother, Clarence Brophy Eckert of San Francisco, the one who came to Fairbanks with Agnes and Minnie back in 1905. Both parents and all of her siblings already had passed. There was no mention of her estranged husband, J. P. Sherman, who was still living in Alaska. Also absent were the three birth daughters whose custody she'd relinquished long ago—Irene Sherman, Frances Burnett, and Georgerene Moore—even though two had visited her in Centralia. Agnes was buried in the city's Greenwood Memorial Park on January 14.

There was reason to wonder, *When did those unnamed survivors finally learn of Agnes's demise?* At least Frances and Georgerene had taken the opportunity to meet her. Perhaps their brief interactions were enough to satisfy their curiosity. They could at least close that chapter.

CHAPTER 31
SIMPLE FAITH - Fairbanks, July 1988
Even though I was tiny, I was supposed to know better

The City of Fairbanks had every right to declare Irene's house and everything around it a public health hazard in 1988, but Irene more than anyone else remembered pioneer Les Nerland's promise and the power behind it.

"Well, they can't because Nerland owns this damn house, you know," she said. "He's a big wheel in town; all I have to do is say somethin' to Nerland and he'd say, 'Mind your own business and leave her alone. That's hers until she dies.'"

That summer day in 1988, I'd driven seventy-seven-year-old Irene back to Graehl from downtown and watched her climb over unidentifiable debris while carrying additional bags of goodies. Entering the tunnel-like entrance, she seemed one misstep away, one broken hip away, from losing her treasured freedoms. But as yet, that hadn't happened. She described what was behind the chained refrigerators and wooden pallets, but did not extend an invitation for me to come in.

"Inside the house I've got tables that's sky high with stuff, dishes and clothing and books . . . God, that's one thing I do a lot of is reading. Then I watch TV and listen to KJNP, that religious station. I'm absolutely gang-busted on that outfit. They been extra good to me and I got myself into their church down here on Third Street. What the deuce, it's nice to belong to somethin'. I come as close to bein' saved as anythin' in that little church.

"Darn it, there's been so doggone many things in my life that's turned me into a pretzel that I've almost hated to go to any of the churches."

Two hours earlier, Wally, Irene, and I had been talking over breakfast when the priest from Immaculate Conception Church strolled into the Black Angus, noticed Irene, and recognized Wally. Father Terrill Heaps veered toward us. "Good morning, Irene. How are you this morning?" he asked. "Happy Golden Days." The priest was pastor of the historic Catholic church on the banks of the Chena River.

In the winter of 1911-12, when Irene just a year old, the church building had been winched onto logs and rolled across the ice from the south side of the river to the north. It was a superhuman effort led by the ambitious Father Monroe, who wanted his church placed next door to St. Joseph's Hospital, so he could minister to the patients there. The frontier hospital is gone now except for the annex added years later. But the church remains.

Hearing Father Heaps' voice, Irene jumped to her feet, amazingly agile, to stand wide-eyed before him.

"Hi, buddy!" she said loudly. "Hello." Irene pumped the priest's hand, her eyes fixed on his face. "Father, I'm a chapel girl, or was. So, by gosh, I'm one of you guys."

"Good for you," said Father Heaps. "You look as elegant as ever." Then he turned to discuss local happenings with Wally. They didn't get far before Irene interrupted.

"Hey, Father. You know something? It's sure nice to see one of you. Cause I'm a chapel girl. I used to help clean the chapel . . ."

"Uh-huh, uh-huh . . ." Father Heaps nodded along.

". . . and help the nuns get the flowers and that sort of thing."

"Uh-hum."

". . . and get the altar fixed and this, that, and the other thing."

I could see that Father Heaps didn't want to brush her off, but likewise had nothing to say in return. He smiled pleasantly, and then continued his conversation of about-town news with Wally.

Irene sat down long enough to take a bite of toast, then looked up and interrupted again, talking through her toast.

"By the way, Father, how you doing on the church deal?"

"What do you mean?"

"How you doing on the church deal?"

"What church deal?"

Wally intervened: "How's your congregation? . . . She's trying to check into your business." He smiled and so did Father Heaps. The confusion cleared, the priest answered with something I sensed had been an automatic answer in many a conversation: "Oh, we just plod along year after year, trying to do the Lord's work."

"Well," Irene said, "I'm a chapel girl myself."

"We're going to have to start getting you to Mass more often," the priest responded.

"Yeah, by God, that's the truth. I was a chapel girl."

Irene was far from conventionally religious, but an ample chunk of her growing-up years were spent with the Sisters of Providence or the Sisters of the Good Shepherd. Her core beliefs were Catholic. And inside her quarters, she had her radio tuned to the Reverend Don Nelson on KJNP (King Jesus North Pole), an evangelical Christian mission radio station broadcasting from the city of North Pole, about twelve miles south of Fairbanks, as "Your Gospel Station at the Top of the Nation."

Irene went to church when she felt like it, sometimes at Immaculate Conception, sometimes at the Assembly of God Church. But somehow, no matter how many services she attended, Irene seemed unable to offload her burdens and memories, and instead took on the transgressions of others, accepting what was done to her as though it was her own fault. Irene's God was a vengeful deity.

"What I've been given by the Lord is a punishment for a misdeed that I did that I shouldn't have done," she told me. "Even though I was tiny, I was supposed to know better."

Even more than seventy years after the fire, I recognized that the woman sitting across from me was permanently altered by the events of November 28, 1916. The fire, what happened before it, and what followed, marred her deeply, far more than those visible scars. This was the Irene that the swarms of friends rarely met. Introspective. Accepting.

"My burns has been my crutch that I've got to hold dear to me to make me know what I'm supposed to do—and what I ain't supposed to do," she said. "And when I go out of that realm, then the Lord has a way of *zapping* you. The way the Old Man takes care of you, you ain't going to get away with nothing. Especially if you get a damn brat from another home that don't give a hoot—that more or less throws lit matches and that sort of thing all over the place."

I remembered those words much later, long after Irene's home was torn down, the lot was smoothed over, and she was in her grave. In my hand was a fifty-year-old envelope measuring nine-by-thirteen-inches that in 1977 had been mailed to Irene from the office of then-Governor Jay Hammond. It was worn, folded, and dirty. The envelope and some other ephemera had been rescued by some of Irene's many friends, pulled from the debris of the wigwam before it was bulldozed. Surviving the years inside the envelope was a note from the governor's now-late aide, Larry Holmstrom. He'd mailed Irene an enlarged photo of the Queen posing with the governor at a bridge opening in 1977.

"Governor Hammond thought you might like to have this picture as a memento of your participation with him in the Steese Highway dedication ceremonies," Holmstrom had written. The photo was long gone, but Irene had used the envelope as scrap paper. On the back side, a message in fine cursive from a local couple invited Irene to come for Thanksgiving dinner. Don and Mary Ann Berry had included their phone number and urged her to call ahead for a ride.

Below that invitation was another message in Irene's loopy, childish handwriting: "I am there walcome gest and friend and pall May God take care of us allwees My hort is with God allwees I Love You For Ever."

※ ※ ※

Sharon Johnson Boko has long been active with Pioneers of Alaska Fairbanks Women's Igloo No. 8. At eighty-plus years old, she clearly remembers Irene walking or biking through her childhood neighborhood toward downtown. Boko was also a faithful member of the Assembly of God congregation, a church that Irene loved.

Although Irene was a cradle Episcopalian with a strong sprinkling of Presbyterian, during her years at the Home of the Good Shepherd in Seattle, she'd asked the nuns if she could convert to Catholicism. But as a minor lacking parental consent, she was denied. In Fairbanks, the little Pentecostal church on Third had an open door and welcomed her. Boko remembered well, because she was the church secretary during a ten-year period when Irene was a regular at their

Sunday night services. In 2022, Boko recalled how week after week, Irene did business with God, petitioning and confessing in private prayer at the altar. Regardless of the time for an altar call, she'd go forward to wordlessly pray, tears running down her face. Occasionally when Irene was pouring herself out, the pastor would make eye contact with Boko. With a nod, he'd send her to Irene's side.

"It was like, 'Go down and see what I can do to help her,'" Boko recalled. "And she would always, either stand up then, or sitting, put her arms around me, pull me into her chest, bury my face . . ." Holding back a smile, Boko paused, then began her story again. "And you just have to imagine . . . the odor . . . Sometimes I thought, 'I'm gonna die!'" With that, we shared a suppressed laugh. *Say no more*, I told her. *You're a good woman.*

To show her appreciation for Boko's kindness, Irene sometimes came by with gifts, like statuettes of the Virgin Mary or the Sacred Heart of Jesus. Boko had been a practicing Catholic at one time, and knew the significance of Irene's gifts, and yet hers was a full-gospel Pentecostal church. She asked her pastor, "What do you want me to do with these?" Wisely, he answered, "Put them on your desk, put them on the window sill. She'll be back to visit." And she did come back, gratified to see her gifts on display, Boko confirmed.

"We all love the same God. We just have different tenets," said Boko.

※ ※ ※

"Hey! KID!" Irene's bullhorn voice cut the soft summer air like an arctic blast. "*Git* down off there!"

Belly down, a little girl was peering over the edge of the retaining wall surrounding the "Unknown First Family" statue in Golden Heart Park along the Chena. Irene's urgent words were lost in the pounding water at the statue's base. The child did not move. The statue had been installed in 1984 in celebration of Alaska's twenty-fifth anniversary of statehood. Not far from this spot, in late August 1901, E. T. Barnette and all his trade goods had been dumped off the *Lavelle Young* and onto the river bank. There's a sign about it.

"Damn brats. Damn kid's gonna fall in there and nobody's watching 'em," Irene muttered. "HEY!" she shouted again, fully engaging her diaphragm.

Again, her calls went unnoticed. Few people were paying attention to her, instead focused on incoming runners. This morning, the downtown park was the finish line for a sixteen-mile footrace along the Steese Highway that began in the remote hills up where Felix Pedro found gold so long ago. The half-marathon was a popular event on the calendar for the weeklong Golden Days festival. Race officials, well-wishers, and other finishers watched for runners, offering congratulatory applause under the warm sun.

In her flashy Golden Days purple cape, red feather boa, and tattered fancy hat, Irene would not be overlooked. Folks glanced at her when she shouted at the child, but brought their focus back to the oncoming runners. So Irene decided to march her oversized winter boots into the finish chute. Two runners patiently loped around her to reach the finish line.

Visiting with Irene that July day in 1988, I noticed that she was thinner than she'd been in years. Weight loss and some short-term memory problems were causing concern for friends. She was slightly confused at times, but still making her rounds, still checking in. And in this community, in this part of the twentieth century, Fairbanks held a relaxed view of their favorite bag lady. She had extraordinary freedoms given behavior that may not have been tolerated elsewhere. Sure, Irene had some medical needs, but those were being addressed. Otherwise, thanks to her friends and tolerant strangers, she was still a free agent, a beneficiary of the grace and goodwill of many who populated the "Golden Heart City."

Perhaps most tragic were the blank spaces surrounding memories of her only child, Robert P. Hartman, Jr. On a day when she seemed glib and the stories were flowing, I decided to wade in and ask about her son. *Where was Robert these days?*

"Well, I did the best I could for the kid," Irene responded, growing agitated as she worked to retrieve any details. I felt a soapbox delivery coming on, deflecting the question. "What I like to do when I have a child is to keep him in ONE SPOT." Fixed on my face, she was practically spitting with the emphasis on her last words. "And if you're roaming from one damn place to another, *uh-huh.*" She wagged one stubby finger and continued, "That just isn't gonna do. And by the time you get the house warmed up and everything else, that child is just about ready to catch the flu or some damn thing or another. That's what happens to children." I sensed that her talk was addressing more than one child that she'd been responsible for.

"I was bound and determined to make a gentleman out of him. Instead of a damn hoodlum. Well, after he grew up so he could get loose from me, he was gone like the wind."

Listening to old-timer Clara Rust's recorded memories later, I gained some insight. According to Rust, Irene never had the opportunity to fully raise her son. When she came back to Fairbanks from Healy with the boy, her parenting was scrutinized.

People were concerned that Robert wasn't fed regularly or dressed warmly. Irene was partying too much. Rust said Irene lost her son "because she wasn't treating him right."

I guessed that Robert must have been eleven or twelve when the territory removed him from Irene's care. He would grow up in a foster home about two hundred miles south of Fairbanks. As a teen, he excelled in Palmer High School's class of 1953 and made the National Honor Society, while joining the chorus, ski club, and student council. In his senior photo, Robert had a broad smile, thick hair, and friendly eyes like his mother's. Later, the young man entered Alaskan mining ventures at Goodnews Bay and Nome, and lived in the Seattle area for a while. He stayed in touch with his Aunt Frances, and he wrote his mother wherever he went, his letters formal and often about the weather. He sent letters and platinum nuggets to his Aunt Frances. Even Georgerene's kids in California remembered meeting at that World's Fair rendezvous in 1968.

I found a letter of Robert's among Irene's papers that a friend had withdrawn from the wigwam before its demolition. He was writing from the remote mining camp of Platinum, Alaska, on the Bering Sea, more than six hundred miles from Fairbanks. Robert's letter, dated April 17, 1963, began . . . *Dear Mother,*

Am enclosing a $100.00 money order in
this letter for you. We are having a cold spring, but
I think the weather should break any time now. I
was lucky to catch a cold in Seattle while I wasn't
working. I've been here ten days and haven't come
close to catching a cold. I guess I am immune for
five months anyhow.

Today was a great improvement over past
weeks, and I do hope that the last days of this
month improve equally well. From what I can hear
on the radio, you are having a lot of snow up there.
We've had snow, north winds, south winds, west
winds, and blizzards.
Well, I had better close now with best wishes for
you, mother.

Love x son,
Robert

I couldn't help but notice that sweet little x that he'd inserted between "Love" and "son." A kiss for his mother.

Robert's note was not a one-off. He'd sent many cards and letters through the years, recognizing their unique relationship. In response to this letter, it seems Irene had purchased a present valued at forty-five dollars, and sent it back to her boy. She'd stapled the gift receipt to his letter that she'd kept.

And yet during my interview with Irene, while I was hoping for stories of her son's childhood, Irene gave me an insightful talk on the essentials of parenting.

"I hope I had an impression on him, anyhow," she said earnestly. "Cause I wanted him to remember everything he was taught.

I wanted him to be a gentleman. And somebody that, when a lady met him, he'd know how to handle that. And when a gentleman would catch up with him, why, he'd know how to handle him, too. And be his own man's man."

Robert would be about fifty now, I figured. I asked his mother if he'd ever married, and she spat out her answer: "Damned if I know. I never can seem to catch up to him. When he got away from me, that was the end of that. And I don't know where he is. I wished to hell that somebody'd let me know. I don't know whether the kid's alive or not. That's what's bugging me."

Robert P. Hartman, Jr. Palmer High School, 1953. He made the National Honor Society and loved sports.

"I'll talk to you later about that," Wally muttered, but somehow we never managed to talk about it again.

After a few days, I was back in Anchorage and ensconced in the public library's Alaska Collection, scrolling through microfilms as I searched for more about Irene's son. His Aunt Frances had suggested diabetes was the cause of Robert's death. What I found rendered me breathless and tearful. I stared at the screen for several minutes, rereading the same six-year-old news item about Robert P. Hartman Jr. The fifty-year-old man's skeletal remains had been found about twenty-five miles outside of Anchorage on April 7, 1982. Most recently he had been employed on a Nome gold dredge, but he'd also worked at Nenana, Lake Minchumina, Goodnews Platinum Mine, and other gold claims around Fairbanks. Irene was the only survivor mentioned in his obituary. She asked for donations to the American Diabetes Association.

I phoned the coroner for more details. Following an inquest, the coroner's jury had ruled his death a suicide. His date of death was unknown. Irene's dear son was buried in Birch Hill Cemetery in an unmarked grave, or so I was told. But visiting the Find-a-Grave website, I found his name attached to a memorial page with a photo of a giant lilac. Near it was a rock that seemed to be sinking into the soil.

What part did Irene have in either the lilac or that rock? I didn't know for sure. I did know that in 1982, Irene had already suffered the agonizing news of Robert's death. And that by 1988, she'd mercifully forgotten it all, leaving only anxiety in its wake as she mulled his whereabouts. The people closest to her, like Wally, would not remind her. Why deliver such unfathomable sorrow again? She'd already had more than her share.

Golden Days, July 1982 (*News-Miner* Archives)

CHAPTER 32
IRENE'S WAY - July 2021
Do you know where this sign came from?

On a sunny summer day in 2020, Jonathan Johnson was happily wetting his fishing line in the Chena River, but it wasn't fish he was after. He'd attached a powerful magnet at the end of the line and was fishing for metal, a favorite hobby, pulling out curiosities that otherwise would have been buried in silty mud for years to come. Johnson was having a good time while doing a good deed for the environment. His growing collection of finds included the benign and bizarre, like rusted-out handguns, a decades-old pickaxe, bikes, and many, many railroad spikes. Even a fifty-cent coin from Fiji.

That summer, twenty-six years after Irene Sherman died, he'd fished out a metal street sign that read "Irene's Way." Of course he remembered Irene from his childhood, as did hundreds in his Boomer generation, all of whom had grown up around Irene on their downtown streets or in her neighborhood, near the "castle" that had once threatened to overflow onto Front Street. After pulling out the sign, Johnson got the attention of a local television station, which sent over a reporter to interview him and document his find. A couple of weeks later, the sign and other unique items in his collection went on display at the Fairbanks Community Museum.

Johnson told me how he'd grown up seeing Irene's ragged collection of old refrigerators, washing machines, pallets, chain, cardboard and such lashed together as fencing around her fortress in Graehl. His family lived nearby, and he was used to the place, but like all kids, he was more than curious about what was inside. He'd seen her climb up and over heaps of garbage and into at least one tunnel-like entrance. Even though she was on the short side, she'd had to bend slightly to enter and balance on what was underfoot.

One day, little boy Johnson and his friend decided to sneak inside Irene's place and have a look around. They'd figured she was out walking or pedaling somewhere around town. Their hearts pounding, the boys poked their heads inside and their feet followed. Little by little they edged in until . . . *"There she was!"* he remembered, and even now his face lit up as if he were nine. "She was right there, inside there, sleeping!" Bug-eyed with fear, the boys turned and scrambled toward the light before Irene could stir. On the street, they didn't pause, but kept on moving out, too scared to mention the encounter to anyone but their closest friends, swearing them to secrecy.

It all came back to Johnson after he pulled that metal sign out of

Jonathan Johnson and his mystery sign, which he donated to the Fairbanks Community Museum. (Courtesy Sarah Hollister)

the river and put it on display in the town museum. That's where I was, looking at all the metal on the display table, when he asked me, "Do you know where this sign came from?" I thought I did.

Among the photocopies from my long-ago research was a published story about Irene, but I couldn't remember the source.

Eventually, I figured out these were pages from Joan Kopenen's book titled *Building from Within*, about unique homes around Fairbanks and the Alaskans who built them. She'd recorded Irene in 1978, asking about her house as she walked the perimeter of the property. But soon Irene had stepped off Koponen's line of inquiry to talk about the value of friends in her very survival through the years. As Irene chatted, she remained alert to the people driving by and exchanged waves without losing a beat.

Friends were everywhere. Some knew her from the stores or streets; others from the bars. Olympia Beer was her brand. Oly. Oly-Pop. If you tried to fill her mug from a pitcher of something other than Oly, watch out. "You know I don't drink that crap!" So you'd buy her an Oly, assured her friendly tongue-lashings were nothing to be afraid of, or were they?

"I've often wondered how in the name of Sam Hill I managed to hang on tough as good as I did, outside of havin' all the guys I had behind me and all the ladies that became my friends," Irene said. "I'd get in with these boyfriends and they'd sometimes bring home food and such, and when I got hold of some gosh darn loot, I'd do likewise.

"Lord a-mighty, it was just hit or miss then. Of course, you had to pay for coal or wood, or scrounge it out in the woods." The previous Christmas, Usibelli Coal had gifted her a ton of coal, she said. "That's the way us people are for each other up here, you know."

With so many friends and the occasional boyfriend, Irene seemed to keep loneliness at bay. Men came and went, as had so many other people in her life. But none was inclined to keep a serious relationship going, so Irene's loyalties were not strained when the next "pal" came along.

"Of course, I try to be a pal . . . like with a gold miner friend who married a damn jane that wasn't doin' him any good. She'd shut down on him and wouldn't let him touch her or anything. And he wasn't gettin' his quota of good will and love and understandin' that goes with marriage. Well, Jesus, that don't make sense. So I take compassion on the poor son of a gun and I give him a little kindness. We get out and go dancin' together and talk over things that pertain to us and what have you, and I always try to be a pal of his."

The reflection led to a confession of sorts: "Right now I've got another new [boyfriend]," she said, "but he's becoming hopeless, too. He don't drink, that's the hell of it." Irene paused and chuckled. "I do."

As her conversation with Joan wound down, Irene rearranged the laundry bundle she'd been loading. She fixed her hat that was decorated, Joan noted, with "ancient feathers and campaign buttons."

As she pedaled away, Irene passed a street sign that had stood since September 12, 1977, when the nearby Steese Highway Bypass bridge officially opened. On that day, Irene, who'd been appointed "project manageress," had pinned a flower on Governor Jay Hammond's lapel while news photographers snapped photos. Jointly, the governor and the bag lady cut the ribbon allowing the first car to cross. Nearby, the newly installed sign read "Irene's Way."

Aboard her three-wheeler in the 1985 Golden Days Parade, Irene was treated like a celebrity, drawing smiles, shouts, and waves. (*News-Miner*

CHAPTER 33
WHAT WAS AND IS - Fairbanks 2022
We were a new cast in a made-over theater

One dusky midday in January, when downtown Fairbanks traffic was practically non-existent, I slowly rolled my rental car down a snowy, one-way Cushman Street from Sixth Avenue toward First and the Chena River bridge crossing. I wanted to examine the cityscape today compared to the Fairbanks I had come to know well in studying Irene's youth. When an account from one of the early newspapers mentioned a location, I could only picture how it looked in 1978 and later. Now I could practically map what had been there in 1915.

I had booked my Fairbanks trip at the perfect time. For weeks, the daytime highs had been lingering at minus twenty Fahrenheit or lower, but when I landed, things had warmed up to minus five. The Interior had seen an overabundance of snowfall that winter. I was warned that broad, thick patches of glacier-like ice remained even after the snow plows did their work. It was dangerous ice that threw cars around, jarring suspensions and teeth.

When I was handed my rental key at the airport, how could I know that the car hadn't been moved in weeks? Sure, it was plugged in and should start without issue. But as I examined the vehicle for dents, I was standing on a berm created by consecutive snowfalls that had been brushed off the car. My feet were higher than the bottom of the car door. I managed to unplug, and then wrestle me and my fluffy coat between the frame and door to slide inside. Backing out would take several rocking attempts. I was about to surrender and humbly go back inside—*why did I mention that I used to live here and knew how to drive on snow and ice?*—when I finally breached the ice wall behind me.

Through VRBO, I'd rented a little house on Fifth Avenue in a downtown neighborhood. Although daylight was in short supply, I was free to walk around, but I was much too lazy and liked warm cars. I'd fully softened to the milder temperatures of Anchorage, where it sometimes dropped below zero, but nothing like Fairbanks. So I drove

In the 1940s, the art deco-style federal building anchored Cushman Street. Beyond it, what was once called the Patten building is visible. Sometime after this period, Woolworth's occupied that block between Third and Fourth that was once the site of the Third Avenue Hotel. (Burnett Family Collection)

and circled and explored the downtown core of Irene's city. Five below was warm enough to roll down the car window for the photos I wanted. I cranked up the heat and set out to see what had filled the places that had been eradicated over time.

The Main School building had been erected in 1907 on Cushman between Sixth and Seventh Avenues. After it burned in 1932, a lovely art deco structure took its place. No longer a school, it now housed Patrick B. Cole City Hall. Two more blocks north, between Fifth and Sixth, I saw a furniture store where J. C. Penney used to dominate. The retail favorite had stood there since 1966 when the corporation razed dozens of old cabins and frame homes to build the multi-level store and parking lot. Just a year later, when the Chena flooded into the city streets in the infamous 1967 flood, the store's second level was a shelter for displaced people. Archival photos show a helicopter on its roof; cars in the parking lot visible only by their roofs. On the other side of Cushman Street, the two-story Eagle Hall had once reigned in Fairbanks social circles. In 1914, John H. Patten had been installed and deputized as Grand Worthy Chaplain of the Fraternal Order of the Eagles Aerie No. 1037. It was there that Agnes had routinely danced the night away as tongues wagged. It's where Searl and Ethel Burnett fell in love at first sight, and the place where the Sherman and Porter children were transported for triage after they were pulled from the fire of November 1916. Eagle Hall closed in 1969 and was demolished in 1970. I saw some irony that the hall had been destroyed in a controlled burn for firefighter training. Borough busses now circled a modest transit center built on the site of many a concert, feast, and dance. It took me several interviews with old-timers to fully grasp where people had entered the hall, which side faced Fifth, and where the stage and stairs were.

Once there was a store, warehouse, and cabins across Fifth from the old Eagle Hall. Today I found a dead zone—the emptiness of a full block of parking spaces. It was here that Gordon's dry goods once sprawled, its inviting picture windows facing Cushman. Behind it, in 1916, there were a couple of small storage buildings, then the Sherman rental cabin, directly across from Eagle Hall. Now it and everything around it were gone. I took a picture of the empty spot—strange, I knew—aware of how I might look to anyone watching. But it was an important location in my narrative of Irene's life.

Back on Cushman, I rolled a little further toward the frozen river to see what stood on the footprint of the lavish Third Avenue Hotel, destroyed in that 1914 fire. John H. Patten had rebuilt a two-story structure with shops on the first floor and offices above. They had called it the Patten Block. Now the space between Third and Fourth Avenues was occupied by a cement-block children's museum with parking in the back. I remembered an attractive Woolworth's there when I was a young woman. The terms "five and dime" and "lunch counter" still generate warm thoughts.

Neighboring the children's museum on the northwest side of Cushman, the entire block between Third and Second was filled with that multistory art deco landmark that has anchored downtown since 1932.

This was once the site of a simple courthouse and jail, the first built on land donated by E. T. Barnette and dedicated in 1904 by Judge James Wickersham. The judge was scratching Barnette's back when he moved the Third Judicial District's headquarters from Eagle on the Yukon River, inland to Fairbanks just a year earlier.

In 1932, on that same lot, this building opened as a courthouse, jail, post office, and home to other federal offices. Had men actually been executed by hanging in what is now a stairwell, or was that urban myth? In the post-pipeline years, the post office had been replanted a few blocks away, a new Alaska State courthouse was constructed to overlook the Chena River, and an imposing federal building went up on Twelfth Avenue. On this winter day in 2022, the old federal building, as sturdy and elegant as ever, was in private hands and filled with professional offices. If there were jail-cell bars on the basement-level windows, they were gone by now.

Finally, across Second Avenue from the old federal building, where it seemed a bank had always been, a bank with a different name still claimed the corner. For many decades, the image of a digital time and temperature sign on that corner, affixed to the First National Bank of Alaska, was the most photographed in Fairbanks history. Really? Minus sixty-five degrees? In personal photos as well as postcards mailed Outside, it was proof that Alaskans could take whatever Mother Nature threw at us. KeyBank now sprawled over the entire block between First and Second. I'm told there was a great outcry when the old bank's temperature sign was removed. KeyBank put up its own.

I had closely studied photos from 1906, when the corner of Cushman and First was occupied by Dawson stampeder and pharmacist John A. McIntosh with his mining partner, Ralph Kubon. Failing as get-rich-quick miners, together they opened a popular drug store. The oversized McIntosh & Kubon thermometer on Cushman arrested the attention of every passerby, and newspapers reported its readings. Fire took down that business in the 1930s. But McIntosh had also invested in the success of the nearby college, what would become the University of Alaska Fairbanks, my alma mater.

The buildings, the people. We were a new cast in a made-over theater. But our history was young. The early citizens rested in the pioneer cemetery or had journeyed back home. They had not been forgotten. Their names were on streets, parks, tribal halls, and university dormitories. Even the scoundrels like E. T. Barnette and Dr. Mahlon Hall had streets named after them. If you made an online search, you'd find the stories behind those names, people who'd dedicated lifetimes to working and raising their families under phenomenal circumstances, always making time for play. Some came from among the First People, exerting their presence and authority from the ages. Others were military folks who fell in love and stuck around at the end of their service. Miners, homesteaders, business people, entertainers, farmers, clothiers, purveyors of spirits, bankers, riverboat captains, and pipeliners, united in their endurance. Delivering some semblance of order to beautiful madness.

In 1979, I'd helped paint a graphic swirl of a mural on one Second Avenue business. It was overpainted long ago, but others from that downtown beautification project remain. A slice in time, the false-fronted (former) Empress Theatre is a staple on Second. Built by Alaska's first millionaire, media mogul Austin "Cap" Lathrop, the Empress was a jewel in his empire. In a later life, the building held the Co-Op Diner, and now was anchored by a restaurant and filled with small businesses, a coffee shop, and the Fairbanks Community and Dog Mushing Museum. It had been "The Co-Op" for most of its life, and was often still referred to that way. Over the years, thousands (including Irene Sherman and me) had used the building as a pass-through, a chance to duck out of below-zero temps and warm up in a slow indoors walk from Second to Third Avenue before next ducking into Nerland's Home Furnishings on Third to find respite strolling through luxurious home décor on the way to Fourth Avenue.

Charlie Creamer was a pioneer dairyman whose grain fields became a wildlife refuge, a choice place to view migrating Canada geese and Sandhill cranes. The No. 1 engine from the old Tanana Mines Railway, later the Tanana Valley Railroad, was lovingly restored by local steam enthusiasts and now glowed inside the Tanana Valley Railroad Museum. The retired narrow-gauge engine had moved miners and freight to and from outlying creeks from 1904 onward.

In 1967, the centennial year of the U.S. purchase of Alaska from Russia, communities all over the state celebrated. In Fairbanks, leadership decided to build a park recognizing various aspects of its history: mining, aviation, transportation on rivers and rails, and Native culture. More than a dozen historically significant cabins were relocated from downtown to the Alaska 67 Exposition park to create Gold Rush Town. Among the relocated buildings was the old "Wickersham House," the cabin that the Burnett family had long ago purchased from Judge James Wickersham. And there was the First Presbyterian Church that Minnie and John Patten had helped found. For decades, it's been a popular marrying spot in the park. Also here, a couple of cabins that were once part of the famous Fourth Avenue "line" for the working girls. The park was later renamed Alaskaland and more recently, Pioneer Park.

Dominating downtown is Golden Heart Plaza with its fountain and centerpiece sculpture of the "Unknown First Family." Across the Chena stands the imposing Immaculate Conception Church. Nearby, an art installation belatedly honors Walter Harper, the young Koyukon Athabascan man who first summited Denali in 1913.

All the places and markers are reminders, but mere symbols of our past, not living and breathing. Maybe that's why Irene Sherman was regarded with such warmth and respect. She was Fairbanks history, walking, walking, walking through the decades and rolling with the changes, until her death in 1995.

CHAPTER 34
AFTER ALL THESE YEARS – Fairbanks, 2020s
You call her 'Mrs. Sherman.' Do you understand?

Facebook has long been the watercooler meeting place for like-minded people to talk about issues of the day, but it's also where sentimental people meet to recall earlier days of the good ol' hometown. One private group that's populated by nearly fourteen thousand Fairbanksans, former and current, is called "You're Probably from Fairbanks If You Can Remember . . ." Of course, I signed on years ago. A few regulars put up historical pictures and ask for new or missing dates and places.

One of the most popular subjects is Irene. Group member Jim Ritter recalled: "Irene Sherman. She would come into the burger place

Irene's annual birthday events were well-attended and often covered by the local press. This 1971 party was held at the Big I, a favorite watering hole. The *Pioneer All Alaska Weekly* reported flowing champagne, flashy decorations, a smorgasbord of delicious food, many gifts, and a beautiful birthday cake. (Courtesy Colleen Redman)

at the Gavora Mall where I worked in the '70s. I told my dad that Old Irene came in. He said, 'You call her Mrs. Sherman. Do you understand?' When my dad died, she came to our house to pay her respects. Tough-as-nails lady. Nice lady. Kind lady. I learned to not judge a book by its cover." And yet another who remembered her said, "That woman was mean."

Of course, Irene wasn't the lavender-scented church lady who said, "Here's a nickel, be a good boy." The Boomers of Fairbanks remembered mostly friendly exchanges; others not so much. The police blotter showed Irene reported vandalism more than once, like the rock-throwers breaking windows or lights outside her house. And one summer, some kids lit fireworks and tossed them into her property. So I asked her, "Do you ever give advice to teenagers now?"

"No, I usually try to stay away from them."

"You like kids, though, don't you?"

"Just so long. Just as long as they keep their damn mouths shut and don't give me too much YAP. Otherwise, then I ditch 'em. Try to ship-ahoy 'em back to their own parents."

In 2019, Jim Ritter logged onto Facebook and posted a picture of a three-wheeled adult-sized bike with the tease, "Who remembers the eccentric lady who used to ride around town on one of these three-wheelers? She was quite the fascinating character. I remember her name. Do you?"

If the saying is true that "You live only as long as the last person who remembers you," then Irene is not yet dead. The public response from that simple "Do you?" was a steady stream of storytelling about a key figure in his generation's childhood. I recalled Michelle Moore's plaintive question when she first wrote me about Irene: "I can see we are too late," she wrote. "Is there anybody what would remember her?" *Oh, no, not too late*, I assured her. Facebook proved my point. One post resulted in nearly six hundred responses, even twenty-five years after her death, as the grown-up Fairbanks kids unleashed their memories, good, bad, scary, and touching. I noticed that in some cases, as in the old days, misinformation was still moving around on a new kind of party line.

My brother and I, as young kids, we often saw Irene walking around town with her trolley carts and many layers of old furs and clothes to stay warm. We'd walk by her home and wonder what went on in the ramshackle pile of boards, boxes and old refrigerators she had assembled into a 'shack' on a plot of land not far from the river. I'm ashamed to admit many of us kids avoided her and made up stories about who she was and why she was covered in burn scars.

In January 1977 we were having a cold snap of -50, and one afternoon my brother and I came home from school and found Miss Irene laying on our couch. To say we were stunned would be an understatement. My mom introduced us and said she saw Miss Irene walking in the cold and realized she had no heat in her hut and would be staying with us until the cold subsided. My brother and I were shy but polite and I did my best not to stare or act uncomfortable, but I was 11 or 12 so I'm guessing we retreated to our room for most of her stay. Irene was there a week, eating my mom's home cooking and taking showers and doing laundry. Behind her at-times gruff-sounding speaking voice was a very sweet person who told us many stories of her years in Fairbanks and the house fire that devastated her family and scared her as a young girl.

By the time she left, our eyes had been opened to what an incredibly strong woman she was, and looking back I realized how thoughtless and selfish I had been for ever thinking she was less-than. After she left we would often run into her walking the streets and she'd always smile and give us a big hug. I can still hear her voice belting out 'Ed-DEEE!' as she grabbed me.
Looking back, I'm ashamed I ever felt embarrassed by the situation. My mom passed years ago, but I always remember her incredibly kind heart and compassion, something that stays with me and compels me to always think about the needs of others no matter how strange or difficult the situation. I hope there's a special place in Heaven for both of them. — *Edward B.*

Way back in 1973-74, I worked at the Firelite Room next to Tommy's [Elbow Room] on 2nd. Irene would come to the back door and get bag of food to take home. Also if it was real cold outside, I would drive her home. The house was real funny with hardly any openings. She seemed to always know when I got off work. Fairbanks folks kinda looked after her. — *Joann W.*

Irene. I remember her; used to ride her bike all over town as a kid I'd see her she would wave. I heard they found over a million dollars stashed away in bed mattress walls, etc. That's what I heard . . . — *Toni H.*

Once I tried to follow Irene home, because all of us children heard the rumors and stories about this strangely dressed woman with a burn disfigurement. I saw her walking once, and I just wanted to know the truth, so I asked my dad if I could go talk to her and he said yes. But as I followed behind her, I just couldn't find the nerve. Yet I couldn't stop following her, my curiosity just wouldn't relent, so I persisted following Irene hoping that I could at least find out where she lives. She finally sensed my presence behind her and she turned around and said to me, 'Did your parents say it's OK to follow me?' I can't remember my reply, I think I said a squeaky scared 'Yes' and then turned and ran home as fast as I could! — *Eric F.*

She was a nice woman; the Nerlands took care of her. My first beer after I got to Fairbanks was on 2nd Avenue. Irene came up to me with a plastic mug and said, 'Buy me a beer.' Sweet woman, had a rough life, but Fairbanks took care of her. — *Norma M.*

Yes and still remember the cruel, brutal things said to her. Sad.
— *Genevieve G.*

In the mid-1980s, Irene was photographed with fellow partiers at Tommy's Elbow Room on Second Avenue. (Courtesy Sean Lynch)

I remember Irene very well; she had a heart of Gold to me if she liked you. But don't get on the bad side of her. She could make your life bad and she would cuss your name to everyone she knew. I used to give her ride when she was caught in the rain and other times when she needed help. — *Michael I.*

Yep, that was Irene. Nothing subtle about her (then again, how could there be if someone has a beer mug strapped to their hip!). Nice to know the Nerlands did that. — *Jim R.*

She was badly burned in a house fire and family pretty much abandoned her, I think her sister still lives in Fairbanks. — *Norma M.*

Irene Sherman . . . nicknamed by some Gripsack Annie, a true piece of Fairbanks town . . . she wore her drinking mug on her waist belt . . . her many layers of clothes and her ol' floppy hat . . . she would come in the ol' Goldrush Saloon on 1st Ave . . . next door to the Arctic Pancake House . . . that woman could drink and hold her liquor well. I am humbled and honored knowing the likes of such people. — *Phillip R.*

I remember Irene well. At one time, she and I shared a room at the old hospital for a period of time. I'd had surgery and she was having skin grafts done on burns she had received. Nurses told me the first couple of days after my surgery if I made any noise, like in pain, etc., Irene would ring for them, no matter what time day or night. After I was able to do a few things, I would help her with her meals as she had bandaging on [her] hand. She told wonderful stories and it was a true joy sharing those days with her. — *Julie C.*

I remember one time in the Big I with my husband and some friends. One of my friends accidentally spilled a drink in my lap, and Irene happened to be walking by and she slapped him. He turned around to hit whoever it was, and it was Irene, so he said, 'Oh, hi, Irene.' She said, 'That's no way to treat a lady,' referring to spilling the drink. My friend bought Irene a drink. — *Barbara P.*

I can still see Irene's place with all the refrigerators piled around it. — *Jim R.*

Irene is a legend. A person I was raised to respect in our community. I also had the privilege of filling her mug at the Big I . . . more than once. — *Eric J.*

I met Irene at the Tanana Valley Clinic when this lady walked over to my wife and took my young son into her arms and lovingly held him, while we were dumbfounded at the time. She was so tender with him. I'll never forget her!
 — *Timothy L. B.*

I was the bouncer at the Flame Lounge. She knew me quite well. She saved my life. One night a guy had pulled a gun on me and she'd come up behind him; had her gun trained on him and said 'I would hate to shoot both of you.'
 — *Dave G.*

Fairbanks was a unique city full of people from all walks of life whose lives intermixed into a Fairbanks melting pot. I lived a few homes [away] on the corner of 1st and Graehl. Irene was always happy-go-lucky with a good attitude of those around her. It seemed she never met a stranger she couldn't be friends with. Even on 2nd Ave, which we frequented, I as a young Iñupiaq Eskimo Native boy sell newspapers and Irene, always her jovial self. I often wondered why she had a string around her neck with a cup tied to the string. I found out later as I walked through the bars (we were permitted to sell papers in the bars during the 1950s). Irene would go to the bar; people would buy her drinks. She had the bartender fill the cup which she would drink from. Irene always had a seemingly loud tone to her voice.

When you saw Irene on the streets she would seemingly always be upbeat to everyone she saw on the streets; she was always quite the walker.

It was during these times I last saw and talked to Irene Sherman on 2nd Avenue. She looked at me and said, 'Who are you?' I explained to Irene who I was and I once lived next door to her on First and Graehl. She didn't remember me. It seemed Irene was humble and scared at the same time, as if she lived in another world. I walked away saddened and thinking, 'Will I be like this when I get older?' — *Chris K. Sr.*

My mother was a friend to Irene and I'm sure like many others would drop her off at her home. One winter, I would say 1973 or 1974, Irene spent some of the winter months in a nursing home recovering from some injuries, and because it was close to the home we lived in that didn't have adequate heat, I would regularly visit her to get warm, but it grew to be more than that. She was not happy to be spending time in the rehab/nursing home but always seemed happy when I showed up. — *Colin C.*

In the early to mid-'60s, she lived in a shack close to the river off Hamilton Ave. Was a sad place, with much stacked everywhere. As a child if you went to her home, it was a bit scary, yet she was always nice to us. She almost froze to death one winter there in that shack. Lucky for her, people gave a DAMN. When she was not seen for a couple of days, they sent the law to check on her. Her life was far from pleasant. She had many hurdles each day. — *Mickey L.*

In 1971, turned sixty, and Peggy Goldizen of Market Basket grocery store offered her birthday wishes in icing. Every year, the bakery ensured Irene had a birthday cake, and often the news photographers were invited to snap a photo to mark the occasion. (*News-Miner* Archives)

CHAPTER 35
CHAIN OF CARE

The irreconcilable truth was that those busy feet had been stilled

Until just a few years before I met Irene at the Polaris, her memory was clear, Wally Burnett told me in July 1988. Although her recall powers had slightly diminished in her seventies, her intelligence and wit were still sharp. Dates, years and ages, she avoided. I decided to wade in and ask about her parents. She was frank, as always.

"Our parents tried to keep a tab on us pretty close, but my mother was more or less the rebellious kind. She wanted to get foot-loose from those kids. That's what caused most of the damn trouble."

"She must have felt terrible after that fire, though," I said.

"Well, she never automatically looked upon it as a crisis because she didn't realize that being . . ." Irene filled her lungs and unleashed a word torrent: "She didn't do what Dad wanted her to do!"

I still had no timeline for the years or months she spent with one parent or another, in what town, which remote cabin, anything. Her mention of J. P. sent me down that trail, asking about her father.

"Well, I used to help Dad with the dog teams and everything else. I'd sit on top of the damn sled and let them drag me for a while. And then I'd get out and help them get the sled dislodged and stuff."

"What happened to your Dad? When did he pass away?"

"Well, I guess he got into a home," she said, "and old age crept up on him and that was it."

"Was he in a Pioneer Home?"

"I don't know. I guess so," Irene said. "Well, with his family getting cut off from each other and that sort of thing, it sort of dislodged him and the like. And he got a little careless and didn't take care of himself right, and that was it. When you don't have your spouse around to see that you eat, that you're kept clean, this, that, and the other thing, you're automatically shot in the head. And Wally, you know what that means."

His response was snappy: "You got me."

Wally was Switzerland in this conversation, just letting the Queen forge ahead. He'd already cleared up that his grandmother Blanche had taken in Frances, and he confirmed that no matter what Frances did for Irene, it wasn't enough. Especially when she was drinking hard, Irene bitterly downgraded her sister's charity.

You might say that Irene expected everyone else to be as generous as she was. In the memorable words of one observer, "She'd give you the shirt off her back, all four of them."

※ ※ ※

"Was your father an old man when he died?" I probed again.

"I don't know where the heck Dad died."

"You lost track of him, too?"

"Yeah, we got separated, and Mom and I got separated. Course we should have been separated a damn sight earlier. Well, she was sort of eccentric in a way. She didn't altogether love Dad anyhow, to tell the truth. She liked getting out and partying, raising hell, and so on and so forth. And these goddamn kids was showing up every time she turned around. And that sort of put a kay-bosh to some of her ways that she wanted to live."

Once more, Irene repeated her favorite "family history in a nutshell" phrase: "And she was German-French Canadian-Scotch. And Dad was Irish-wooden-shoe-Holland-Dutch and English. He tried to chop her off on a lot of things, but he didn't do very good."

With some digging of my own, I found that J. P. Sherman, the stubborn, hard-working miner and trapper of the Totatlanika, had lived an extraordinarily long life, dying at age ninety on April 26, 1969. J. P. finished out his days at the Pioneer Home in Sitka, established as a rest home by and for the old-timers of the Yukon and Alaska gold rushes. Back then, it was the only one of its kind, and residents had to be a member of the Pioneers of Alaska to live there. I didn't imagine J. P. as a joiner. Even so, he would have had to fill out an application and list his arrival date in the territory. If that was Valdez in 1900, it would have meant sixty-six years as an Alaskan. At one time there was a minimum number of residency years to qualify as a pioneer and enter the home; now you don't even have to be a member of the Pioneers. Just one continuous year in Alaska gets you into any one of six locations, if there's room. All over the state, Pioneers of Alaska membership rolls have dwindled. My contact at the state office spoke with regret. It seems that younger people aren't as interested in this or other fraternal groups, he said. He had a hunch that J. P. had registered at Nenana Igloo No. 17, the closest to his mining claims in the Bonnifield. But at the Nenana Igloo, like those all over the state, the oldest applications were long ago destroyed by fire, flood, or sometimes just tossed. At one time, Nenana's Igloo No. 17 had its own building for meetings and entertaining, but the group eventually dissolved. The old Pioneers of Alaska building there had stood until around the turn of the new century, when at last it collapsed. The paperwork was gone.

The tattered marker on J. P. Sherman's grave lies in the Pioneers of Alaska section of Birch Hill cemetery. The land for the cemetery was once a field farmed by J. P.'s father-in-law, John Patten. (FindaGrave/arcticamy)

When J. P died in 1969, his remains were flown to Fairbanks for burial in the Pioneers section of Birch Hill. No doubt members of Igloo No. 4 had served as pallbearers and saluted the old miner. I was warmed to learn that even now, members do not forget their own.

In 2022, I'd sent a photo of J. P.'s beat-up memorial plaque to my new friend at the group's state level. "Is that a recent picture you took?" he asked. "The Pioneers have funding to replace it. We'll have a nice granite gravestone installed next summer. We can do that."

※ ※ ※

Photographer Myron Rosenberg's 1987 portrait of Irene Sherman is one of many art pieces in the hallway connecting Denali Center, the residential care facility, with Fairbanks Memorial Hospital. Printed on blank notecards, the image has sold more than a thousand copies, and even today can be found on grocery stores and gift shop card racks throughout the state. There is Irene, posing on the rooftop of Wally and Ruth Burnett's Polaris Hotel in 1987, looking directly at the camera with one hand on her thick waist. She's wearing a men's shirt with a ratty green sweater over it. Red garters hold up each sleeve. A wool blanket wrapped around her hips serves as a skirt. But her statement piece is the "I [heart] Fairbanks" button affixed to a black hat. No doubting that sentiment.

In the years before Irene was placed in residential care, Wally Burnett had ably served as Irene's friend, confidante, accountant, chauffeur, and favored nephew. However, when he was no longer able to look after her affairs, she wasn't set adrift. Others stepped up. Some in Irene's chain of care were friends; others were court-appointed helpers or professional caregivers.

Local radio personality Gayle Maloy hosted a program on KFAR in which she interviewed pioneers each week. Irene had been on more than once and was a favorite, although the station manager hovered, worried about her unleashing foul language over the airwaves. "She had a mouth on her," they said.

After getting to know Irene well, Maloy began intentionally watching for her around town. So did the owners of the Coin Shop, the Steak & Pipes, the Big I, and other places that she frequented. They'd know first if something was wrong, if Irene didn't make her rounds.

Yet, as she approached eighty, deteriorating health care issues caught up with Irene. Dementia was altering the way she interacted with her world. Redirecting her was harder. Fears of falling were in the minds of many who knew about her home place.

Finally, one day Irene did break her wrist, not at the wigwam, but in her room at the Polaris. When she was found, she had no memory of how the accident happened. Now she required skilled nursing. Irene was finally admitted into residential care at Careage North, where she met Lorraine Russell. Soon that facility became Denali Center with its connecting hallway to the hospital. Whenever Lorraine escorted Irene to a hospital appointment, she'd spy her portrait among the artworks and warmly erupt, "Hey, that's me!"

In this stage of her life, Irene could not have had a better friend than Lorraine, who nearly forty years later still remembered the Irene days with affection. She credited the entire caregiver team for helping extend Irene's life, keeping her warm, fed, and as happy as possible.

"She was very challenging, because she lived . . . ," Lorraine hesitated. "You always worried that someone would take advantage of her or something, but you couldn't keep her contained. You'd like to have her stay in the building, but she would have no part of that.

"That would have been the first time I worked with Irene in care, and then over time, they petitioned and got her a guardian. The Office of Public Advocacy started looking after her. Some did a good job and some did not-such-a-good job."

Lorraine had first met Irene in 1977, right after her move to Fairbanks from the East Coast to attend the University of Alaska. "I happened to be downtown looking for some gifts to send to friends, and I ran into her in the Coin Store on Second Avenue."

"What was your first reaction?" I asked, remembering my own when I first met her.

Popular notecards featuring Irene are still sold by photographer Myron Rosenberg through his website and in shops around the Alaska. For Irene's caregiving team at Denali Center, they were a useful tool. (Tricia Brown)

"It was a little startling, and she certainly liked her curse words," she said. "But she was very friendly. She kind of latched onto me, called me Kid, talked to me in her Irene fashion. I remember her telling me she was the Queen of Fairbanks."

A couple of years later, Lorraine's parents visited, and as tourists, they met the Queen face-to-face at the Steak & Pipes restaurant. Irene was working the crowd, going table to table to say hello and chat. Sometimes she didn't make any sense, Lorraine said, so if there was a lag in conversation, or nobody offered a beer, she'd move on to another table. If a pitcher was tipped, well, all the more reason to stick around and offer some Fairbanks history, cold-weather stories, mining stories. Lorraine's father, a New York Police Department captain, took the bait and bought her a beer. She fascinated him for as long as she stayed, until she up and moved to the next table. It was memorable visit for the cheechakos. "I don't think she recognized me," Lorraine remembered, somewhat relieved.

Little more than a decade later, by 1990, Lorraine had assumed the role of Irene's social worker and primary caregiver, an important player in the series of people who formed her safety net.

"There always seemed to be like this patchwork quilt of people, many of them longtime Fairbanksans who would kind of step up in one manner or another," Lorraine remembered. "I remember Wally Burnett, and there was a connection. I think when that ended, I wanna say that Jerry Cleworth stepped in—he was on the city council, the coin store guy."

With the natural attrition that happens in cities, the places on Irene's rounds were drying up. "I think she was kinda left on her own," Lorraine said. "Nerland's furniture store closed down, Steak & Pipes went away, there was the Coin Shop. The downtown bars over the years got destroyed. It kinda coincided with Irene, because of medical problems, really losing her ability to continue her lifestyle. The Big I continued. I think she got her beer and food there."

After Irene broke her wrist in 1990, poor Wally realized that even the Polaris was not safe for her. But to get Irene into skilled residential nursing care, he'd have to formally evict her so she'd be homeless in the legal sense. Those who knew Wally also knew how heartbroken he was. But once Irene gained admittance, she was in good hands with Lorraine.

The years leading up to Denali Center had been rough, not only for Wally, who was no quitter, but also for the city and many others who'd kept an eye on her. Irene had begun trespassing, even shoplifting, and upsetting people around town. In Wally's hotel, she'd accused a tourist of stealing from her in a loud and very public encounter. She'd become incontinent and was soiling the lobby chairs. She was speaking senselessly in what one social worker called "word salad," her speech more aggressive than ever and salted with hostility. Wally's business suffered.

Irene had undergone surgery for skin cancer on her face and more recently survived a bout of colon cancer, all while her cognitive abilities were diminishing. A psychiatrist diagnosed her with paranoid schizophrenia with increasing paranoia, along with dementia.

Talking with Lorraine, I wondered aloud about strange questions that I'm sure others had pondered, too. For one, what was the condition of Irene's feet after thousands of miles slogging around in ill-fitting, hand-me-down footwear?

"A lot of times they were men's boots and could have been different sizes," Lorraine said. "I remember her feet being small and tough. Under all those layers, she was small."

We talked about the skin grafts that were taken from her father, J. P. Sherman, just a week after the fire, and that the procedure was done right there in a frontier hospital . . . way back in 1916! I recalled the newspaper reports about the innocent little girl that began that year. Interest never waned as the papers went from blaring "Irene Sherman on the edge of death" to "Little burn victim is holding on" to "She will recover." And that was her second brush with death. There was the time she had nearly frozen at age two.

"Even as a young child, and whatever else she endured prior to that . . . her *tenacious* nature," Lorraine said with admiration in her voice. "She would talk about Seattle and the nuns, and her face. Her face always hurt. You don't get burned that badly without . . . It hurts in the cold. We would put different creams on it. But I just think she had chronic pain from it years and years after."

Clearly, Irene's relationship with Lorraine was complex, a melding of both professional social worker and intensely personal friend. Lorraine was not satisfied with using medications to make her job easier. She would not watch Irene finish her last months or years sitting quietly or napping, no longer a "nuisance."

"She defied all of the traditional rules," Lorraine said. "We spent quite a lot of time about what to do and how to do it. It was the day when congregate care was heavily hitting people with psychotropic medications, and that wasn't going to work. It didn't make a difference. In my opinion, it took away part of her. And we just said, 'We're done with this. We're not going there.'"

Lorraine and her team came up with creative ideas to meet Irene's needs, especially her powerful desire to get outside and walk. There was the time when Lorraine and a coworker signed up themselves plus Irene in a charity walk. The trick was suggesting to their patient that she was going to be in a parade. The old woman was still physically strong, thanks to all those years of getting around on foot. She couldn't be tamed, no matter what, and they understood that. So they used their wits to allow freedom while protecting her. That morning, crowds gathered in the J. C. Penney parking lot, and Irene was getting lots of attention, back among people who knew her as the Queen. Then the walkers headed down Cushman to First and west along the river to the finish celebration at Alaskaland, as the city's Pioneer Park was then called. Irene was loving it. At the park, they were milling around and enjoying the day when suddenly Irene made a beeline toward the Chena River. Lorraine's associate had stepped in to use the restroom, so poor Lorraine was on her own.

"I'm trying to turn her around and cajole her," Lorraine remembered. "She wasn't going to have any part of that. She got angry. She turned around and started to beat me up!" Looking back, what annoyed Lorraine most was that a couple of Alaskaland grounds workers stood by, just watching and laughing, enjoying the show. Right then, Irene's second caregiver appeared, and together they managed to redirect and calm the old woman.

When Irene was still somewhat new to residential care, with the support of her doctor, the team's action plan was to make good use of those blank note cards with Irene's portrait on them.

"In order to keep her safe, but let the town know who to call, we got a bunch of those Myron Rosenberg cards, and we wrote out a little blurb with our phone number," Lorraine said. "We followed her for a while to see what she would do. Red lights and things, Irene had that down. It was still connected: when to go, when to stop."

When Irene left the facility for a walkabout, a Rosenberg photo notecard hung on a lanyard around her neck. Inside was a handwritten message: "Irene Sherman now lives at Denali Center. As summer is here, Irene would like to return to her familiar street routines. We expect that she will be frequenting the downtown area and businesses." And while Irene was not "as robust as she once was," the note said, Denali Center was trying to "maintain that difficult balance which recognizes Irene's lifelong habits, yet keeps her as safe as possible."

The message appealed to business owners, asking them to pay attention if she visited. If she seemed distressed, would they please call Denali Center's nursing station? If she wanted to go back to Denali Center, would they please call her a cab? Fare would be paid upon arrival. The note finished with phone numbers for Irene's court-appointed guardian and for Lorraine at Denali.

That worked for a while. But in increasing numbers, some locals were less tolerant as Irene's behavior declined. By 1991, someone might call the police to have her gently escorted away, like the time she joined a business meeting, taking a seat at the conference table and injecting nonsense commentary. Or folks might report at which intersection she could be found sitting in the grass, wet and cold. Once a family saw her outside their apartment building at an odd time, hours after she should have been back at Denali Center. They knew who to call. If not the police, then her caregivers would come.

"Eventually she ended up unable to manage," Lorraine said. She remembered getting calls from the Alaska Department of Health and Social Services, and realized Irene was in a new phase: unaware that she was no longer safe. "Early, when we made the cards and she did her thing, I think we let down some of our professional boundaries to recognize and appreciate who she was," Lorraine said. "I was very fond of her, as were a lot of people in her care team. So while you have to retain your professional boundaries, Irene had no boundaries, so . . ."

Irene's team also knew that seeing friends was always good for her, inside or outside the facility. People continued to stop by—she was not forgotten. Talking with Lorraine by phone in 2022, our conversation turned back to that 1987 Rosenberg portrait in the hallway from Denali Center to Fairbanks Memorial. I'd recently bought one of the blank notecards of Rosenberg's in the greeting card aisle of my Anchorage grocery store. I gazed at Irene's placid expression. "She looks so poised and relaxed, almost at peace."

Irene's old friend and caregiver had a different take. "For all of her challenges and sadness in her life, she was really just very— I wouldn't say at peace, because there was a fire in her—but I think she looked forward to every day."

※ ※ ※

In September 1992, Georgerene was living in Santa Ana, California, and about to write Irene a letter. How long had she stalled and what had actually stirred her into action? Her kids say she knew about Irene, but they'd never even talked by phone, let alone met in person. Years after Irene's magazine profile was published in 1988, Georgerene had found a copy and learned more details. Now she was acting.

How does one write such a letter to a stranger, especially without knowing their address? Georgerene threw out a wide net, writing to the top man in the Fairbanks postal service. Dated September 14, her letter traveled 3,300 miles before it landed on the desk of J. C. Thomas, postmaster and operations manager. She had enclosed a second letter— one for Irene Sherman's eyes—and asked if anyone there knew of her. Was there some way he could get that letter to her? Georgerene signed her missive "Pauline Agnes Sherman."

Immediately, Postmaster Thomas sat down and wrote back, beginning with "Dear Ms. Sherman." It was one of the few times that Georgerene had been addressed by her birth name as an adult. "Today I received your letter requesting that a letter be delivered to your sister, Irene Sherman," Thomas wrote. "We do know where Irene is and I will personally carry the letter to her place of residence.

"Irene is well known in Fairbanks," he continued. "When I was a letter carrier, I delivered mail to her home. Enclosed are two articles from our local newspaper that will give you some idea of how she is faring these days. She has been living at the Denali Center for about two years." He noted the center's address and added a final "I hope that this is helpful to you."

That letter was the beginning in a series of poignant discoveries for Georgerene. Yes, Irene was still alive. She had reached out in time from that perspective. But no, Irene probably wouldn't know who she was. Dementia had robbed the old woman of most memories. Postmaster J. C. Thomas was good for his word, and personally brought the mail to Denali Center, to Lorraine Russell. Now armed with an address, Georgerene sent Irene another letter, and another. Finally, Lorraine's response informed Georgerene of harsh reality in the kindest way. She began, "Dear Pauline."

"I'm writing for your sister Irene. We received several of the letters you have sent to Fairbanks, and are very happy to hear that Irene has family. I work with Irene as her social worker. She is a patient at Denali Center, which is an extended care facility here in Fairbanks. Irene has lived at Denali Center for the past two years. She has several medical problems which make living independently no longer possible or safe for her. Irene led a very active and unique lifestyle. She is a legend here in Fairbanks. Somewhere in her life the title Queen of Fairbanks was given to Irene and she is widely known as this.

"Irene came to Denali Center after being in the local hospital for several reasons. She had broken her wrist, was losing weight, and was unable to care safely for her needs or herself. She is experiencing symptoms of dementia, which was recently diagnosed as Alzheimer's type.

This has caused a gradual loss of intellect, memory, and language skills. Presently Irene needs a high level of supervision and guidance from staff. Her physical condition is

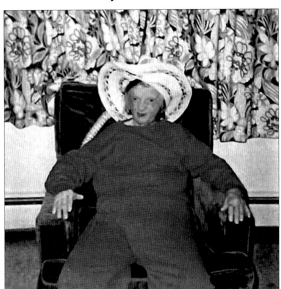

Lorraine Russell snapped a Polaroid of Irene on November 30, 1992, to mail to Georgerene. The old woman was down to one layer of clothing. She was warm, well-fed, and unconcerned about her old home place. (Lorraine Russell Photo/Moore Family Collection)

good. She is strong and [has] no other major medical problems. I have read your letter to Irene many times since it arrived. She listens intently and remarked you are 'a good egg.' This is very much how Irene describes things for as long as I have known her, which is approximately the past ten years. She also has read parts of your letter out loud to me and I keep a copy in her room.

"I hope this news is not too sad for you. I think it's great that you thought of Irene and sought her. I'm enclosing a picture of Irene as well as copies of newspaper pictures from years past. Irene has been featured in the news, at least one book also enclosed, and on a card. She also posed for an oil painting."

Russell had sent a series of three Polaroids showing a much thinner Irene in sweatpants and a pullover sweatshirt, all in red and only one layer. In one picture, she's lifting her hand in a wave; in another, she's wearing a flouncy wide-brimmed hat and even a trace of lipstick. She looks slightly vacant, but clean and content.

Lorraine continued: "Irene is fondly a part of Fairbanks history and well looked after at Denali Center. . . . Please write and tell me your family history so I can share your memories with Irene. Have a wonderful holiday, Pauline. Lorraine Russell, Social Worker."

※ ※ ※

Linden Staciokas knew about Irene, because who didn't if you lived in late twentieth-century Fairbanks? Linden had seen the bag lady around town for years, well before she became personally involved in Irene's life as the latest in a series of state-appointed guardians and conservators. By the summer of 1992, the declining, elderly woman had been at Denali Center for two years, unaware and/or unconcerned about what was happening at 740 Front Street. Wasn't it time to make good on Les Nerland's promise to transfer the land to the borough?

The city and borough were ready to finish the bridge and road that would require demolishing Irene's former home. More important, the structure's roof had caved in during one heavy snow year. The decaying piles and everything around them were now a public health hazard. Teenagers were making it an adventure destination.

It was time to tear down the wigwam. But the next essential question was, *What was inside?* Were there genuine treasures amid the trash? Did she have a stash of gold from the mining days with her dad? What had she done with all the finds she'd brought home that actually might have value?

On July 10, 1992, Linden legally waived her client's claim to the property, officially dropping the flag for demolition. Irene was oblivious to the decision that many viewed as right and necessary, despite their misgivings about the real action that was coming. Bulldozing the house that Les Nerland had constructed for Irene—clearing the lot completely —would mean the borough could go forward with building the road to the Island Homes subdivision.

When Lorraine Russell learned that the property transfer was a go, she asked Irene if she wanted to go over and gather up some belongings. Irene refused. She just didn't care anymore. In the two years that she'd been living at Denali Center, she had disconnected. The idea of the home place coming down had no emotional response.

Even so, Irene had friends who thought it was important for the city to move at a slower pace. On Thursday, July 16, at 740 Front Street, emotions had ratcheted up between 9:00 A.M. and 2:00 P.M. Neighbors stood in the street, agitated or saddened, but avidly watching. Some friends mobilized. A group advocating for Irene went to court requesting a delay in the demolition action. They wanted more time to sift through the debris for valuables. However, before Superior Court Judge Jay Hodges could even schedule a hearing, the city's Public Works Department and the Fairbanks North Star Borough voluntarily pushed the hold button.

Earlier in the week, a few neighbors who'd known Irene for decades had already crept inside her home and collected a few items, fearful that they'd be lost forever. One woman found some antique mining tools, photos, and newspapers. She told the *News-Miner*, "I say it's history; they say it's garbage."

One of those who wanted to slow things down was Karen J. Erickson, who early on had made an appeal directly to Linden Staciokas, Irene's guardian/conservator, writing, "It is my feeling there is much Fairbanks memorabilia and ephemera to be uncovered with a little commitment. Irene's clothing, hats, pins, Olympia beer mugs are

On June 25, Marty Russell-Hade was among those trying to rescue anything salvageable from Irene's place. Vandals had been exploring the property, alarming neighbors and friends. Demolition was on the horizon. (*News-Miner* Archives)

all items which should be put on display at the Pioneer Museum or other designated area."

Karen Erickson agreed with Linden that the property truly was a public health hazard, dangerous and ever more attractive to kids as a creepy, abandoned home, but she wanted a few more months to catalog anything salvageable.

Linden was not the bad guy in this scenario, but she did have to make tough, unpopular decisions. In preparation, Linden had made three advance trips to Irene's place to find anything worth keeping. She'd contacted the University of Alaska Archives and invited them to send someone to look for salvageable items. Also, she'd checked in with Lorraine. Since Irene had moved into Denali Center in 1990, Irene had come over with Lorraine on occasion, looking around and grabbing a few things. Most of the time, it was junk.

"We would go by there and she would disappear," Lorraine remembered some forty years later. "It was like a hobbit hole. I went in, too . . . it was a bunch of blankets and tarps, and it was very low, so you kinda had to hunker down to get in the main part." While Irene allowed Lorraine to go into the tarp-covered outdoor space, she never went inside the actual frame building that Les Nerland had built.

"[Her home] was a place to be reckoned with," Lorraine remembered. "Here Irene would come out with bad, smelly things and bring them back [to Denali], and we'd have to slowly get them from her and eventually throw them away. Sometimes it was old, nasty deteriorating clothing, one time it was photos, which we helped her keep. I just remember the odor."

Lorraine made a scrapbook of Irene's pictures and copies of newspaper clippings, including many of the birthday celebrations Irene loved so well. Each year there had been a round of pictures with friends and a cake from Peggy Goldizen at Gavora Mall's Market Basket. "She had her sheet cake every year," Lorraine said, "long after Gavora's went out of business."

That red scrapbook of memories that Lorraine assembled would become Irene's lifeline to the past. "It was calming for her, like when she was in a bad mood or something, we'd say, 'Hey, give her the red book,'" Lorraine said. "Then she connected, 'cause the long-term stuff does stay with you even when the short-term goes away."

The next day, *News-Miner* reporter Lin Gale filed her story, writing, "Besides the old wooden cart Sherman pulled around town to do her collecting, and a pile of 1955 newspapers, Staciokas pulled little from the rubble. It consisted mostly of old timbers, empty beer cans, and plastic shopping bags."

Even with all of the preambles to demolition day, when the backhoe arrived on Front Street on Thursday, July 16, Linden was taken off guard by the speed with which the city and borough had responded. Neighbors gathered to watch, horrified at what was happening to the landmark that had stood among them for so long. The bystanders wondered aloud if Irene knew what was happening, and what she'd do if she knew. One man said, "I thought she'd be back. I now know that Irene will never be back."

Linden waved at the backhoe operator to please pause. Could she look through the boxes that had just been uncovered? As in other searches, most of what she found was rotting. Over the previous days, Linden had conferred with Lorraine at Denali Center, and had gathered a box of things that Irene might like. She'd already dropped them off.

Naturally, in speaking of the gold-miner's daughter, there were those who speculated, "Where's the gold?" And the collectibles. It had to be an archival treasure trove in there. As Karen Erickson had written to Linden, "[Irene's] living situation is certainly not conventional but her 'collecting' habits over the last forty years deserve more respect than what the scoop of a bulldozer can offer."

"She was not a museum curator," Linden told the newspaper. They found no gold. Or, perhaps Irene had conformed to the habits of other miners, tucking her poke and nuggets into a Hills Brothers coffee can and burying it in the dirt beneath her feet. Had that happened? Friends say probably not. There were only the stacks of stinking, rotten debris with narrow pathways between them. Walking on stuff to get to stuff. What once may have had some value, no longer did. As for the supposed gold stash, whatever she and her father had mined in Healy

The July 19, 1992, issue of the paper delivered the stark news. For some, it was welcome; others protested through the courts. (*News-Miner* Archives)

very likely had stayed with him. J. P. Sherman would have sold or spent whatever was left of his assets before admittance to the Pioneer Home in Sitka. There he spent his last days dying in 1969. J. P. now rested up on Birch Hill.

On Friday, the court appeal to delay demolition was denied. One of Irene's supporters told the paper, "All I wanted was a week. They wouldn't give it to us. I'd die a happy woman thinking I'd saved some of Irene's treasures . . ." Back at Denali Center, Irene was her benignly happy self, barking out her hellos and wearing only one layer of clean clothes per day on a form that was much smaller. She still liked her hats though. A poster on her wall read, "My Room. My Mess. My Business."

By Sunday the mess at the wigwam was gone.

Irene Sherman was eighty-four years old when she passed away in her sleep at Denali Center on February 20, 1995. Her Old Man Upstairs had finally taken a notion. Once again, she made front-page news.

"I was glad that she didn't die, cold, in the middle of her hobbit hole," said Lorraine, who knew Irene best in this final chapter. "Some of our care team had actually grown up in Fairbanks, so they had that connection of Irene always being a part of Fairbanks." Those friends were tearful as they packed up Irene's remaining things, her "My Room. My Mess. My Business" poster, her red scrapbook, her hat collection, now manageable. And together they made decisions about what Irene would wear in her casket.

"I'm pretty sure we bought what she wore," Lorraine told me. "I'm pretty sure we tried to be true to her. Lots of layers, a hat, she always had her beer stein, I think that went with her. By those days, many of the core group, like Wally [Burnett], the Nerlands, and stuff, they were pretty much out of the picture. It didn't really pass on to the next generation." And yet both Lorraine and I knew that there were others, so many others, individuals behind front doors, local storefronts, city hall, and borough, state, and federal letterhead, who ensured that Irene's long walk ended well.

"You couldn't be so boxed into the medical model to be successful with her," Lorraine said. "Enjoying the end of life, it's an important goal for every patient. We kept her safe. I think her life extended to three more years because of us." The damaged little girl had grown into an independent woman who'd left an indelible mark on a gold camp town. In tribute, City

As scarred as Irene's hands were, first from the fire, and then by multiple surgeries through the years, she remained surprisingly strong. (Erik Hill/*Anchorage Daily News*)

Public Works Director Dave Jacoby deemed it appropriate to reopen the pioneer Clay Street Cemetery for one last casket burial come spring. That "damn brat" burn victim Mary Porter was there at Clay Street, too, among the men, women, and children, most from other places in the world, who rode out the highs and lows of building a frontier city.

Because Irene died in February, the Queen's remains would be stored until spring, when the ground had thawed enough for burial.

When Irene passed, it seemed everybody in town was talking about what a survivor she was, how tough she was, how she was the blood and bone of Fairbanks. People shared stories about their own encounters with her, Irene's unusual ways, her loud speech, her love of Olympia beer, and her hatred of errant rocks. The irreconcilable truth was that those busy feet had been stilled.

Somebody called Frances Burnett in California for a word to include in the obit. Frances remembered Irene as "a very loving and thoughtful woman. She was a very big-hearted lady," she offered. By then, Frances herself was in decline, too, and travel wasn't possible.

A few days after Irene's death, Denali Center hosted a memorial service officiated by the hospital's Catholic chaplain, Father Joseph

Laudwein. Following the well-attended gathering, friends stayed for a root beer float reception and made much of Irene in their conversations. Meanwhile, Denali Center also began accepting public donations for a proper headstone. A local named Lynn Hilton drummed up support, too, sending the *News-Miner* a letter to the editor with an appeal titled "A Gift for Queenie." Hilton's letter asked, "How many have ever seen Irene enjoying lunch with the girls, shopping leisurely at Nordstrom's, driving a sports car, getting her hair and nails done, bowling, skating, buying a pretty pair of summer sandals? Don't you get the feeling even the ordinary things passed Irene by?

"I ,for one want her to have something brand new (not secondhand or second-class) to call 'mine.' Her very own for once: the prettiest headstone in the Clay Street Cemetery. . . .

"Anyone and everyone who ever shunned, ridiculed, or made hurting remarks to her owes her this kind and last consideration."

Contributions for Irene's bronze marker came in from all over; city volunteers oversaw the installation. (Tricia Brown)

In conclusion, Hilton wrote, "This is how I think of Irene: the happiest people seem to be those who have no particular cause for being happy except the fact they are so."

Months later, once the Clay Street Cemetery ground had sufficiently thawed, Irene's burial was scheduled for 2:00 P.M. on Monday, May 8. Father Terrill Heaps and Sister Mary Soucy, CSJ, led the graveside prayers before Irene's simple coffin was lowered. I wasn't there. But reading about it, looking at pictures thirty years later, I remembered that interview with Irene, how she'd leaped to her feet when Father Heaps came into the Black Angus restaurant. "I'm one of you!" she'd exclaimed. I was warmed to hear that after the graveside service some old friends met up at the Big I bar to tell stories and toast the chapel girl.

Within weeks, Irene's resting place was identified with a lovely bronze marker reading: "Irene Sherman, 'Queen of Fairbanks' 1911-1995, God Be With You Until We Meet Again." Dozens had pooled their donations to purchase a marker that was laid by volunteers from the city's Public Works Department.

Cycling through my own Irene remembrances, I recalled a long-ago conversation when she told me how she heated her home with wood or coal (just as her parents had so long ago and others still did). In that moment, I flashed on the image of her very flammable hovel. How reluctant I was to ask Irene the hardest question in my reporter's notebook. In the end, it came out naturally: "But Irene, aren't you afraid of a fire?"

The old woman drew herself up. She had her private fears, I was certain, but right now she was maintaining her public face as a no-holds-barred Alaskan.

"Oh, hell, that don't worry me none!" she spat impatiently. "Now, listen!" Irene raised a scarred, upward-pointing finger in my face. "I am extra careful! I don't have any fires that's out of hand. I believe in keeping my fires down to a minimum, or less than a minimum!" And with that, the subject was closed.

So when I learned that conservator Linden Staciokas had asked Irene a similar question toward the end of her life, I was curious. What was her answer to "Are you ever afraid?"

"I will never forget what Irene cackled," Linden told me. "She said, '*Lady, fire got in a fight with me once, and I won.*'"

※ ※ ※

Georgerene never did get to meet Irene in person. But three years after Irene's death, their paths actually crossed in a bizarre, almost supernatural way. It was in 1998, not long after Georgerene had had hip replacement surgery. Her kids told me that she'd always had a mindset to fight back against infirmity, even when her body said to slow down. So after surgery, even though she lived at elevation, Georgerene would grab her walker and set off down the draw to town. It was her self-prescribed physical therapy with spiritual benefits.

"I usually pray when I'm walking," she told her kids, "that Jesus would send someone good to stop and pick me up."

One day a couple did stop as Georgerene crept along the shoulder with her walker. As usual, she was wearing her big, bulky green wool coat. She had combed her hair back from her face. She was eleven years younger than Irene, now seventy-six years old, yet there was very little gray in her hair.

A car pulled over, the window came down, and a woman asked, *Can we give you a ride?* Georgerene cheerfully accepted and learned that the couple was fairly new to the area, having recently retired.

Driving down the draw, the woman kept stealing looks at Georgerene. Finally, she asked, "By any chance, do you have a sister in Fairbanks?" Surprised, Georgerene replied, "Why, yes, I did, but I never met her." The resemblance between the sisters was so strong, it was impossible to ignore. As they conversed, Georgerene was astonished to learn that the couple had retired here from Fairbanks. And that back in Alaska, this woman had once been on Irene's care team.

That night, she shared her shocking story with John and Michelle. How was it even possible? Days later, they all met at a local steakhouse for dinner: the Fairbanks couple, Georgerene, her son and his wife, and their two boys. They marveled at the strange and wonderful circumstances and took pictures together. In the photos, someone whose face is off camera is holding a decade-old copy of *Heartland* with my Irene story inside.

Photos from that evening were stored in the same box of memorabilia that held original letters from the Fairbanks postmaster and Lorraine Russell. Georgerene had tucked them away, and her kids hadn't touched the box. It had been years since her death.

Who were those people who'd stopped to pick up Georgerene along the road? There were no names on the photos, and after all this

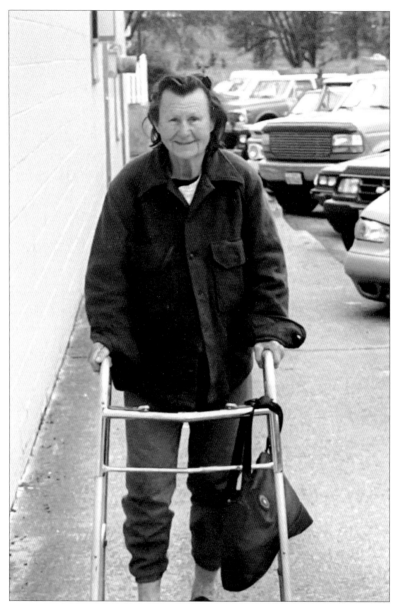

Georgerene and her signature baggy coat became a familiar sight to the people of Kamiah, Idaho, as she determined to bounce back after hip surgery. (Moore Family Collection)

time, John and Michelle couldn't remember. Looking into the woman's face, I first wondered if this was Lorraine Russell, who'd written those gentle letters in response to Georgerene's query. I hadn't yet located her and I wouldn't for months to come. When I did find her, I texted Loretta the retired lady's photo and asked, "Is this you?" No, she said, but she'd try to reach back in time for a name.

I made private inquiries around Fairbanks and shared the picture with many long-timers, still making no ground. I'd already decided against blasting the private photo on a Facebook page, although that might have delivered a fast answer. Everyone who stared at the photo said the same thing: "She looks so familiar." But no one had an answer. I showed it to a member of the Pioneers of Alaska. Nope. Lorraine came back saying she thought the woman had been a certified nursing assistant at Denali, but couldn't say for sure.

I sent the picture to a former columnist at the *News-Miner*. He'd been a copy editor and had written a "hometown" column. His wife had worked with me in features. Between them, they knew everybody. Yet neither one had a name for the retired woman from Fairbanks. My former coworker wrote back: "She looks so familiar. . . . I don't recognize anyone in the photo, except for Irene."

Of course that was not Irene in the photo. It was Pauline Agnes Sherman, aka Georgerene Irene Coover Moore, a dead ringer minus the burn scars.

Georgerene died six years after Irene, on June 12, 2001, in Orofino, Idaho. *Interesting place for the death of a gold-miner's daughter*, I thought. In Spanish, Orofino means "fine gold."

CHAPTER 36
THE ROAD HOME - Fairbanks 2022
So many spilled tears watering that land

Driving nearly four hundred miles to Fairbanks for Golden Days, I think about how empty the city seemed as my father, stepmom, and my outrageous, gold-digging sister were all resting up at Northern Lights Cemetery. My aunt and uncle who'd transplanted here from Guam in the early 1970s had retired Outside and she'd passed away, too; other siblings, their kids, and grandkids were scattered around Alaska and beyond. Inside, Outside, but (thank goodness) no more Morningside.

It wasn't just me. Golden Days, especially the Grande Parade, wasn't the same for Fairbanks people of certain generations, who used to watch for their flashy, layered-up Queen to bestow us, her subjects, with love as she wheeled by on her trike. Still, even though the colors are slightly dimmer for me, my love for this city and its enlarged sense of community is unchanged. Here I find my place among old friends who drag me out of history and into the present, where I do actually live. I've reserved a booth space for the Street Fair again this year. Tomorrow I'll be setting up a tent canopy with my back to the First Family statue in Golden Heart Plaza, ready to meet my readers and sign books. I'm keenly aware that in 1988 I posed Irene for a photo on that very spot.

Driving north from Anchorage, I slow and park on the shoulder of a lonely stretch that didn't even exist until 1971, the year that the Anchorage–Fairbanks Highway opened. The road has a number—Alaska Highway 3—but as visitors soon learn around here, people refer to the highways by their names, not their numbers. It was renamed the Parks Highway, or the Parks. Roughly paralleling the Alaska Railroad tracks, the road honored former Governor George Parks, one of the many territorial officials through the years who knew Irene on a first-name basis. Tourists would be hard-pressed to call all of the Parks' road-miles a "highway." It's mostly two lanes, with occasional passing lanes, beginning in more urban areas then wending from one climate zone to another, from Southcentral Alaska to the Interior, from the "banana belt"

It's hard to capture Denali's scale and grandeur in a photo, but on good days, Parks Highway drivers can view it from the road. Better still is this view from above. For J. P. and Irene, Denali was a neighbor. (Tricia Brown)

to the too-cold in winters, too-hot in summers, center of the state. In summer, fuchsia-colored fireweed rises brilliantly against birches that are still standing, but blackened, following a not-that-long-ago fire north of Willow. Further on, on good days, Denali looms in my windshield when conditions are right. Watch for moose; watch for caribou; watch for "'Bagos," as all RVs are called in the generic use of Winnebagos.

North of Healy, I pause at roadside for some landscape pictures: patches of scraggly black spruce poking out of dwarf willows, and in the middle distance, Jumbo Dome, supposedly shaped like an elephant's head. Not far from here, Agnes Sherman had stumbled through the snow for more than thirty hours, leading to the death of her baby, Jeanette, and Irene's near-death. Not far from here, J. P. had "rattled rocks" and extracted unknown amounts of gold, and nineteen-year- old Irene had joined him in mining and trapping. Where the Shermans had lived at Healy Forks, passing railroaders had chucked rocks at a big boulder near their cabin, aggravating Irene enough to pick up a shovel and bury the boulder rather than risk life, or at least a broken window, from a ricocheting rock.

Another sixty-three miles north, I stop again at the Nenana train depot along the Tanana River. I cup a hand over my eyes and squint upriver at the railroad bridge, knowing that beyond its footings there once was an Athabascan village and the log buildings of St. Mark's Mission dormitory and hospital, where Agnes had given birth to at least two children. Built on a cut bank of the fast-moving Tanana, it was now all gone, sloughed into the river or washed away in successive floods. Even the mission cemetery was gone. Only the log church of St. Mark's Episcopal survived, rescued early and moved into town. Irene had married there, a short walk from the train depot.

On the north side of the railroad bridge, the spot where in July 1923, President Warren G. Harding had driven the Golden Spike is now on private land. Walking up there is discouraged for lots of reasons. At the depot, Alaska Railroad trains no longer stop for passengers. Inside I find a museum that a small town can be proud of, cared for by railroad enthusiasts who accept donations to keep it going. I look around at the glowing, refinished wooden ticket counters, benches, and wainscoting. This was the very waiting room where Agnes Sherman and Red Cross nurse Dorothy Sleichter, along with two-year-old Pauline and one-year-old Richard, had lingered in December 1924 before boarding the government railroad for their final trip to leave Alaska. Outside for good.

Time to drive farther north. An hour later, I am in Fairbanks and parking near the gates of the old pioneer cemetery. There I rendezvous with Janet Richardson, a deeply committed volunteer with the city's Clay Street Cemetery Commission. Janet and I had started talking by phone and email more than a year earlier, when I was trying to locate the burial places of the Sherman children. The graves were unmarked, she'd told me. That was also true for the grave of that sweet-voiced neighbor girl, Mary Porter, who'd died shortly after the 1916 cabin fire. Yet, they were not the only unmarked burials in the files. Throughout the last century, markers by the dozens had been carried away or destroyed in any one among a series of annual Breakup floods created by ice dams. Additionally, there were catastrophic floods in 1937, 1948, 1960, 1963,

The landmark Jumbo Dome was visible from roadside at one of my stops near Healy. J. P.'s claims were east of today's Parks Highway, on the Totatlanika and the Platt; others lay in the Susitna Valley. (Tricia Brown)

1964, and finally the 1967 flood that people are still talking about. That's not to mention continuing damage at the cemetery by vandals and routinely severe elements.

Nonetheless, locations of Mary's and Jeanette's graves were recorded in the Clay Street Cemetery books. In one of our talks, Janet declared she could do something about those two missing markers. She had a working list for replacement headstones, and she moved up the names of the Sherman infant and the little Porter girl who'd died just two years apart. Using funds from city bed taxes and private donations, Cemetery Commission volunteers operated ground-penetrating radar and used probes to identify the edges of their graves. They had reset the two new stones just days before I arrived, so I could see them for myself. Honoring these innocents. It is gratifying to trace their names etched

The pioneer Clay Street Cemetery was closed to casket burials many decades before Irene's death, but the city of Fairbanks allowed one more in 1995—one last honor for Irene. (Tricia Brown)

in stone, making the children yet more real to me.

I take photos and try to imagine the physical labor required for those winter burials. It is impossible. As we wander over to Irene's grave, Janet tells me they haven't yet located the grave of her little brother who died in the fire, baby James Day Sherman, but he is on their list, too. She has an idea of where to look. More ground imaging would be required. I read and reread Irene's headstone, pull dandelions, and think about those kind people who'd loved her and propped her up through the years. I thought about others who saw her as a tourist attraction and posed with her for a photo, the ways her clipped compliments probably did make somebody's day, and how her closest friends at Denali Center had so conscientiously chosen her burial clothes to suit her fashion tastes. I flash back to a story I'd heard from ninety-year-old Ron Davis, who'd worked alongside Les Nerland at his home furnishings store for fifteen years. As vice president, Ron's office was right next to Les's, so Ron couldn't miss the times Irene tromped past his door to see her benefactor Of course, Ron could also easily hear everything she said, loud and clear. One time Irene dropped in as Les was preparing to go. He and Mildred were heading to Hawaii.

"Well, while you're there, could you get somethin' for me?" Irene demanded. "I want a couple of those moo-moos . . . no, make it three, three moo-moos, alright?"

Les agreed and was good for his word. Irene's face lit with delight on the day he handed over her presents. But later that same day she was back at Nerland's, striding past Ron Davis's door in a hurry, as always. He couldn't help but hear what she had to say.

"You know, I really liked two of those moo-moos," she said to Les, "but that third one? It made me look tacky."

How Les managed to keep a straight face, nobody knows. In Ron's office next door, people had their hands over their mouths.

※ ※ ※

I drive by Birch Hill Cemetery, the land that John and Minnie Patten had briefly farmed decades before it became a cemetery. Oversized gold stars of the Big Dipper emblazon the property's steep hillside along the Steese Highway. The Pioneers of Alaska section and J. P. Sherman's grave is somewhere up toward the hilltop. I recall that long-ago dispute between J. P.'s father-in-law, John Patten, and the disgruntled worker who'd threatened his life and demanded payment, walking him through the field with a gun at his back.

In downtown Fairbanks, I cruise by what used to be the Polaris Hotel on the corner of Second and Lacey Street, still the tallest building in town at 134 feet. Its eleven stories were once topped by a rooftop aurora-viewing deck and the elegant Tiki Cove restaurant; on the ground floor, the Black Angus Steak House, where I'd met up with Irene and Wally Burnett a long time ago. For years Wally had ensured his unofficial aunt had a second home—with maid service—waiting up there on the ninth floor. The hotel closed in 2000, and little more than a decade later, it was condemned. The Polaris was standing, but in grave decline in 2016 when Wally passed away at age eighty-six. During this

John and Michelle Moore, Georgerene's son and daughter-in-law, carried on her desire to find family. (Moore Family Collection)

trip in 2022, the Polaris had few flaws on the outside as it still dominated the skyline, but its days were numbered. Inside, the once-luxurious rooms and restaurants were in ruins. The concrete "high-rise" was slated fo demolition, with many locals protesting the loss of this landmark. My heart drops a little as I park nearby and take a good look and a few photos before she's gone. I had invited John and Michelle along on this trip, because July means Golden Days, but they were unable to get away from jobs and other family duties. I imagined them joining me at the Fairbanks Community Museum, asking them to stand during my scheduled history talk about Irene and her lost siblings.

I thought they'd relish walking the streets that Irene, Minnie, John, Agnes, and J. P. (and even Great-Aunt Elizabeth) had walked, visiting the Nenana train depot, exploring the land around Healy and maybe flying over the great mountain, the tallest in North America. At times I can see Denali all the way from Anchorage, four hours away by road. Thanks to the phenomenon called "fata morgana," sometimes its shimmering, distant outline is extra-large on my horizon. For Irene and J. P., Denali and its supersized foothills lay just outside their Healy Forks home. For now, it was only in my vivid imagination that John and Michelle were seeing what I was seeing.

I would have wanted them to shake hands with a couple of pioneers, Denny Birklid and Janice Ostnes, a brother and sister who were recently introduced to me. Their parents and grandparents had run a mom-and-pop placer mining operation on the Totatlanika, the same river that the Shermans had mined. I smiled to learn that their Swedish grandfather, Nelson J. Jackson, had been a contemporary of J. P.'s.

"They were on the Platt for a while, too," Janice told me. *Ah!* I remembered, *the creek J. P. was working when he married Agnes.* He was going to sweep away his bride to the Platt by dog team.

Janice spent her childhood summers on the "Totat," as she called it, and when her kids were little, they did, too, playing among the wildflowers, the stunted willows and spruce, while mom and dad worked the dirt. As a wife and mother, Janice had split her time between cooking meals, doing laundry, and running the backhoe and trammel. The years spun out as Janice and her husband worked their Totatlanika claims until 2020, the year he died while they were out at the mine. The very next year, Janice's twelve-year-old grandboy was there when he suffered an accidental death on a four-wheeler. When we talked, she was grappling with grief, not sure she'd return.

"The place I loved for so many years . . . but these last two years, I gotta get past that before I spend any time there," she said.

Mentally, I reviewed the stories of sorrow and loss that Agnes, J. P., Irene, and Jeanette had suffered on the Totatlanika. Two families working the same dirt, generations apart, and hardships that reached across time. I thought about my lifeline intersecting with Irene's on the common ground that was Fairbanks. So many spilled tears watering that land.

※ ※ ※

On this sweet summer day, I roll by the house where my father and stepmother once lived. The grass is high, and the house looks empty, its blank picture window staring across Noyes Slough toward the spot where Irene's fortress used to stand. I remember looking out from Dad's and seeing her junk pile beyond a sparse row of birch. It was not a wrecking ball, but a bulldozer that brought down the hazmat site. The road to Island Homes Subdivision that needed to be extended, was extended, crossing a corner of land where a wall of chained appliances had once guarded Irene's inner sanctum. Today I notice that another had taken up residence on the remaining real estate, not nearly as full of extras to be considered a hoarder, but certainly not a neighbor most would choose.

It is standing room only at the Fairbanks Community Museum the next night when I present my talk and PowerPoint titled "Untold Stories of the Queen of Fairbanks." Gray heads in the room predominate, many of them Pioneers of Alaska who are ready listeners.

When I get to the part about Michelle sending me that first email, I pause, projecting onto the screen the words she'd written me about her mother-in-law, Georgerene. *Click.* "When you see her photo, you will be amazed." *Click.* "When you hear how she lived, you will be even more amazed." And then, *Bam!* the next slide reveals the broad, smiling face of Irene's long-lost sister, Georgerene. In one accord, the entire room inhales sharply. Irene had been their friend. They'd counted her as a neighbor, drank with her, offered rides, had her over for dinner, and watched over her. And here was a younger lookalike, free from burn scars. I feel great satisfaction in that moment as I introduce Georgerene to them. I wish Michelle and John could have shared in it.

What was it about Alaska that sealed itself into Georgerene's very pores? Enough to demonstrate to her son and daughters, *This is how you do it. This is how you survive.* "I was born in Alaska," she liked to proclaim, and by writing that first letter to the Fairbanks postmaster, she was fighting to reclaim that which was taken from her. Traveling to see Frances, traveling to see Agnes, traveling to see Richard, coming away feeling, what? Whatever it was, she didn't share it with her children, nor did she write it down. But she had acted. She had lived out what she dreamed. How she'd wanted to meet Irene in person!

It was not Irene, but Georgerene who had tried to reunite her siblings. Had they met, would these two sisters have liked each other, I mused, each with her wild woman leanings, multiple marriages, hoarding issues, and intense love for their children?

Early on, Irene's security—her physical and mental health—had been destroyed in every way possible through parental negligence. Other factors had undermined her further: violence, homelessness, sexual assault, and base poverty. If not for her pioneer friends and the stake she made in Fairbanks, Irene would have been a lost soul. Some thought she

Always a dog lover, Georgerene paused for puppy play during a drive to Washington state in 1997. (Moore Family Collection)

was, but I don't believe she saw herself that way. Georgerene's first two years with Agnes and J. P. had to have damaged her on some unseen level. After all, they were the same parents who'd twice lost custody of their living children and admitted their short-comings as providers and protectors to the court. Yet, after adoption, Georgerene was comforted by adoring parents, while she cultivated her exploratory mind, a drive to learn, serve, and create. She enjoyed a comfortable income, traveled the world, and collected her treasures. And at the end, she had two grandsons to dote upon, now family men who are learning about their ancestry.

For decades, Georgerene had been the tenuous glue in trying to piece a family back together. And now, her children and grandchildren had picked up the glue stick. They'd begun by sending an email to a stranger in Alaska asking if a sibling of their mother's—or even the child of a sibling—might still be around. The answer, as we'd all learned since then, was no. There's only you and your family, the last of the Shermans. What remained for the Moore family was an enlarged treasure of remembrances, and with it, the knowledge of a city in the Far North where they're still hoarding memories of their Queen.

Irene in 1966
Buried Clay Street
Cemetery, Fairbanks

Frances in early 1940s
Burial place unknown

Georgerene in 1997
Buried San Luis Obispo
Cemetery, California

Birth and death information about the child born between James and Pauline Agnes (Georgerene) remains unknown.

Jeanette and baby James Day Sherman are both buried in the Clay Street Cemetery in Fairbanks. Her marker is new; his grave has not yet been located.

Richard was buried in Fort Rosecrans National Cemetery in San Diego, California.

IRENE MARY SHERMAN'S FAMILY
First Generation to the United States

FRANK JENOTT	JENNIE JENOTT
Francis Lachappelle dit Jenott	Marie-Jeannette Frances Giroux
1825 Quebec–1905 Seattle, Wash.	1838 Quebec–1912 Seattle, Wash.

Born to Frank and Jennie Jenott:

Joseph Lachappelle, 1863 Quebec–1929 Seattle, Wash.

Charles Lachappelle, 1865 Quebec–1951 Seattle, Wash.

Mina Elizabeth Lachappelle, 1869 Ottawa–1929 Kent, Wash.

William Lachappelle, about 1872 Canada–Unknown

Elizabeth Lachappelle, 1873 Quebec–1960 Los Angeles, Calif.

Louisa Lachappelle, about 1875 Quebec–1934 Seattle, Wash.

Irene Philomene Lachappelle, 1876 Quebec–1953 L.A., Calif.

Marguerite Lachappelle, 1879 Quebec–Unknown

James Lachappelle, Unknown–Unknown

Second Generation

MINA "Minnie" LACHAPPELLE JENOTT	FREDERICK "Fred" HENRY ECKERT
May 1869 Ottawa, Canada–July 26, 1929 Seattle, Wash.	September 1857, Ontario, Canada–May 31, 1936 Salem, Ore.
+ 2nd husband John Patten	+ 2nd wife Harriett Farnham

Born to Minnie and Fred Eckert:

John Joseph, 1885 Saginaw, Mich.–1938 Glendale, Calif.

William Frederick, 1887 Hayward, Wisc.–1952 Tacoma, Wash.

Minnie (1888 Hayward, Wisc.–1905 King County, Wash.

Agnes Elizabeth, 1889 Hayward, Wisc.–1964 Centralia, Wash.

Clarence Brophy, 1891 Seattle, Wash.–1972 San Francisco, Calif.

Bessie Mae (Betty), 1895 Seattle, Wash.–1951 Burlington, Wash.

Third Generation

AGNES ELIZABETH ECKERT Jan. 28, 1889 Hayward, Wisc. – Jan. 11, 1964 Centralia, Wash.	JAMES PAUL "J. P." SHERMAN Dec. 15, 1878 Kilbourn, Wisc. – April 26, 1969 Sitka, Alaska

Born to Agnes and J. P. Sherman:

**Irene Mary, Jan. 29, 1911 Fairbanks, Alaska Territory –
Feb. 20, 1995, Fairbanks, State of Alaska •**

Jeanette A., Dec. 23, 1912, Nenana, Alaska Territory – Feb. 16, 1913, near Nenana, Alaska Territory ••

Frances Marguerite, Oct. 11, 1914, Nenana, Alaska Territory – Aug. 17, 2011, Tempe, Ariz. • ⌂

James Day, Feb. 12, 1916, Fairbanks, Alaska Territory – Nov. 28, 1916, Fairbanks, Alaska Territory ••

Unidentified child, born/disappeared between 1920-24 near Nenana, Alaska Territory ••

Pauline Agnes, June 26, 1922 Nenana, Alaska Territory – June 12, 2001, Orofino, Idaho ■ ⌂⌂

Richard DeWitt, Sept. 12, 1923 Nenana, Alaska Territory – March 3, 1959, Los Angeles, Calif. ■ ⌂⌂⌂

- • *Ward of Alaska Territory*
- •• *Died in early childhood*
- ■ *Ward of King County, Wash.*
- ⌂ *Adopted by John F. "Jack" and Blanche Burnett of Fairbanks, Alaska Territory*
- ⌂⌂ *Adopted by great-aunt Irene Coover, nee Jenott, of Los Angeles, Calif.*
- ⌂⌂⌂ *Fostered or legally adopted by Elizabeth Goreska, nee Jenott, of Los Angeles, Calif.*

. IRENE MARY SHERMAN
Jan. 29, 1911 Fairbanks, Alaska
Territory –
Feb. 20, 1995 Fairbanks, Alaska

+ 2nd husband Fred J. Potter

ROBERT P. HARTMAN SR.
May 17, 1892 Tacoma, Wash. –
Apr. 26, 1982 San Luis Obispo, Calif.

+ 2nd wife Olive

ROBERT P. HARTMAN, JR., October 29, 1931, Fairbanks, Alaska
Territory – April 7, 1982, Anchorage, Alaska

2. JEANETTE A. SHERMAN
Dec. 23, 1912 Nenana, Alaska
Territory –
Feb. 16, 1913 near Nenana,
Alaska Territory

**3. FRANCES MARGARET
BURNETT**
[Frances Marguerite Sherman]
Oct. 11, 1914, Fairbanks, Alaska
Territory –
Aug. 17, 2011 Tempe, Arizona

NATHAN "BRICK" JACOBS
Aug. 21, 1909 New York, NY –
Jan. 5, 1995 Reno, Nev.

+2nd husband Walter Bilowas

4. JAMES DAY SHERMAN
Feb. 12, 1916 Fairbanks, Alaska
Territory –
Nov. 28, 1916 Fairbanks

5. UNIDENTIFIED CHILD
Born about 1920-21 Alaska
Territory –
Unaccounted for by Dec. 1924

6. GEORGERENE IRENE COOVER	FRANCIS THOMAS MOORE
[Pauline Agnes Sherman]	
June 26, 1922 Nenana, Alaska	Oct. 5, 1919 Philadelphia, Penn.–
Territory –	May 19, 1992 Riverside, Calif.
June 12, 2001 Orofino, Idaho	

Born to Georgerene and Frank Moore:
A daughter, a son named **JOHN JOSEPH**, and a second daughter

7. RICHARD DEWITT SHERMAN GORESKA
Sept. 12, 1923 Nenana, Alaska
Territory –
March 2, 1959 Los Angeles, Calif.

Fifth Generation

JOHN JOSEPH MOORE	MICHELLE HODGKINSON
1956	1964

Sixth Generation

Born to John and Michelle Moore:
Two sons, **DANIEL** and **JAY**

Seventh Generation

DANIEL and **JAY MOORE** both married;
each is the father of two children.
Irene Mary Sherman would have been their great-great aunt.

ACKNOWLEDGMENTS

Thank you, John and Michelle Moore, for mobilizing me to write this book. Your genuine care and transparency about your mom and her spirit have been unfailing. Thank you to Renette Moore and others linked to the Sherman family, including Daniel and Jay Moore, Barbara Eckert Tripp, Connie Burnett, Jeannine Burnett, and Celeste Burnett Garcia, who allowed me to mine their memories.

I'm grateful to the Rasmuson Foundation for awarding me a 2021 Individual Artist Award fellowship, allowing the financial freedom for travel and research. I so appreciate colleagues who reviewed earlier versions of the manuscript and offered helpful remarks: Andromeda Romano-Lax, Carol Sturgulewski, Nancy Gates, Sara Juday, Kent Sturgis, Debbie Carter, and Dermot Cole.

For sharing your knowledge of Interior Alaska life and history, my thanks to Joan Koponen, Bob Eley, Karen Norris, Roger Brunner and Niesje Steinkruger, Sharon Johnson Boko, Lamont Hawkins, Karen Erickson, Ron Davis, Kate Ripley, Lin Gale, Tom Walker, Gloria Corey, Jonathan Johnson, Denny Birklid and Janice Ostness, and members of Pioneers of Alaska Igloos Nos. 4 and 8.

Many who knew Irene are now gone, but they touched her life in important ways. I want to recognize Harriet Hess, Blanche Burnett, Dorothy Sleichter, A. Leslie "Les" and Mildred Nerland, Wally and Ruth Burnett, Sharron Wasser, and Jen Walker-Mang.

For generously imparting your skills and heartfelt care (to Irene and to me), thanks to Chena Koponen Newman and Gary C. Newman, Lorraine Russell, Irene's Denali Center care team, Gayle Moloy, Linden Staciokas, and Erik Hill. Thank you to my co-laborers in the Irene Sherman Project: Bob Eley, Ron Davis, Virginia Farmier, Mike Cook, Jeffry J. Cook, Tania Clucas, and Angela Linn.

Irene and her life challenges touched public servants at every level. Among them were Jim Hayes, Brian C. Phillips, Dave McNary, Dave Jacoby, and Jerry Cleworth. Local publishers C. W. Snedden of the *Fairbanks Daily News-Miner*, and Tom Snapp and Colleen

Redman of the *Pioneer All-Alaska Weekly* were among the journalists who faithfully kept their readers up to date on Irene's affairs. Thanks for your assistance Janet Richardson and others on the city's Clay Street Cemetery Commission. Also helpful were Leah Hainebach and Abby Focht of the Alaska State Archives; Kimberly Arthur, Erik K. Johnson, and Jan E. Thomsen of the National Park Service, Denali National Park & Preserve; the Pioneer Museum at Pioneer Park; UAF archivist Fawn Carter; and *Fairbanks Daily News-Miner* reporter Kris Capps.

Thanks to all of you Fairbanks Boomers, both those in town and strewn across the country. You've kept Irene Sherman's memory alive in conversation and on social media, and you've introduced her to new

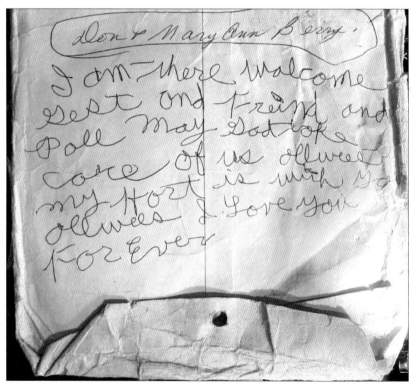

Before Irene's home was torn down, friends seeking to rescue some of her personal items from destruction found this 1977 note written in her hand. Her letter was addressed to no one in particular, but revealed a heart overflowing with gratitude after a dinner invitation from locals Don and Mary Ann Berry.

generations. Thanks to you folks who've relentlessly asked, "How's the Irene book coming?" like Joan Schultz, who helped me carve out time to work. Thank you Pam Stinson for your fresh eyes. For your grace, thank you to my beloved Pedersen family. Finally, my gratitude to Perry Brown, Jennifer Houdek, Kierra Morris, and Braydon and Kelton Houdek for your patience and understanding while I was away in "Irene world," whether traveling or at my desk. I love you dearly.

Mostly, thank you, unforgettable Irene, so true to yourself, and thanks to your baby sister, Georgerene Irene Moore, for your trying journey to connect with family.

740 Front Street in Graehl, Irene's custom-built home place. (Tricia Brown)

ABOUT THE AUTHOR

 **Tricia Brown** writes for adults and children, and has nearly thirty books to her name. Among Brown's titles for early elementary readers, five were selected by the Alaska Library Association for the Alaska Battle of the Books. In 2021, Brown received an Individual Artist fellowship from the Rasmuson Foundation to support her work on this book. In 2023, she was recognized by the Alaska Center for the Book with the CLIA award for Contributions to Literacy in Alaska. Brown also serves on an organizing committee raising funds for a statue of Irene Sherman to be installed in a prominent place in downtown Fairbanks. For more information on the statue project or to join the effort by donating, see ireneshermanproject.com. To learn more about Tricia's other works, visit triciabrownbooks.com.

OTHER BOOKS BY TRICIA BROWN

FOR ADULTS

Alaska Homesteader's Handbook

Icons of the Iditarod

The World-Famous Alaska Highway

Iditarod: Images of Sports

FOR CHILDREN

Bobbie the Wonder Dog

Children of the Midnight Sun

Patsy Ann of Alaska

The Itchy Little Musk Ox

Zig the Warrior Princess

Alaska Native Games and How to Play Them

Charlie and the Blanket Toss

Groucho's Eyebrows

Children of the First People

Alaskan Night Before Christmas

Musher's Night Before Christmas

Interior and Southcentral
ALASKA

············ Alaska Railroad

——— Road System

(2024 map courtesy Alaska Tour & Travel; AlaskaTrain.c